I0812789

IMAGES
of America

BRISTOL

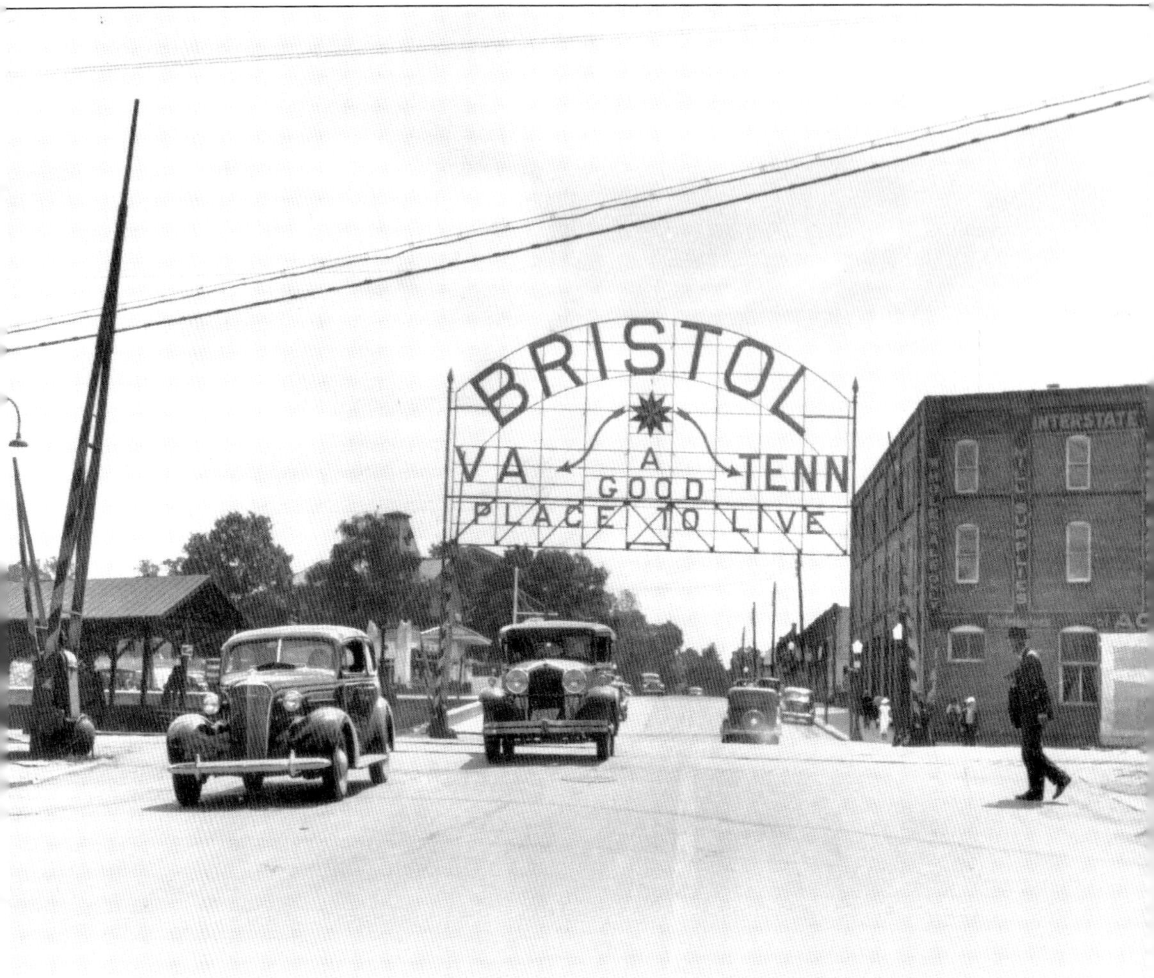

The Historic Bristol Sign was originally erected on top of a hardware store building in 1910. *The Bristol Herald Courier* reported on July 6, 1910, that, at the time, there were only two or three such electric signs in the country. The Bristol sign was moved to its present location in 1915. (Courtesy of Bristol Historical Association.)

On the Cover
S. E. Massengill and his brother, Norman H. Massengill, founded the Massengill Brothers Company in 1897. Norman later left the pharmaceutical company, and the name was changed to the S. E. Massengill Company. Workers are shown in the cover photograph doing what they did best: creating and manufacturing medicine. The company was sold in April 1971 and renamed Beecham-Massengill. (Courtesy of Bristol Historical Association.)

IMAGES
of America

BRISTOL

George Stone and Sonya A. Haskins

ARCADIA
PUBLISHING

ISBN 978-0-7385-4167-9

Published by Arcadia Publishing
Charleston, South Carolina

Printed in the United States of America

Library of Congress Catalog Card Number: 2005928558

For all general information contact Arcadia Publishing at:
Telephone 843-853-2070
Fax 843-853-0044
E-mail sales@arcadiapublishing.com
For customer service and orders:
Toll-Free 1-888-313-2665

Visit us on the Internet at www.arcadiapublishing.com

For Paul Stone, who was my inspiration in producing this book. —George Stone

For Amy, may the memory of your mother go on forever, but your sadness lessen with time. I hope this book brings back fond memories of your life in Bristol. —Sonya Haskins

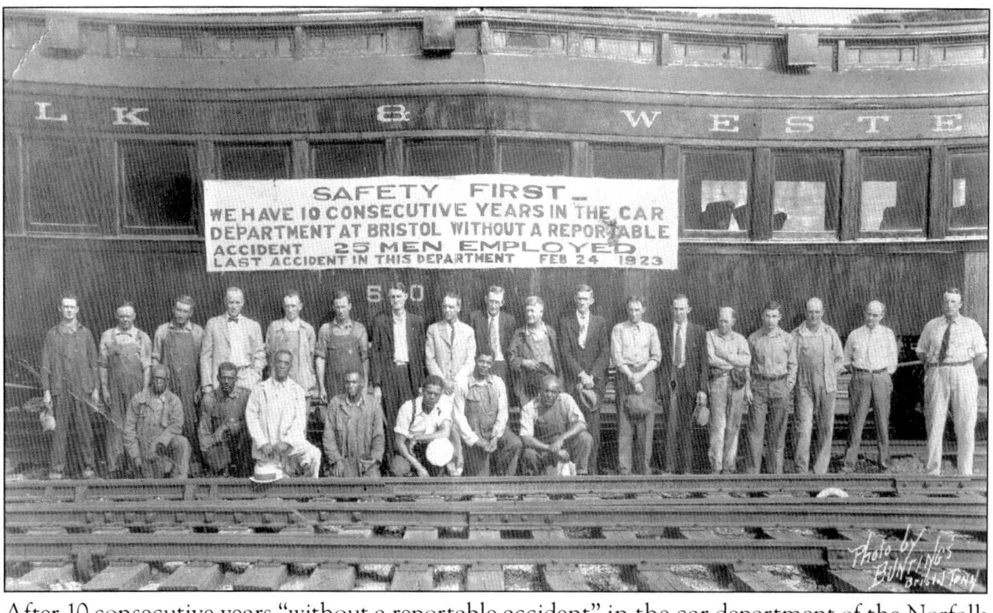

After 10 consecutive years "without a reportable accident" in the car department of the Norfolk & Western in Bristol, the 25 employees gathered for this 1933 photograph. Notice that there were several African Americans working for the company at the time. Many of these men probably had fathers or grandfathers involved in the Civil War, though in Upper East Tennessee, loyalties were divided. (Courtesy of Laverna Long of Bristol Antiques.)

Contents

ACKNOWLEDGMENTS

The authors would particularly like to express appreciation to Linda Brittle, Bud Phillips, Tim Buchanan, and William Wade for their help with this project. You have been available, made photographs and documents accessible, and helped us tremendously with research. Our work would not have been possible without you. Thank you!

We would also like to express appreciation to the following individuals: John Tallman of the Virginia Intermont College library; Walter Doane; Merle Dickert of Virginia Intermont College; Lt. Darryl Milligan of the Bristol, Virginia, Police Department; Tommy Helton and Peggy Brown of the Bristol, Virginia, Fire Department; and Bill Hartley of the Birthplace of Country Music Alliance.

There are also other individuals who generously allowed us to use their photographs and stories in this book. We appreciate your willingness to share your history. The names of these individuals can be found at the end of each caption.

We were extremely happy that the book received the blessing of the Bristol Historical Association, which shared photographs and information with us while having a delightful time in the process. We would highly recommend that other Bristolians support the Bristol Historical Association with monetary donations or gifts of historical value. The historical association will ensure that the items are preserved as part of Bristol's heritage. Carolyn Williams, Bristol Historical Association Chair of Education, History, and Archives Committee, has been responsible for keeping items filed, organized, and accessible to those who need information. We thank her for the commitment she has to the history of Bristol.

Bill and Ruth King selflessly offer space for the Bristol Historical Association to maintain their collection. Bill and Ruth are kind, generous individuals whom we would be remiss to exclude. Thank you for your willingness to give.

Adam Latham, our editor at Arcadia, once again was very helpful and encouraging. It's great to work with professional yet friendly people.

Finally, we would like to thank our families for allowing us the time to work on this book. We love you very much!

FOREWORD

Over the years, many people have speculated how much different life would be in Bristol, Tennessee/Virginia if the state line that divides the city were suddenly moved ten miles. Think about it, one police force, one school board, one high school, a state income tax . . . or not, depending on whether the line went north or south.

Things would certainly be different if Bristol were not split down the middle of State Street. Different but definitely not better, because you see, the minor inconveniences that result in being in two different states at once are part of the charm of Bristol. One can debate long and loud that two states are indeed better than one. It is easy to love these cities and the people who inhabit them.

Most cities with a combined population of around 45,000 have nowhere near the number of distinctions that sets the Bristols apart from their neighbors in Southwest Virginia and Northeast Tennessee. Bristol is indeed "A Good Place To Live."

No city, no matter how many states bisect its borders, can boast of being "the Birthplace of Country Music." That is a title taken seriously by almost all Bristolians, whether they are music lovers or not. From the earliest sessions with Jimmie Rodgers and the Carter Family up until the very successful Rhythm and Roots Festival held each fall, music has always been a part of the fabric of Bristol.

Strangely enough, another unique feature of the Bristols is as far away from the gentle mountain music that wafts down State Street on the acoustical scale as is possible. While the lilting sound of a mandolin or a country fiddle may calm the nerves, the scream of high performance racing engines drives aficionados of motorsports to a new high down Volunteer Parkway at Thunder Valley.

Because you see, Bristol is also home to two of the most storied facilities in motorsports, Bristol Motor Speedway and Dragway.

A trip to these two facilities, originally built in the early 1960s, has become a pilgrimage that all true racing fans must make before their lives are complete. Currently, one of the five largest spectator facilities in the world, the speedway is NASCAR's most popular track, and Thunder Valley is arguably the finest dragway in the world.

But that is not all that happens at the complex. What other facility hosts everything from symphony concerts to outdoor shows and ends each year with what has been judged as the best holiday light show in the Southeast? This is just another distinction that makes the Bristols what they are.

While country music and racing are certainly special, the one trait that no other city or cities, for that matter, can duplicate is the people. The people who live in Bristol appreciate the past but are inspired by what the future holds.

If someone suggests a project in Bristol, it's likely that it will be done. Bristolians have built a new hospital, resurrected an old movie theater and turned it into a state-of-the-art performance center, refurbished the train station, built a new library, and revitalized downtown. If it is something that will be good for the community, Bristolians not only talk about doing it, but they actually do it.

This is what happens when people live in a place they love, and the people love Bristol, both the Tennesseans and the Virginians. Or is that the Virginians and the Tennesseans? It works both ways for most of us.

It is our hope that you can discover the Bristol that we love in the pages of this book. If you are a "local," it is anticipated that the photographs, postcards, and documents in this book will encourage you to develop a deeper sense of appreciation and pride for Bristol. If you are just getting acquainted with Bristol through this book, we hope you will come see for yourself what makes Bristol so special for all of us.

—Jeff Byrd

INTRODUCTION

If Charles Dickens had not already penned his great classic *A Tale of Two Cities*, the story of Bristol could very easily have had that title. With its main street straddling two states, Bristol is rich in history and has been the economic backbone for Northeast Tennessee and Southwest Virginia for over 100 years. Bristol, named for the manufacturing city in England, was christened in 1852 when Joseph R. Anderson bought a tract of land from his father-in-law, Rev. James King. Anderson then proceeded to plan this little town, which sat directly on the Virginia-Tennessee border. In 1856, the Virginia and Tennessee Railroad came to Bristol, and the town grew into a major trading center of the Appalachian region. It was also in 1856 that Bristol received its official charter. Today, Bristol is a city of over 40,000.

Bristol's importance in history was never more evident than during the Civil War, when the town was a vital railway link between the North and the South. Following the Civil War, when wounds had been healed, Bristol would rebuild and grow along with the rest of the war-torn country.

In August 1927, an event known today as the Bristol Sessions took place at the Taylor-Christian Hat Company on State Street in Bristol, Tennessee. Ralph Peer, a talent scout for the Victor Talking Machine Company, traveled to Bristol from New York City to record Southern Appalachian musicians who played what was then referred to as "hillbilly music." Because of the Bristol Sessions, little-known musicians such as Jimmie Rodgers and the Carter Family would soon become household names. As a result of those early recordings, Bristol today is recognized the world over as the Birthplace of Country Music.

No doubt one Bristolian who was influenced by the likes of Rodgers and the Carter Family was a youngster by the name of Ernest Ford. Ernie, as he was more commonly known, spun records at radio station WOPI before embarking on a career in music and television that catapulted him into stardom as a singer and comedian. He would be recognized all over the world as simply Tennessee Ernie.

Any historical account of Bristol would not be complete without the mention of the King family—from the Kings who settled the area as early pioneers to another King family who played a significant role in making Bristol such a successful commercial center.

Bristol has offered young people throughout Appalachia and beyond the opportunity to earn a solid education with centers of higher learning such as King College, Virginia Intermont College, and Sullins College. And not to be overlooked is the deep religious faith of those who call Bristol home, evidenced by the great number of church steeples dotting the landscape throughout the city. Sports also play a major role, from minor league baseball to high school athletics to recreational leagues.

While many names have become household words in the written history of Bristol, it is those individuals whose names have been forgotten who make Bristol the city it is today. These citizens were the shopkeepers, the firemen, the policemen, the mail carriers, and others who spanned the era of the horse and buggy to that of the motor vehicle.

This book is not meant to be a history of Bristol, but rather it is the past caught through the eye of the camera—snapshots of everyday life now frozen forever in time thanks to photographers, some known and some unknown, of decades past who felt it was important enough to snap the shutter and preserve forever a slice of history. Many of the photographs on these pages are being seen in publication for the first time, having been hidden away in family albums for generations.

The year 2006 marks Bristol's sesquicentennial. As Bristolians and visitors alike stroll the rejuvenated downtown district and look east toward the train station, one fact remains. The historic sign that towers over State Street is more than a landmark. It serves as a reminder to all who see it that Bristol *is* A Good Place To Live.

—George Stone

One

Friends, Neighbors, and Families

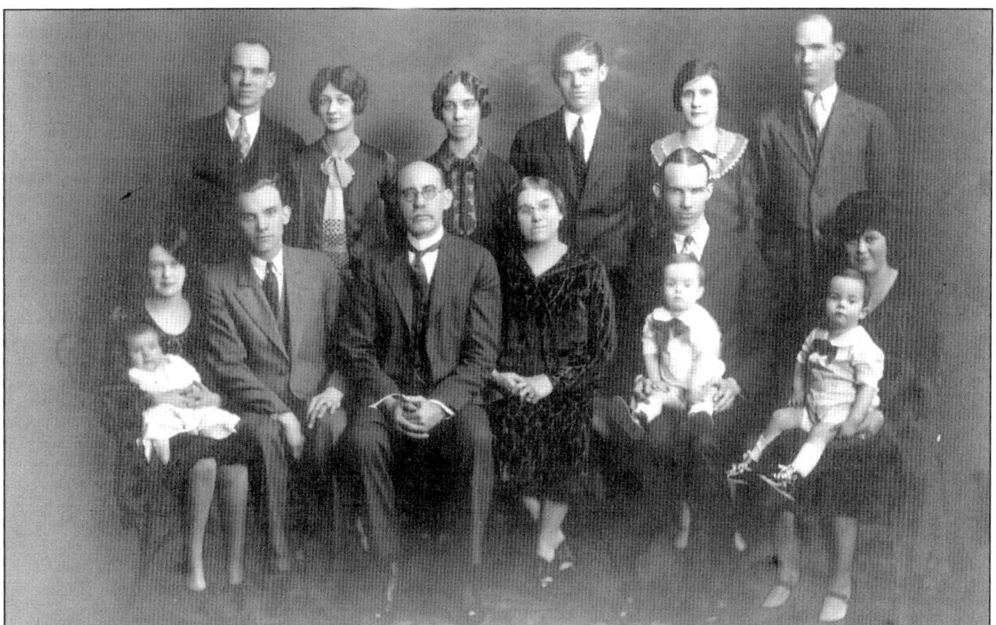

J. D. Faucette came to Bristol to work with Huntsman Brothers in the wholesale grocery business until he established the Faucette China Company in 1899. Faucette (seated center) is shown here with his wife, Jennie, whom he married in 1891, and family. Faucette was a well-known community leader and was active in many religious affairs of the day. He died in 1942. (Courtesy of Tim Buchanan.)

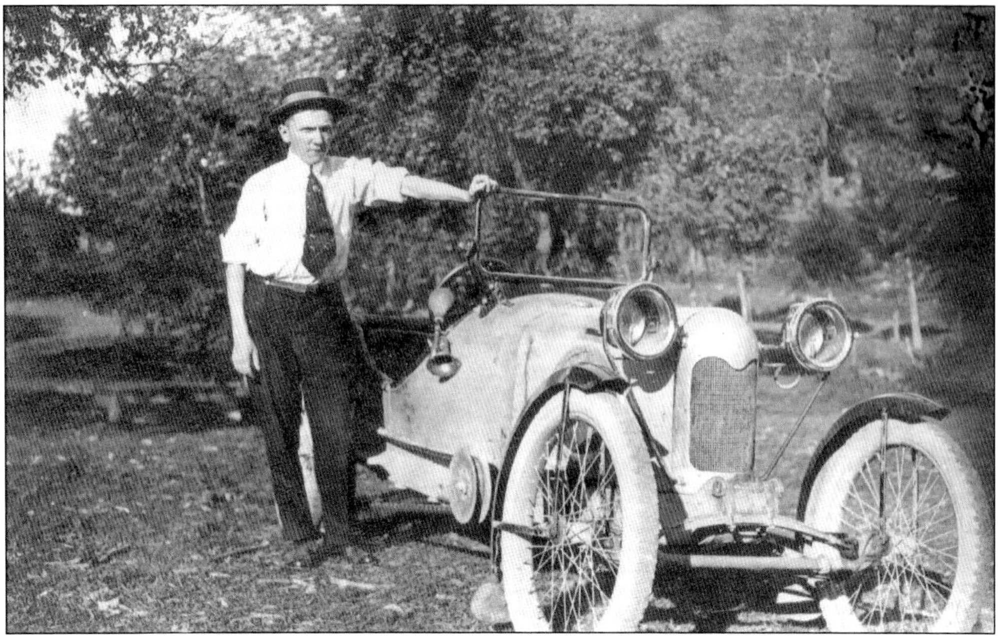

Basil Harr poses in front of a car that is unidentified but probably of foreign origin. Harr owned rare collectibles such as coins, a cigarette case that was presented to World War I flying ace Baron von Richtohofen, and an Iron Cross awarded to a Prussian prince in 1870. The items were kept in a makeshift museum at his home. (Courtesy of Paul Stone Collection.)

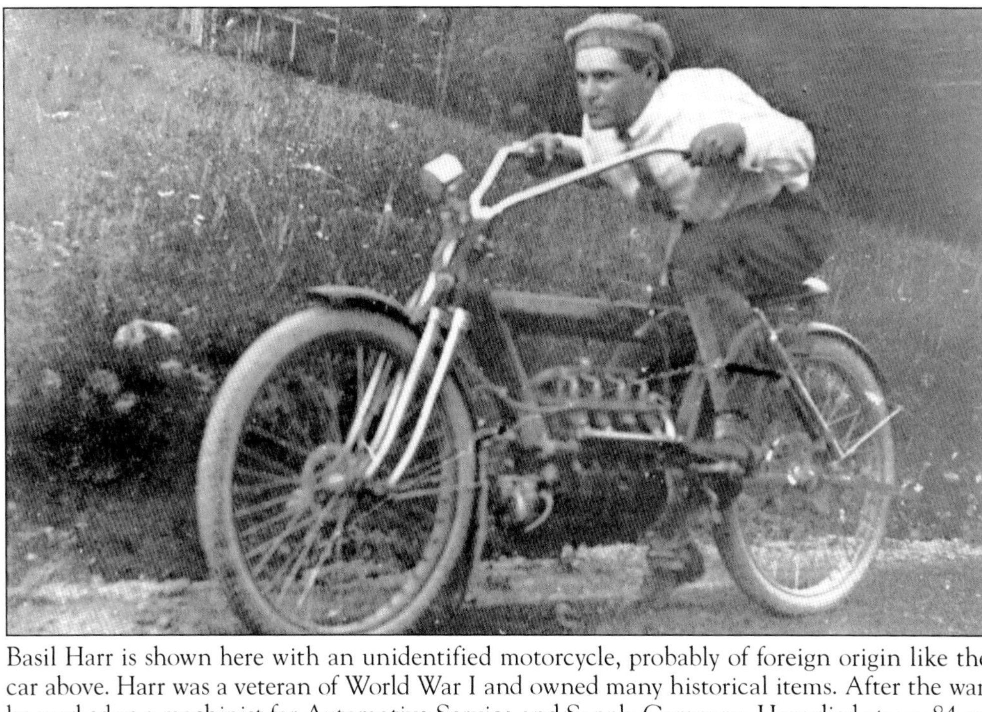

Basil Harr is shown here with an unidentified motorcycle, probably of foreign origin like the car above. Harr was a veteran of World War I and owned many historical items. After the war, he worked as a machinist for Automotive Service and Supply Company. Harr died at age 84 on March 2, 1974. After his death, a fire destroyed almost everything he had collected. (Courtesy of Paul Stone Collection.)

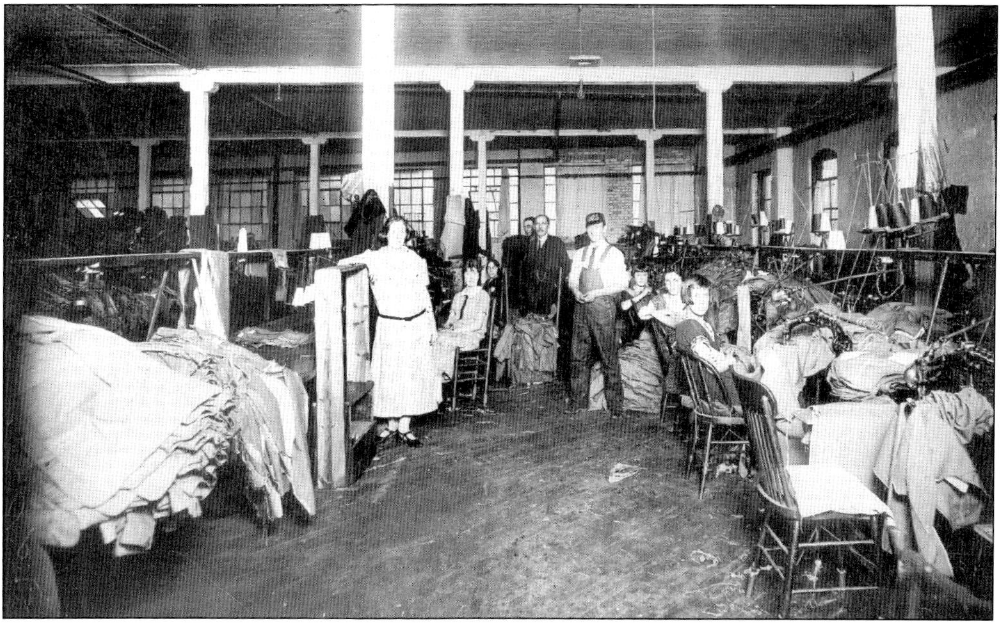

When the Head-Lipscomb-McCormick Overall Company reorganized under the name of the Big Jack Manufacturing Company in 1921, Carroll Kidd served as president and John S. Lipscomb, who had originally founded the company in 1905, served as vice president. Lipscomb, dressed in a suit, is in the center of this photograph taken around 1920. (Courtesy of Mrs. Dick Easley.)

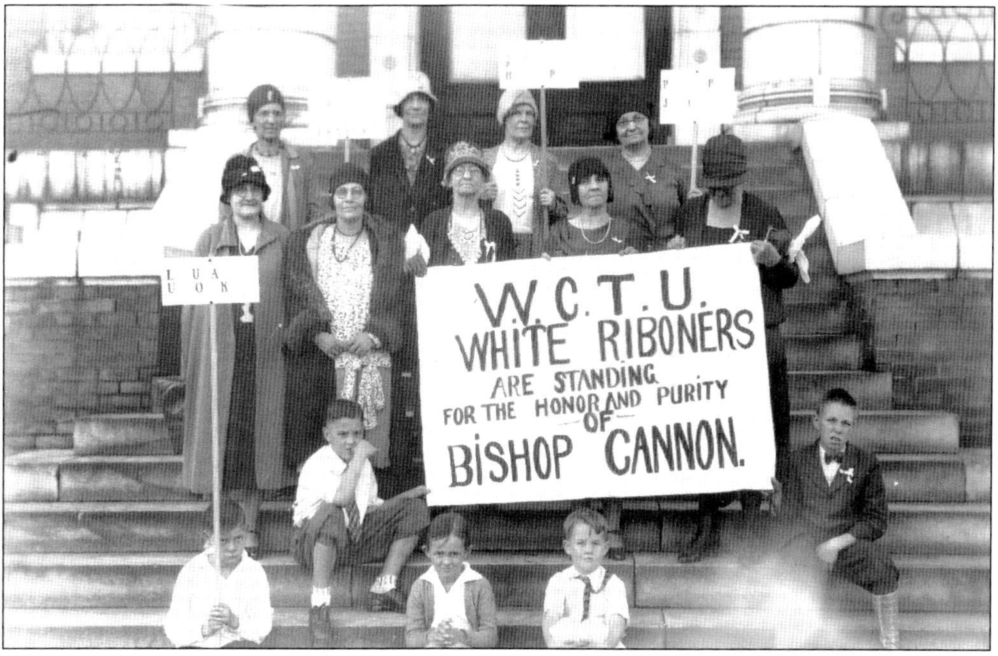

Women, who were not expected to do much in society except be homemakers and wives, actively campaigned to maintain the "honor and purity" of their communities through prohibition in the beginning of the 20th century. Shown here are the officers of the Women's Christian Temperance Union of Bristol with their young children, who most likely went everywhere they did. (Courtesy of Bristol Historical Association.)

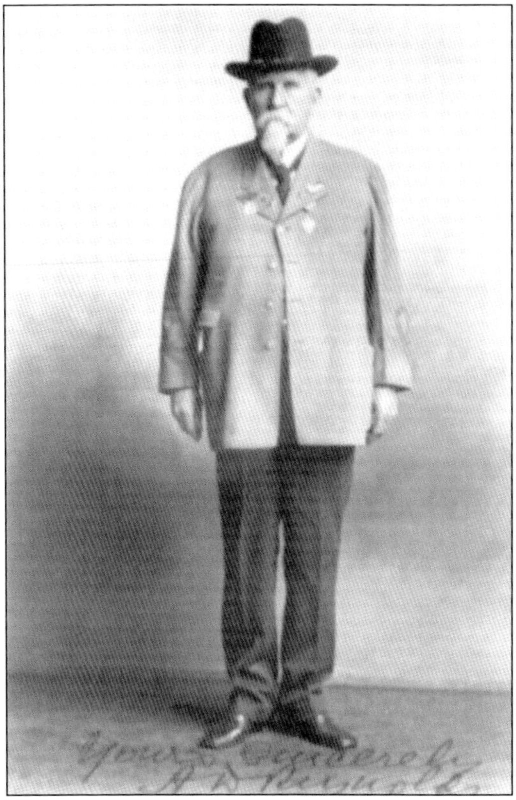

In 1871, when Maj. A. D. Reynolds came to Bristol, tobacco grown in this area was purely for home consumption, and even that was not very common. Reynolds set up a tobacco factory in his home in 1872, although work didn't begin in the factory until 1873. Reynolds was born in Rock Spring, Virginia, on August 13, 1847, and died September 23, 1925, at age 78. (Courtesy of Bristol Historical Association.)

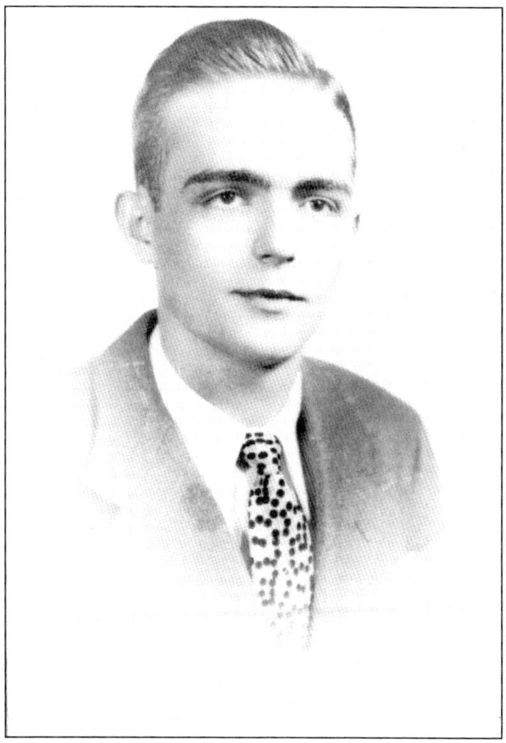

Raymond Honaker retired from Morrison Molding after a lifetime of making fiberglass. His wife's name was Cassie, and they had two children, Bob and Betty. The family lived in the Lakeview community. (Courtesy of David and Angela Gray.)

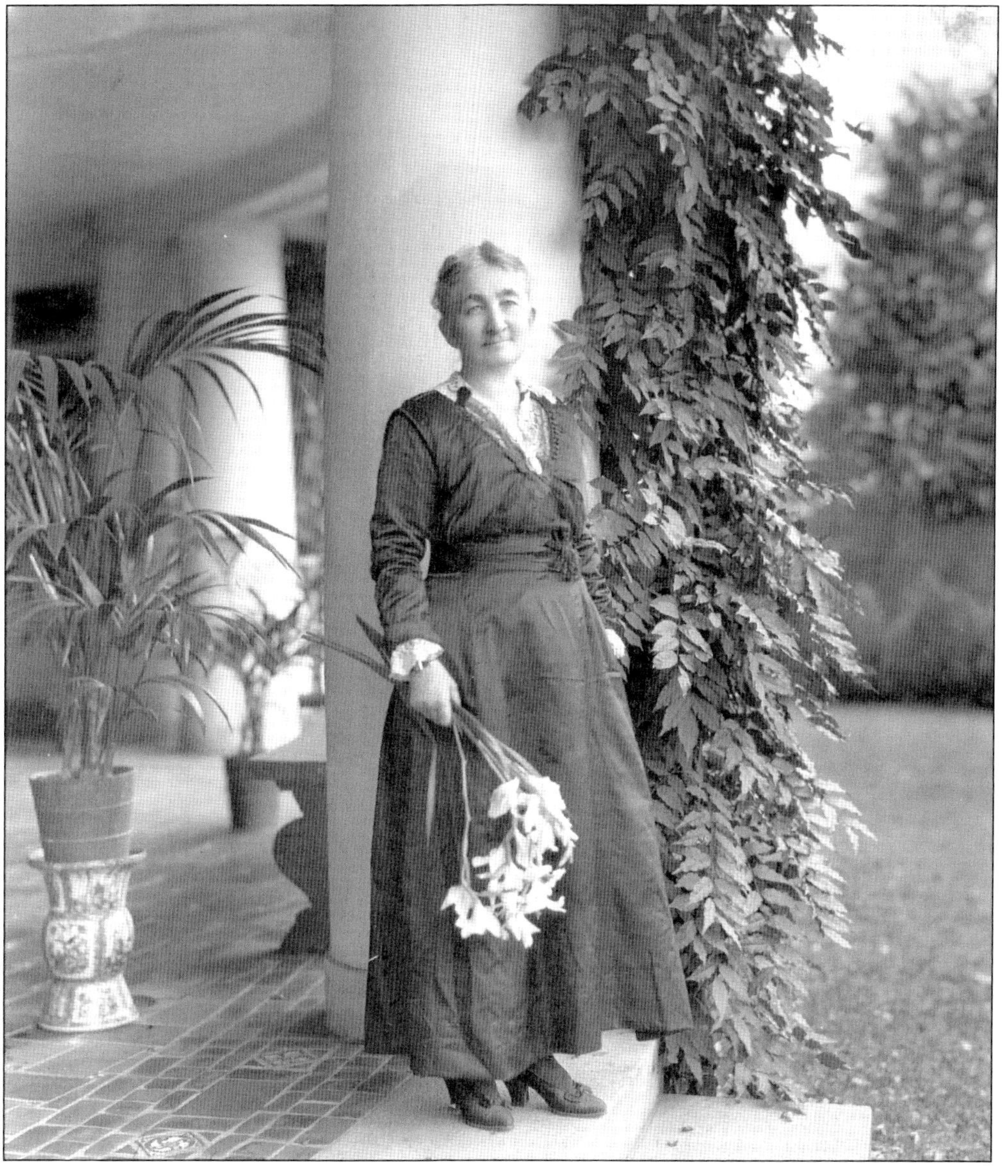

This lovely portrait portrays the dignity of one of Bristol's elite class ladies. Senah Ann Hoge was born July 20, 1849, in Giles County, Virginia. She married Maj. A. D. Reynolds in October 1872, and they had eight children, one who died in infancy and one who died as a young man. Senah Reynolds died October 7, 1925, at her home on Spruce Street about two weeks after the death of her husband. Senah was called the Mother of the Local YMCA because of the work she did for that organization. (Courtesy of Bristol Historical Association.)

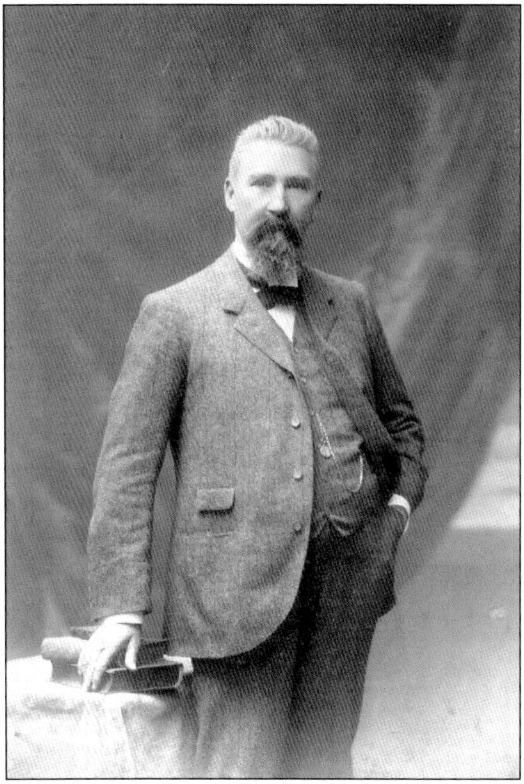

In 1875, Richard Joshua Reynolds, brother of A. D. Reynolds, was only 25 years old when he began a company to manufacture chewing tobacco in Winston, North Carolina (now known as Winston-Salem after the two small towns merged). This was the beginning of the R. J. Reynolds Tobacco Company, once the largest cigarette company in the United States. Reynolds died in 1919 at age 68. Reynolds poses alone in the top photograph and is shown below with his son Richard Jr. (Courtesy of Bristol Historical Association.)

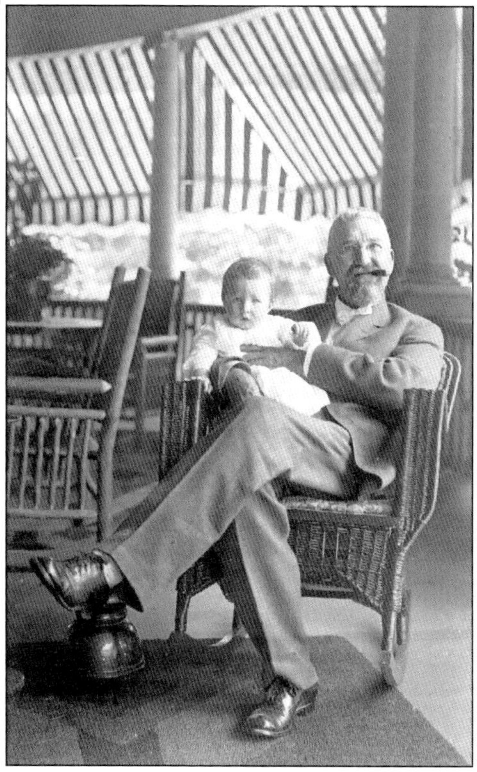

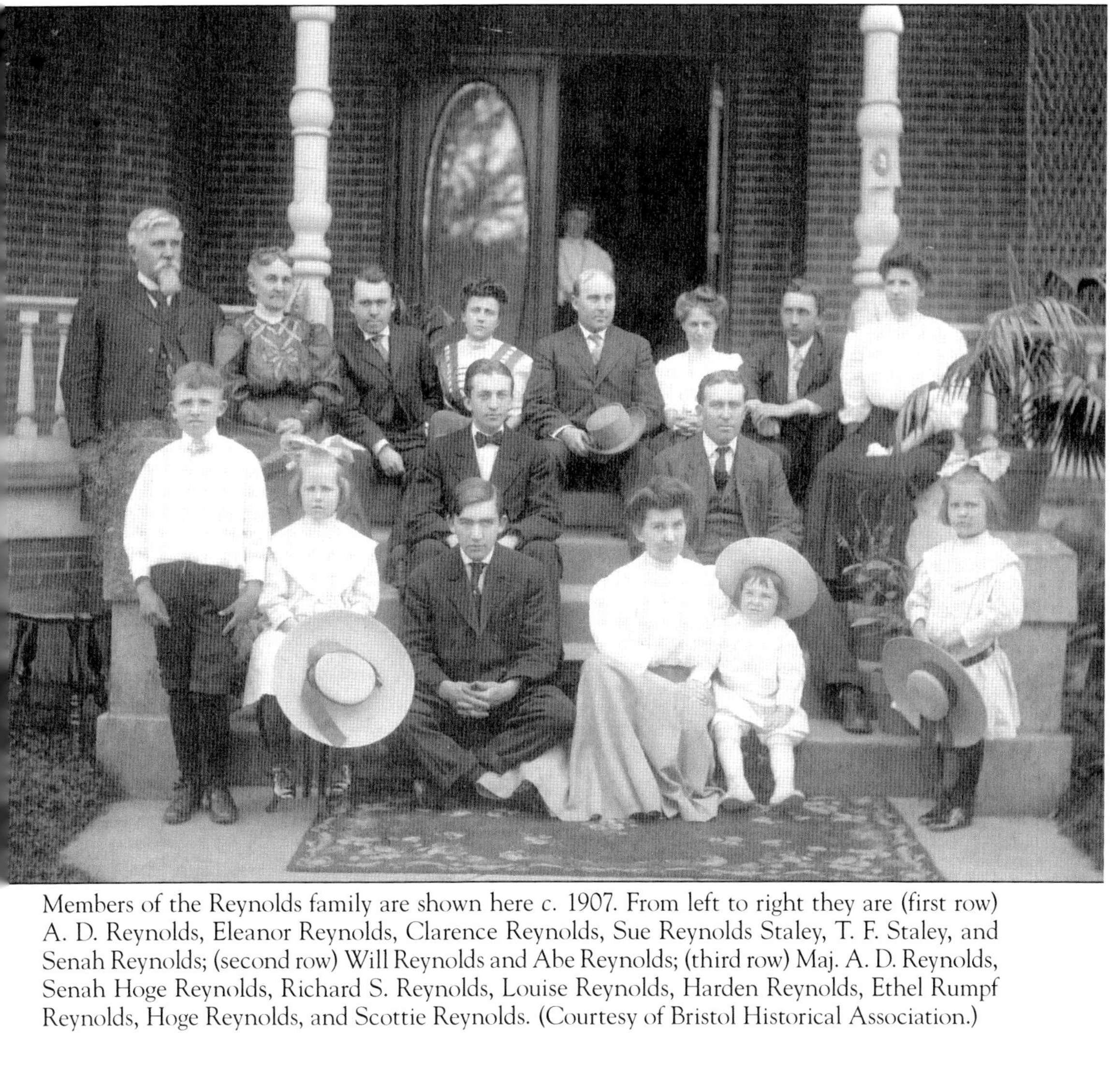

Members of the Reynolds family are shown here *c.* 1907. From left to right they are (first row) A. D. Reynolds, Eleanor Reynolds, Clarence Reynolds, Sue Reynolds Staley, T. F. Staley, and Senah Reynolds; (second row) Will Reynolds and Abe Reynolds; (third row) Maj. A. D. Reynolds, Senah Hoge Reynolds, Richard S. Reynolds, Louise Reynolds, Harden Reynolds, Ethel Rumpf Reynolds, Hoge Reynolds, and Scottie Reynolds. (Courtesy of Bristol Historical Association.)

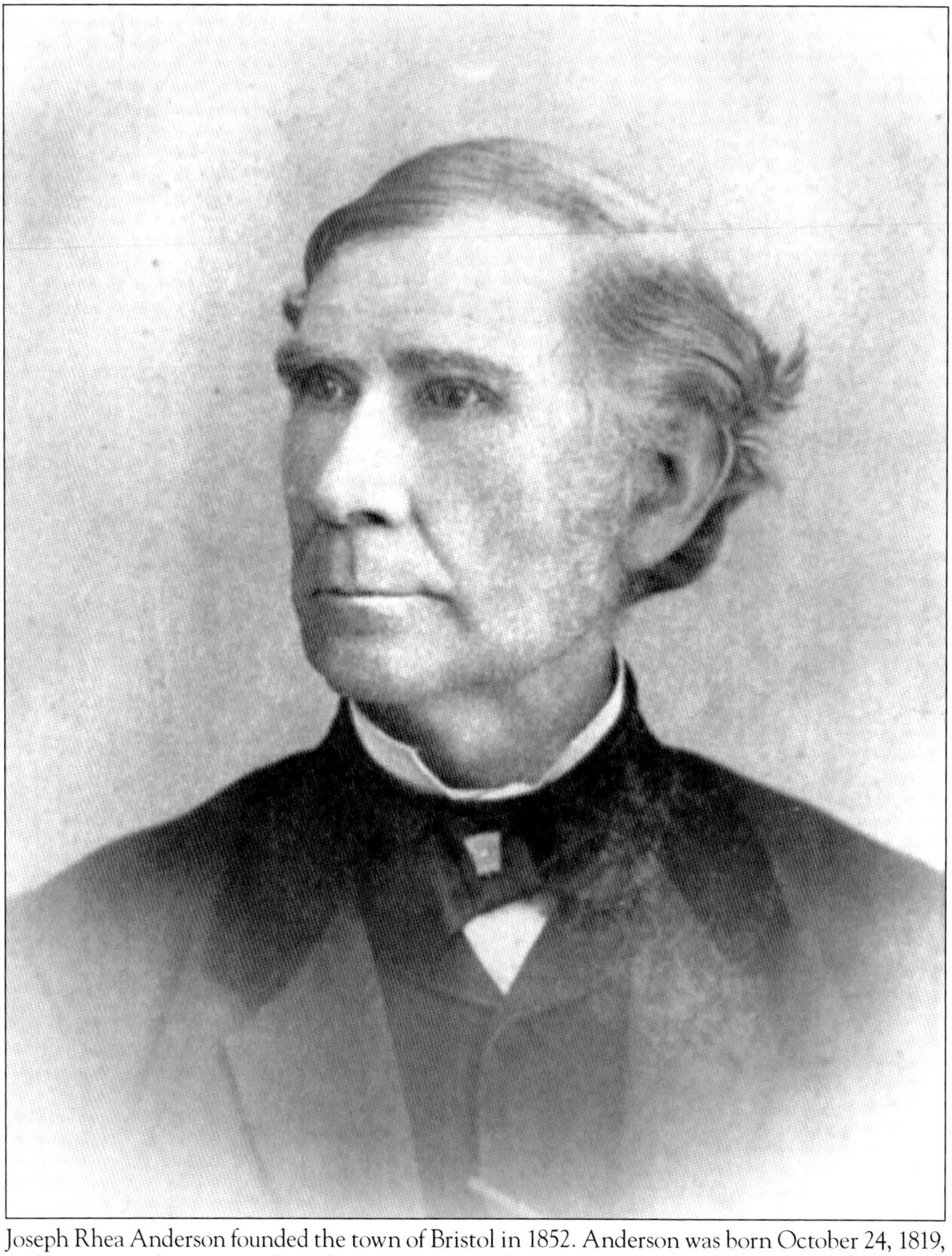

Joseph Rhea Anderson founded the town of Bristol in 1852. Anderson was born October 24, 1819, and went into the mercantile and private banking business in Blountville. He married Melinda King on June 3, 1845. Melinda's father, Rev. James King, sold 100 acres of his land to his son-in-law, Joseph Anderson, upon which the latter founded the town of Bristol. Joseph considered calling the new town Paradise but changed his mind to Bristol after the great iron center in England. (Courtesy of Bud Phillips.)

James A. Moore (October 12, 1884–April 12, 1972) and Minnie Kate Minnick Moore (March 1, 1882–April 9, 1935) are shown here shortly after their wedding of October 18, 1903. James operated an auto repair garage on Shelby Street and co-owned a dry cleaning establishment on Fifth Street with Hill Kestner. James and Minnie Kate lived in the Cross community near Blountville. (Courtesy of Bob and Marie Broyles.)

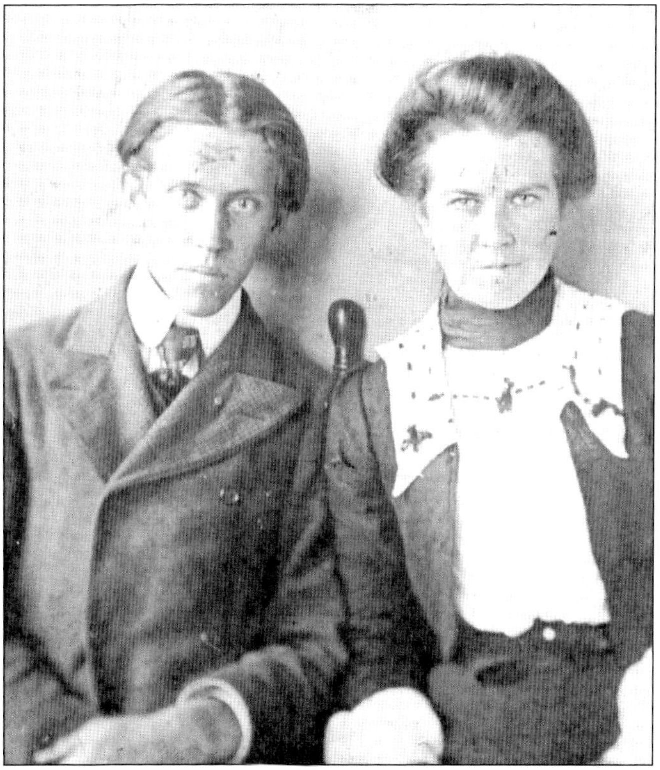

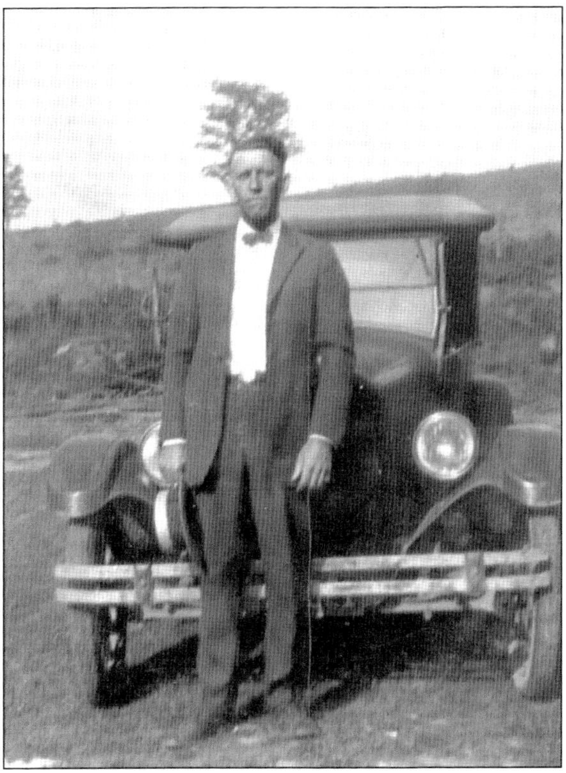

During an era when not every family owned automobiles, James Moore was well known in the Cross community, between Bristol and Blountville, for his cars. It wasn't unusual for Moore to drive neighbors to town or even farther to visit relatives on a Sunday afternoon. Moore is shown here with one of his automobiles c. 1930. (Courtesy of Bob and Marie Broyles.)

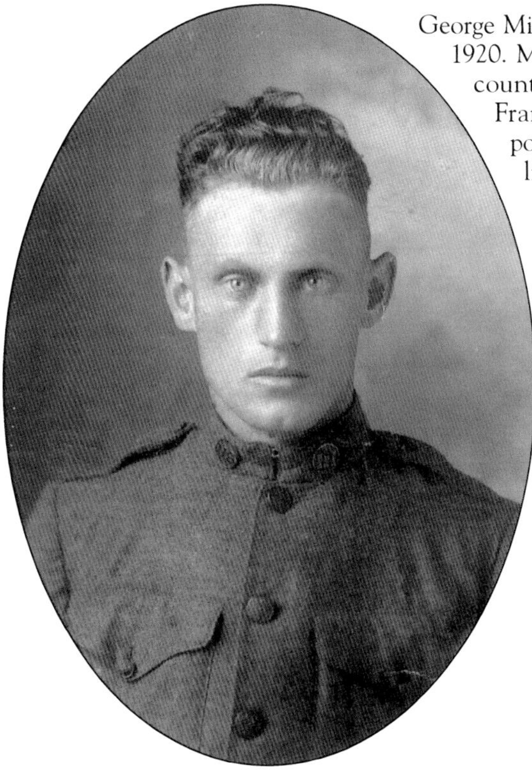

George Minnick is shown here in his army uniform c. 1920. Minnick joined the U.S. Army to serve his country during World War I. He saw action in France and was discharged after suffering gas poisoning, which troubled him for the rest of his life. After his discharge, Minnick could always be found in the Union Shoe Shop on Front Street repairing customers' shoes. (Courtesy of Marie Broyles.)

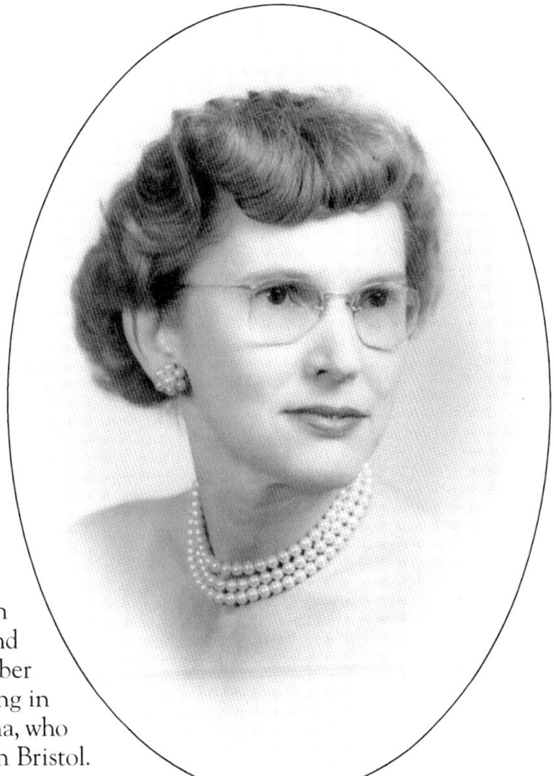

Edna Haskins taught piano in her home on Anderson Street for over 40 years to numerous local children, including her own three sons, Eugene, Bradley, and Michael, and several of her grandchildren. She is a member of First Presbyterian Church, where she sang in the church choir for more than 50 years. Edna, who is almost 100 years old, continues to live in Bristol. (Courtesy of Eugene Haskins.)

Olive Dungan, born in 1880, graduated from Virginia Institute in 1898. She married John S. Lipscomb in 1905, and they had two children, Elizabeth and John S. Lipscomb Jr. Despite this dainty photograph from 1902, Olive would often accompany her husband to Big Creek, now part of South Holston Lake, to help clear land in preparation of the dam that would be built there. Olive died in 1964. (Courtesy of Mrs. Dick Easley.)

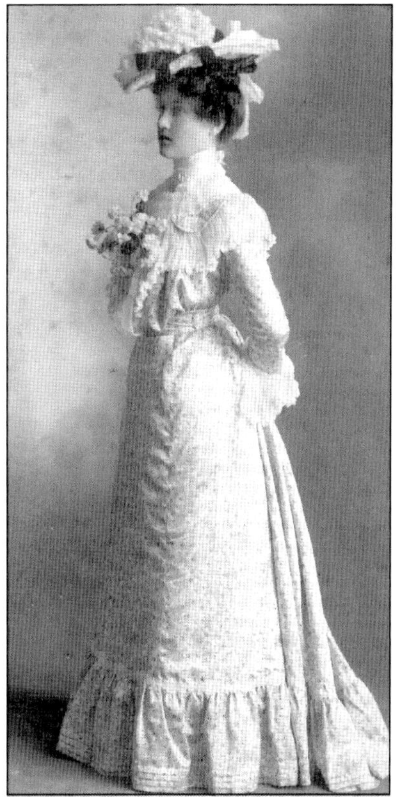

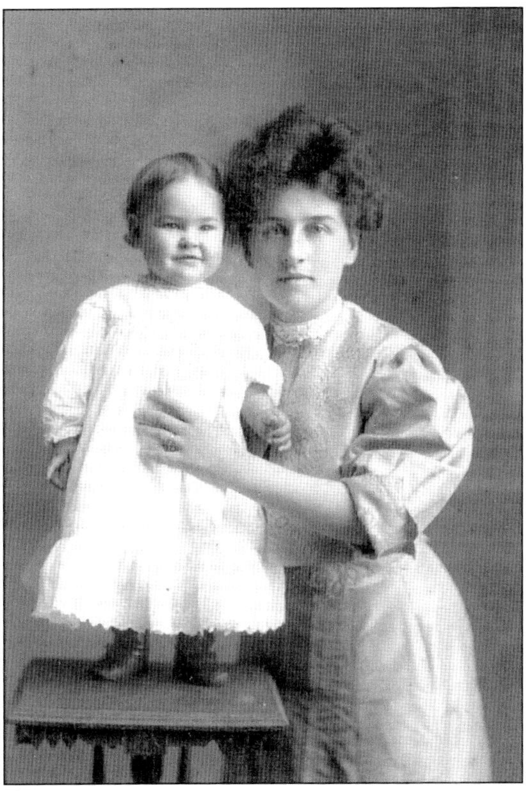

Olive Dungan Lipscomb poses with one-year-old daughter Elizabeth in this Hodges Art Gallery photograph from 1907. Olive was the wife of Big Jack Overall Company founder John S. Lipscomb. Elizabeth, a graduate of Virginia Institute, became the wife of R. M. (Slim) Easley, who owned Easley Insurance Company. The Easleys would have two children, Dick and Rachel. (Courtesy of Mrs. Dick Easley.)

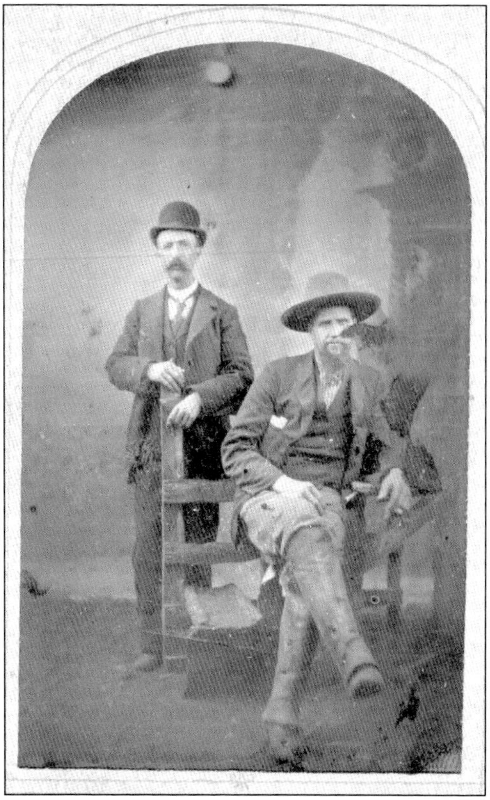

This tintype image is of a young J. L. C. Smith and likely his father, Lewis Smith. J. L. C. Smith came to Bristol with the railroad in 1872 and was the engineer between Bristol and Radford from 1876 to 1890 from the Bristol yard. He married Martha Alice Hagy of Abingdon and, following his retirement, was a well-known merchant established under the name of Smith & Waskey. (Courtesy of Tim Buchanan.)

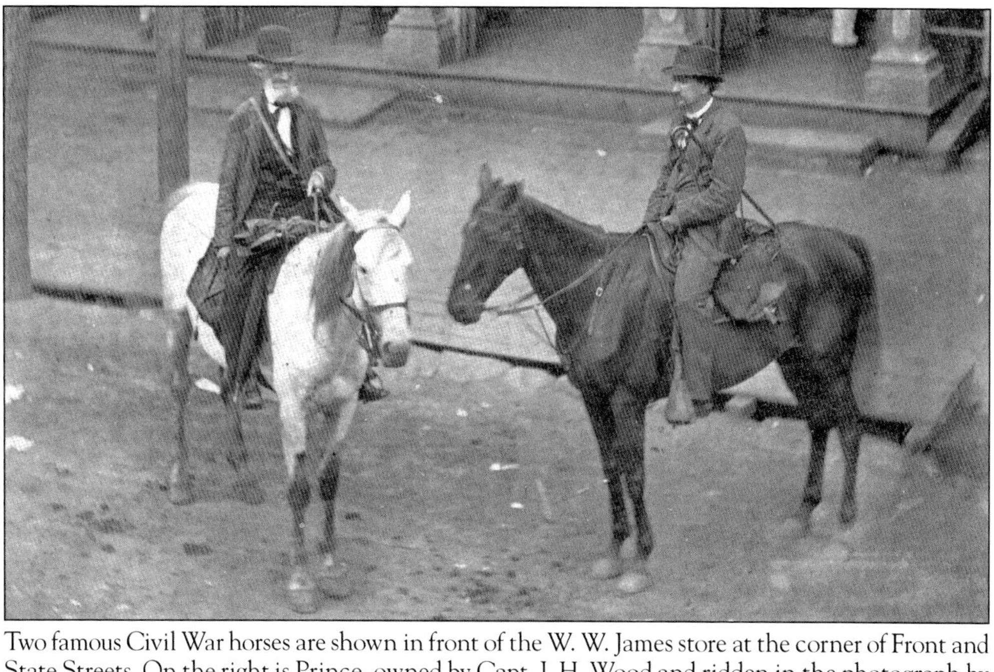

Two famous Civil War horses are shown in front of the W. W. James store at the corner of Front and State Streets. On the right is Prince, owned by Capt. J. H. Wood and ridden in the photograph by Maj. W. T. Brown. On the left is King Richard, known as Bristol's last surviving Civil War horse, ridden by Jacob Susong Carmack. King Richard died in 1896. (Courtesy of Bud Phillips.)

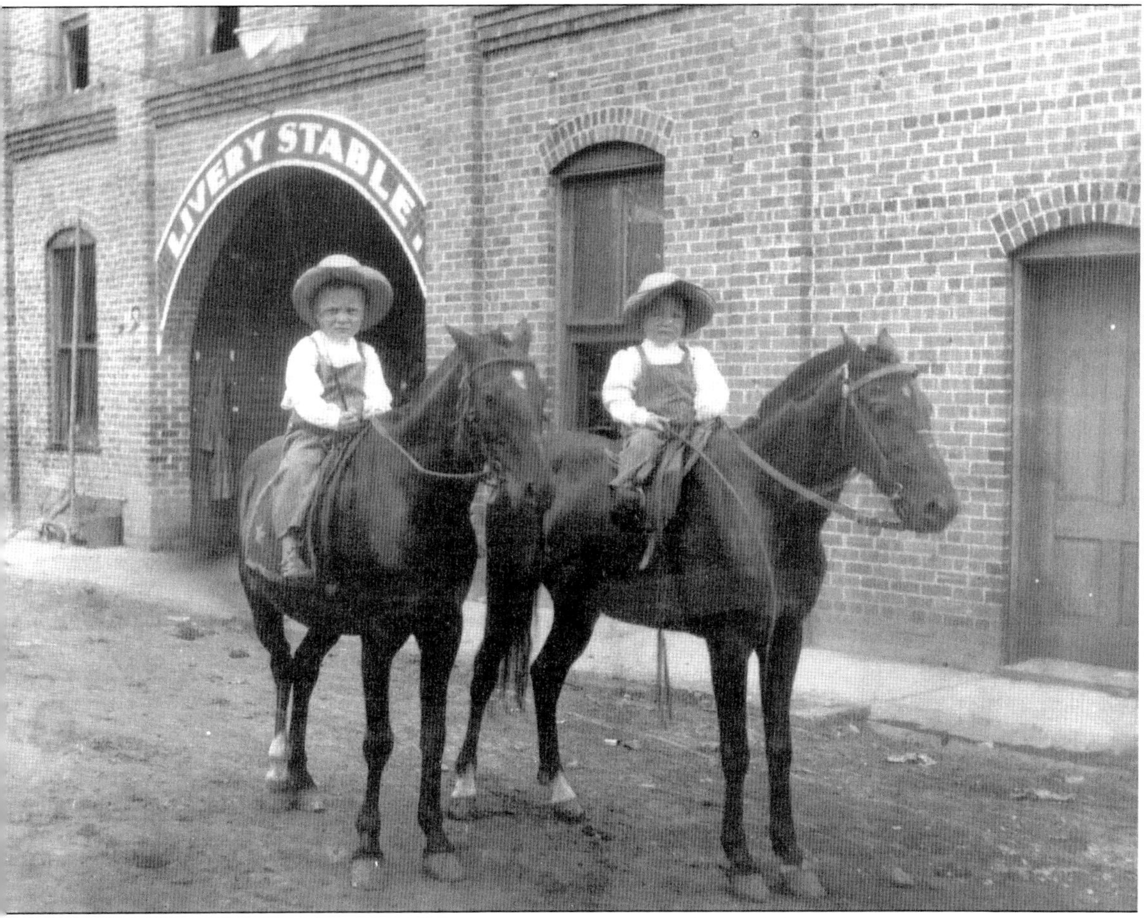

Pete (left) and Pat Moore pay a visit to their father's livery stable on Water Street in this 1906 photograph. C. P. Moore ran the livery stable for several years and later would go into the automobile business. Pete began Pete Moore Appliance in 1946, and his grandson Dudley still runs the business today in the building that once was the Lee Theatre. Pete's daughter, known as Monkey, owns Pete Moore's Antiques. Pete died in 1984 at the age of 81 and Pat (C. P. Jr.) died in 1957 at the age of 55. (Courtesy of Bristol Historical Association.)

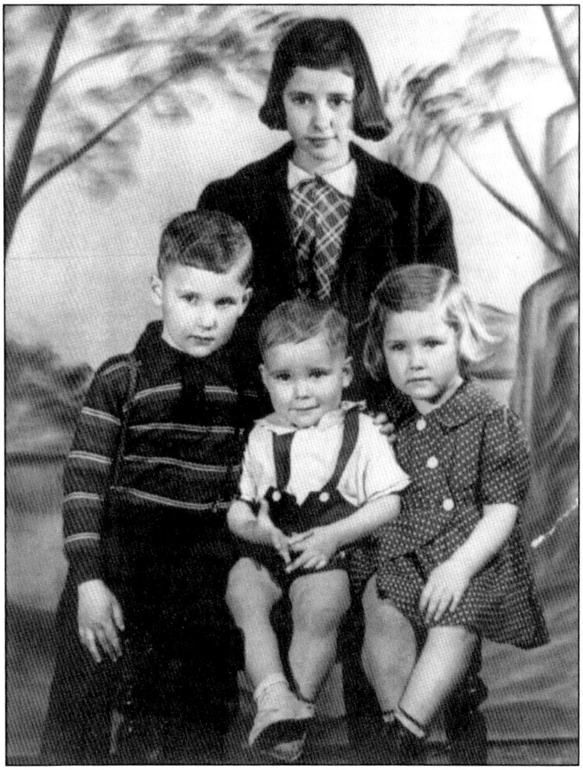

D. A. and Ida Allison were the proud parents of eight children. Shown here in 1943 are the first four. From left to right are (first row) Dewey Jr., Jerry, and Joyce; (second row) Lila. D. A. Allison came to Bristol in 1927 from Saltville, Virginia. Lila, Jerry, and Joyce still reside in Bristol, but Dewey Jr. passed away in 1985. (Courtesy of Joyce Kistner.)

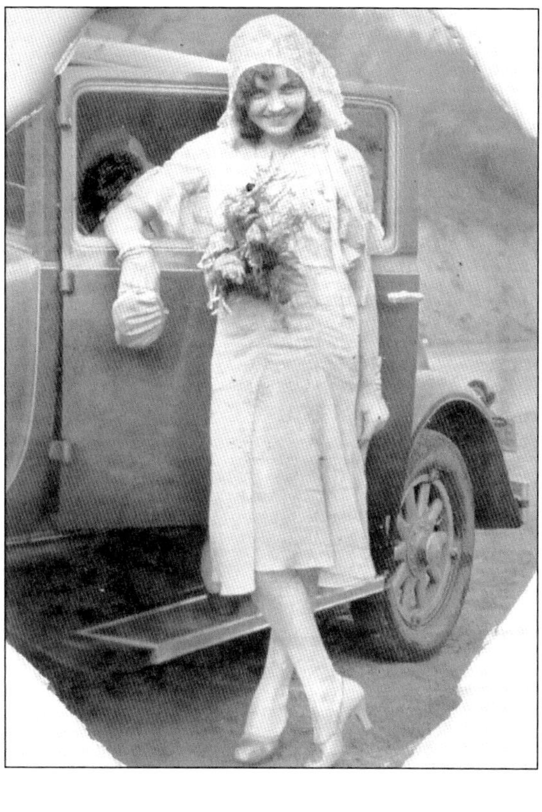

Ethel Cawood posed for this photograph during Easter *c.* 1931. Ethel married R. T. Helton in 1932 and later owned Bristol Antiques on West State Street. (Courtesy of Barbara Jane Maust.)

C. M. McGee, shown here *c.* 1915, lived at 332 Seventh Street and was a dealer for Wyrick Mineral Water. The water arrived in 55-gallon drums from McGee Mineral Spring Company of Crockett, Virginia. McGee then sold the water in five- and one-gallon containers. McGee died in February 1933 from injuries sustained in an automobile accident on the Bluff City Highway. (Courtesy of Lois Nolley.)

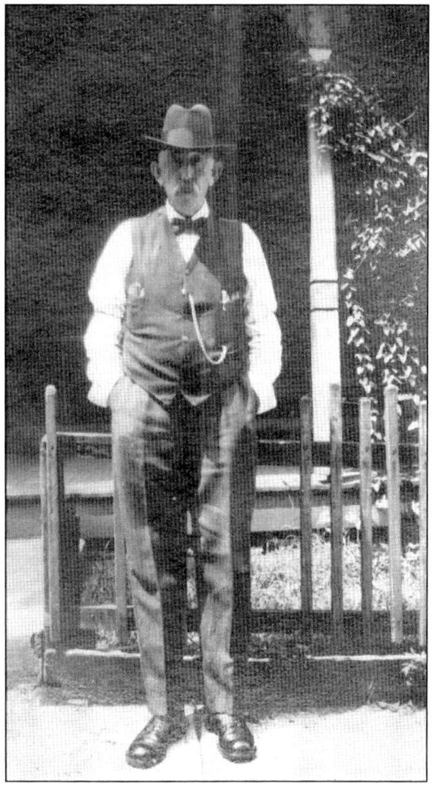

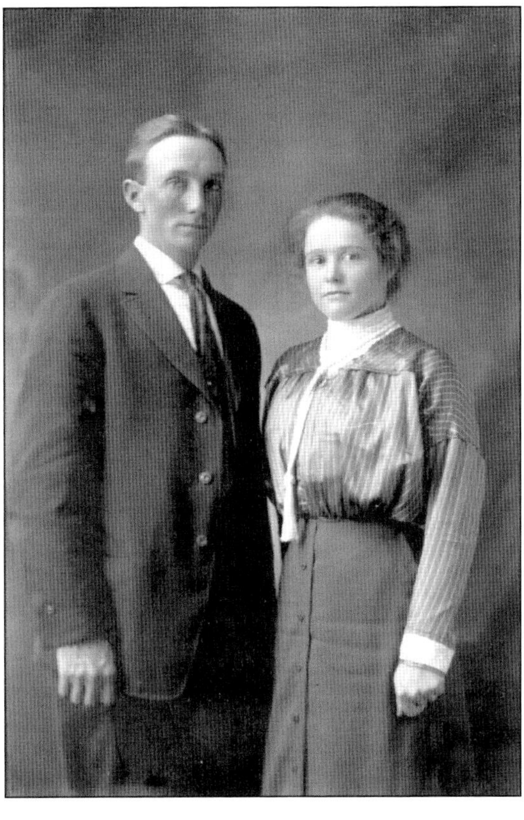

As it is today, the celebration of a marriage was a popular time to take photographs. Nettie Newland Grubb and Ira Jasper Phillips Grubb were married on October 28, 1914, when this photograph was taken. Nettie worked for Rutherford Freight Lines. The couple had nine children, one of whom only lived four days. (Courtesy of Beth Grayson Taylor and Patt Grayson Phipps.)

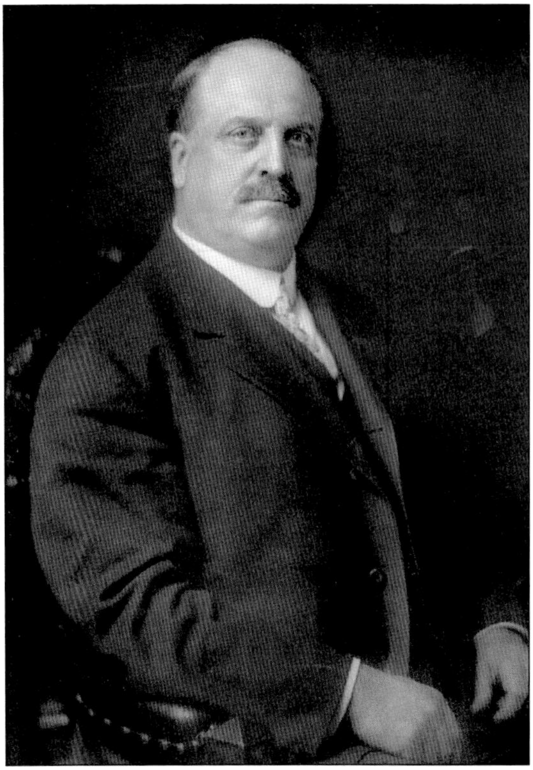

Benjamin Lewis Dulaney III was a Bristol businessman responsible for the organization of Virginia Iron and Coke Company as well as the Black Mountain Coal Company. He served as commissioner to the Paris Exposition of 1900 and the St. Louis Exposition of 1904. Dulaney was also one of the founders of the Boy Scouts of America. He lived from 1857 to 1930. (Courtesy of Rocky Mount Historical Association.)

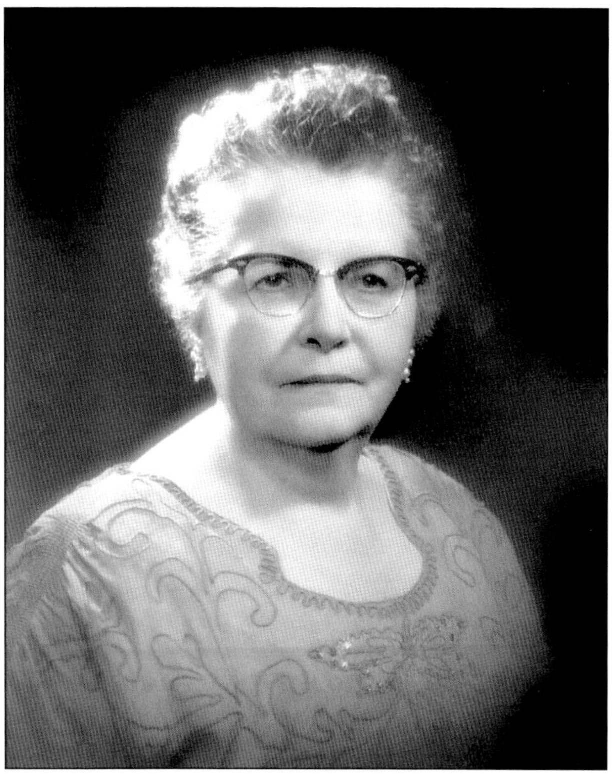

Pauline Massengill DeFriece is remembered for her commitment to the community, particularly in the areas of education, religion, local history, and business. She served as secretary-treasurer of S. E. Massengill Company, chaired the committee that secured a location for Bristol's first public library, helped organize an outpatient clinic at Bristol Memorial Hospital, and was an elementary school teacher. She was chairman of the Bristol, Tennessee, School Board and fought for equal pay for black teachers. One of her greatest contributions came when she supervised the preservation and development of Rocky Mount, which opened to the public in 1961. (Courtesy of Rocky Mount Historical Association.)

J. W. Lynn served as mayor of Bristol from 1926 to 1928. He was also president of the Chamber of Commerce and president of the First National Bank. (Bristol Historical Association.)

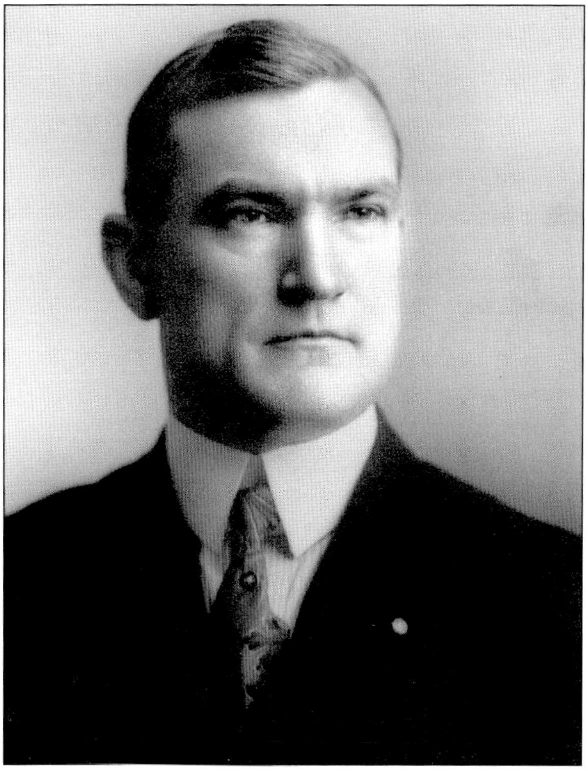

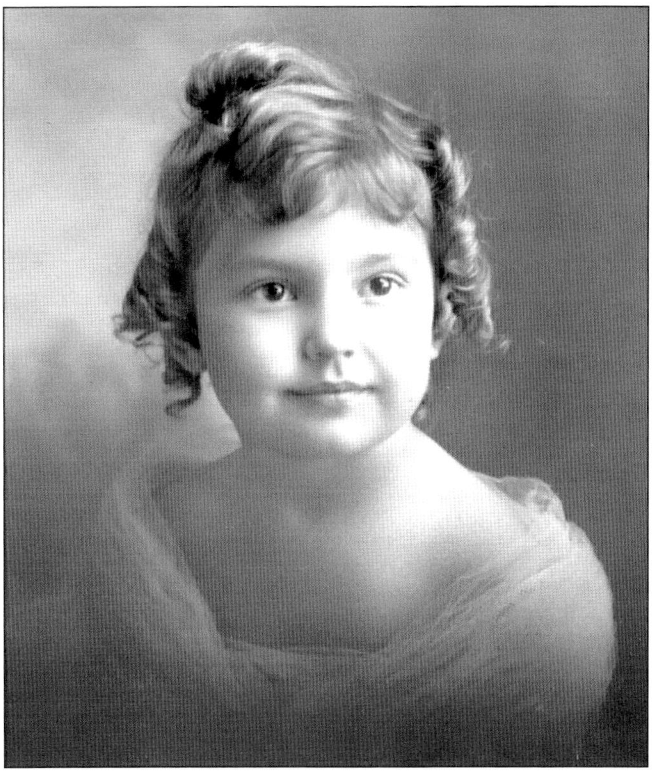

Evelyn Shankel, shown here c. 1918, was born and raised just outside of Bristol near the Clay Pot off Highway 126. She married Robert Baskerville Sr., who operated a Gulf station on Ninth and State Streets. Evelyn worked as a credit manager for several businesses and died on July 4, 1976. Their son, Robert Jr., owns and operates the Clay Pot Greenhouses today. (Courtesy of Bob Baskerville.)

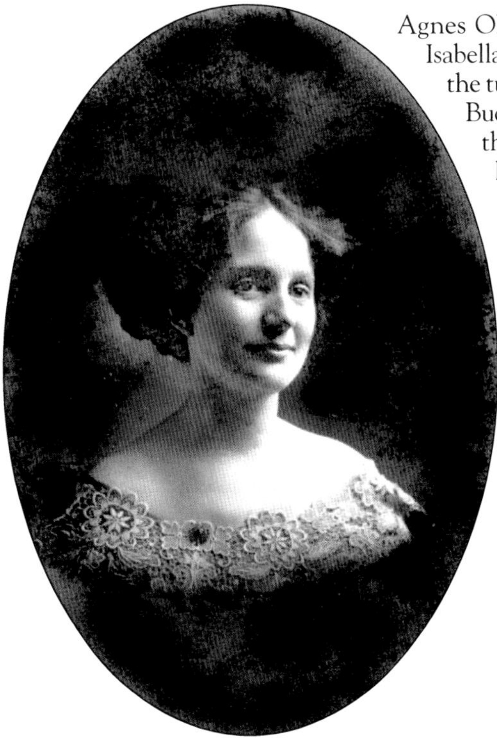

Agnes Oliver Buchanan and her parents, Richard and Isabella Oliver, moved to Bristol with the railroad around the turn of the century. In 1903, Agnes married Preston Buchanan, who served as vice president/treasurer of the Faucette Company for over 50 years. The couple lived most of their married life on Lee Street and reared four children. Agnes, known for her kind hospitality, died September 8, 1970. (Courtesy of Tim Buchanan.)

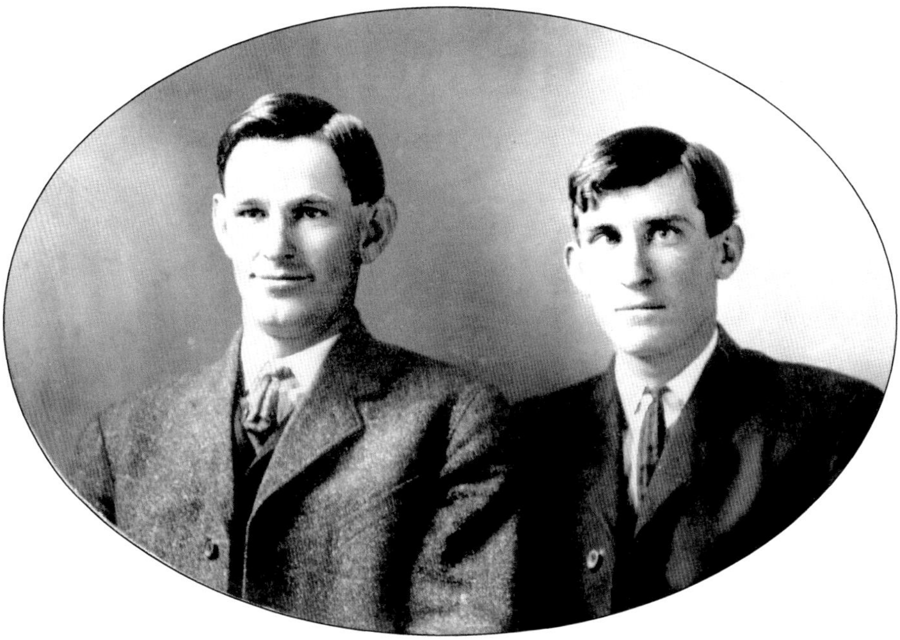

J. M. Shell (left) and J. M. Phipps (right) were brothers-in-law. Phipps worked for the railroad in Bristol. This handsome photograph was taken c. 1906. (Courtesy of Beth Grayson Taylor and Patt Grayson Phipps.)

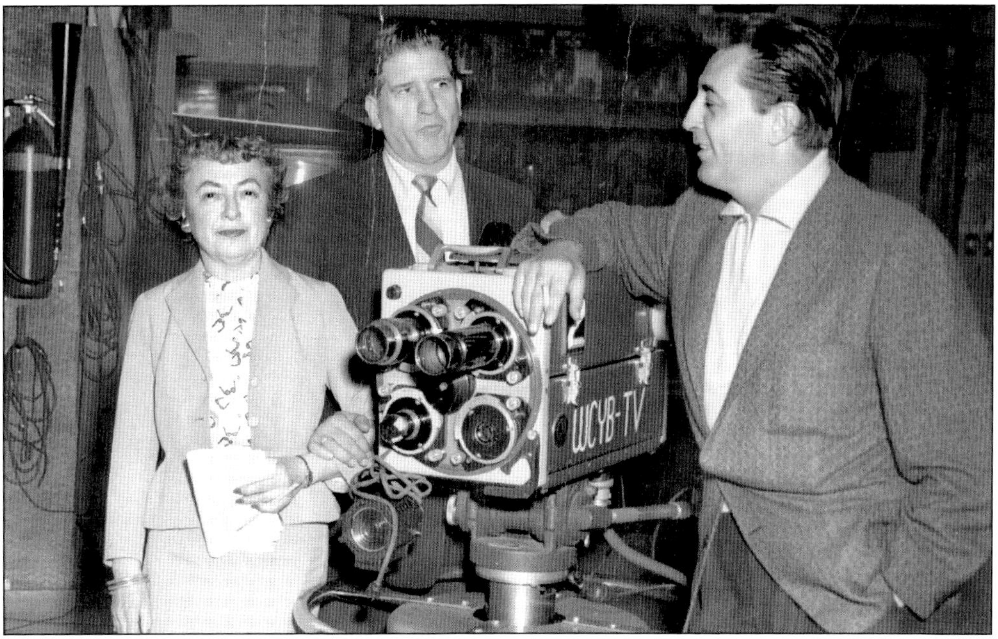

Robert and Mary Porterfield (of Barter Theatre fame) are shown here with actor Robert Mitchum (far right) at a March of Dimes Telerama, which WCYB produced from the late 1950s through the early 1980s. The telerama differed from most fund-raisers because it was locally produced. WCYB programmed all 18.5 hours, from 11:30 Saturday night through 6:00 p.m. on Sunday. (Information courtesy of WCYB; photograph from authors' collection.)

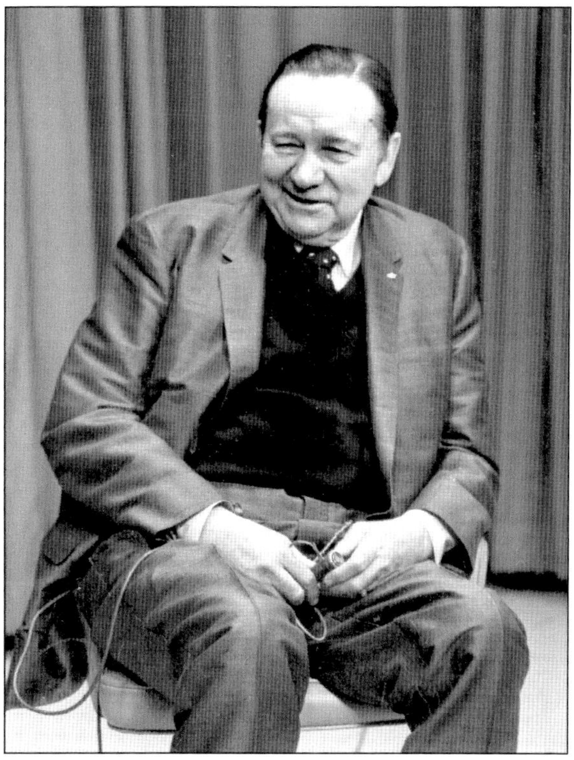

Through WCYB's teleramas were produced locally, the station did bring in nationally known hosts such as Pernell Roberts, Michael Landon, or Ken Delo (*The Lawrence Welk Show*). Local talent performed throughout the program, the news team gathered and read pledges on-air, and the host kept the program moving. Shown here is country music singer and actor Tex Ritter, probably from a telerama. (Information courtesy of WCYB; photograph from authors' collection.)

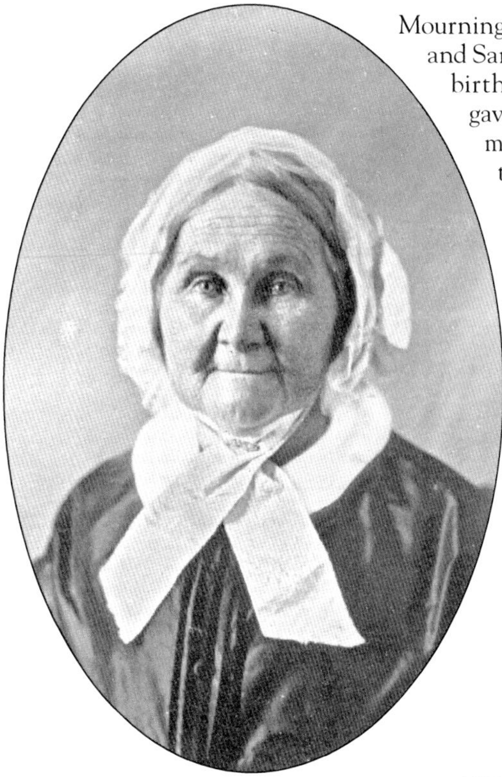

Mourning Micajah Watkins was the daughter of Micajah and Sarah Watkins. Micajah died before his daughter's birth in 1796, and his widow, then in mourning, gave her the unusual name. At age 16, Mourning married James King, who had just purchased a vast tract of land, which now encompasses much of downtown Bristol. Their sixth child, Melinda Williams King, married Joseph R. Anderson, founder of Bristol, on June 3, 1845. (Courtesy of Tim Buchanan.)

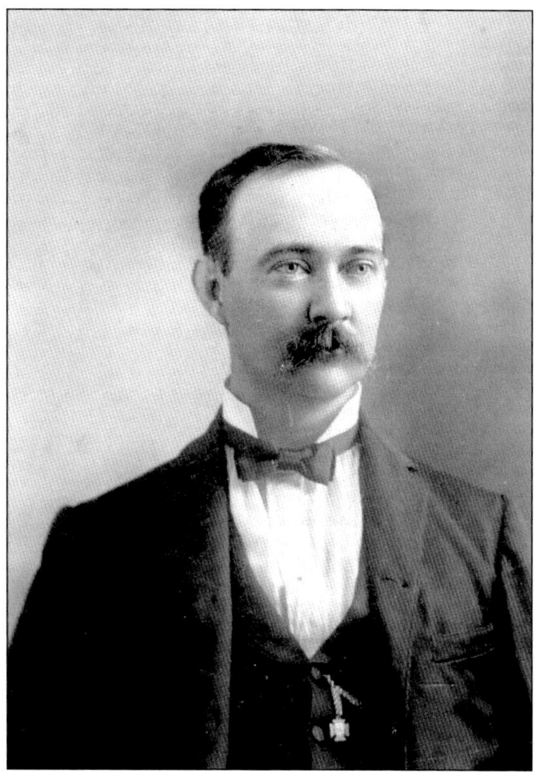

Col. Samuel Lee King, born July 20, 1863, was the grandson of the Reverend James King, whose land was used as the foundation of Bristol. The Colonel, as he was called, served as Bristol, Tennessee, mayor and president of the Bristol-Goodson Water Company. King married Annie Phipps in a grand wedding in Kingsport on June 6, 1894. The couple had four children. King died November 27, 1928. (Courtesy of Tim Buchanan.)

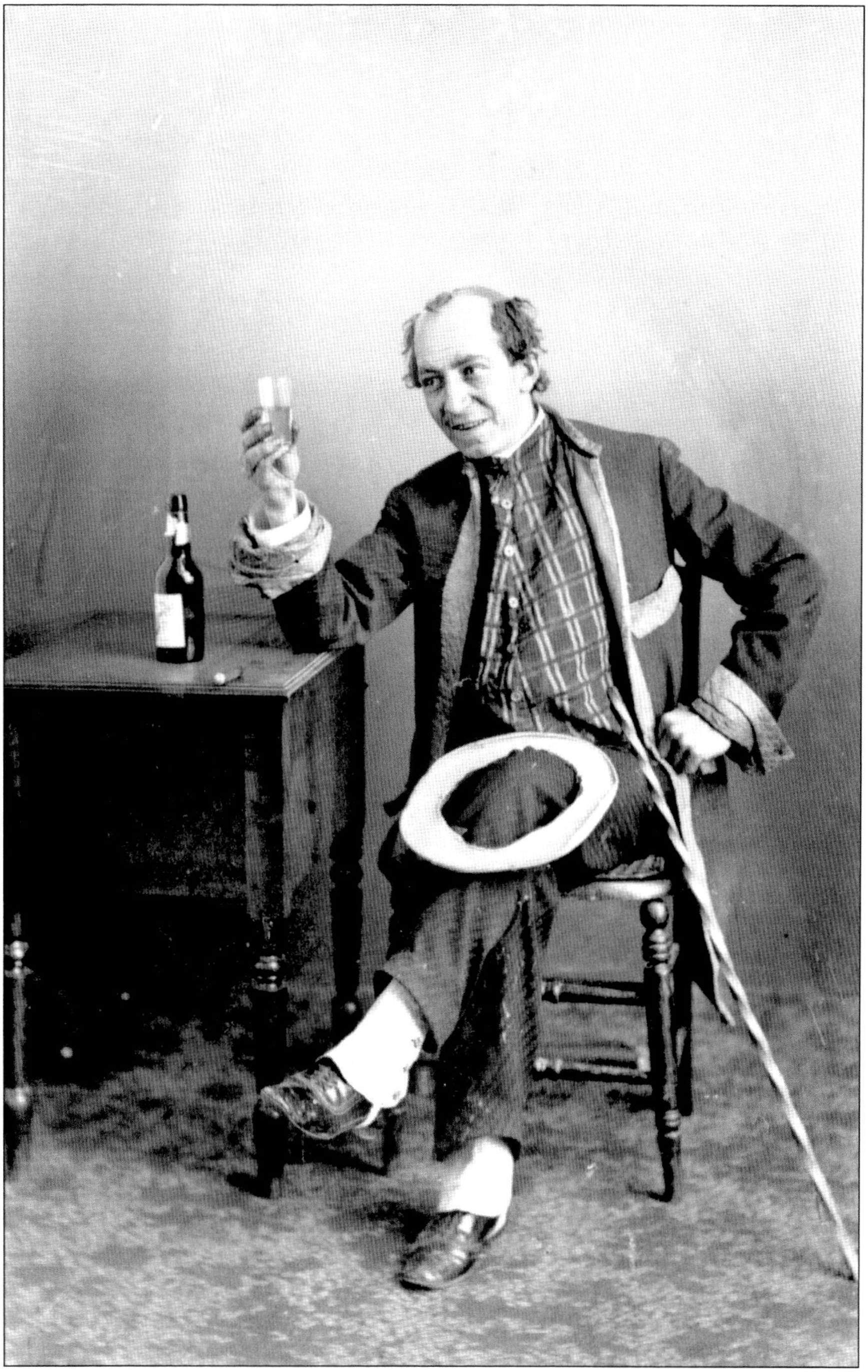

Oliver Taylor Sr. was an actor and playwright around the turn of the 20th century. Most of his acting, which took place from 1886 to 1913, could be viewed at the Harmeling Opera House located on the second floor of a building in downtown Bristol. Taylor also traveled all over the country playing Shakespeare. He died in 1923 at the age of 61. The Harmeling Opera House and Taylor were instrumental in having Robert Porterfield come back to the region to start the Barter Theatre in Abingdon, Virginia. (Courtesy of Bristol Historical Association.)

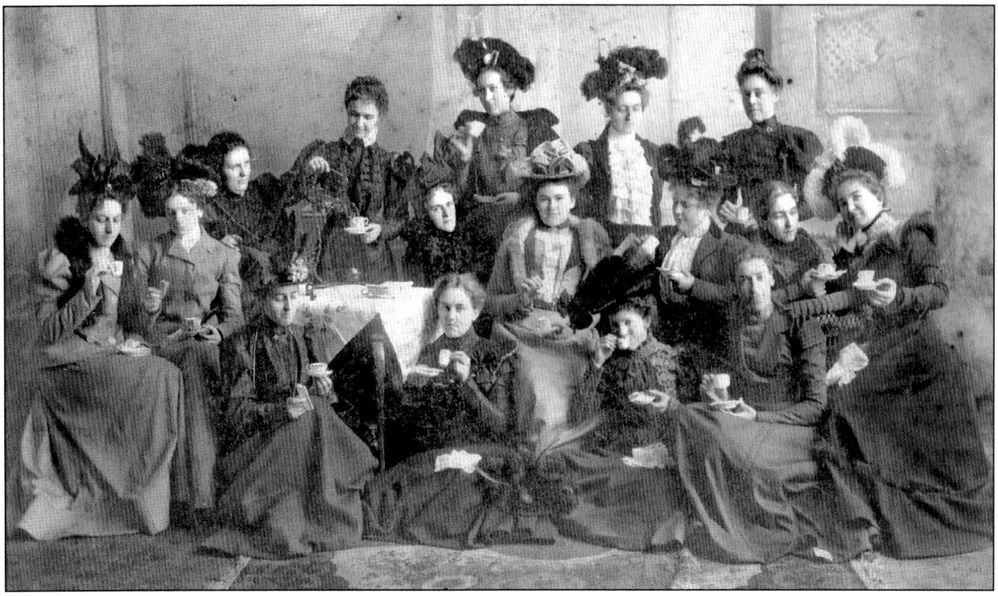

Fannie Williamson came from Winston-Salem, North Carolina, to become Mrs. John C. Anderson in the late 1800s. Mrs. Anderson is shown here with some of her best friends at a tea party comparable to a modern-day bridal shower. John was president of the First National Bank in Bristol, Tennessee, and served as mayor. (Courtesy of Fan Hepburn.)

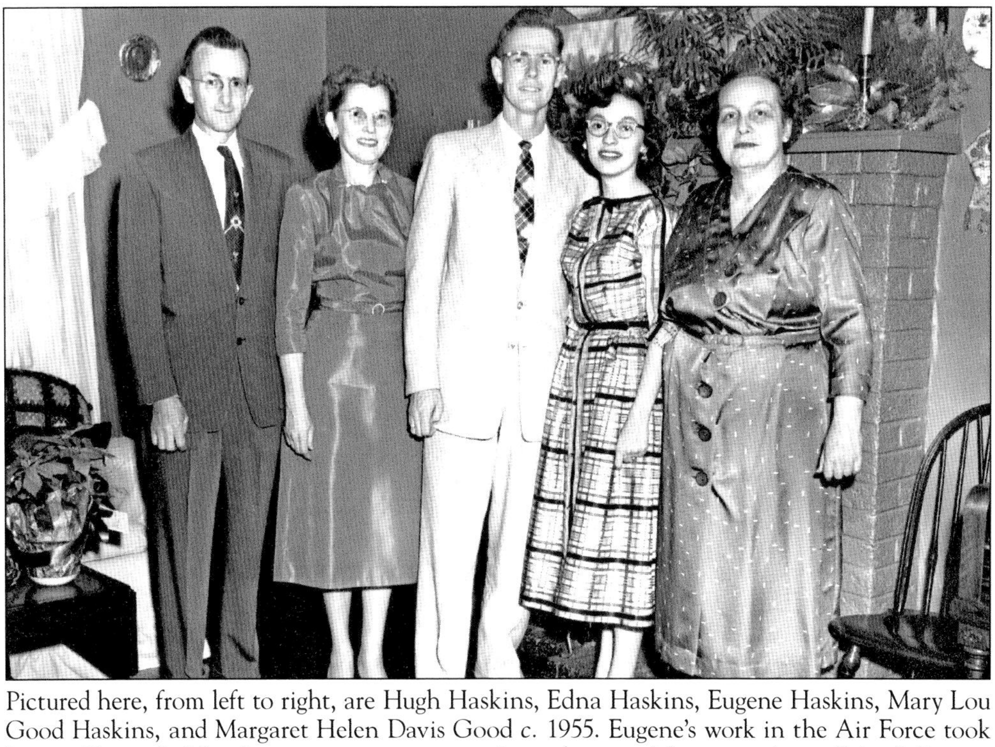

Pictured here, from left to right, are Hugh Haskins, Edna Haskins, Eugene Haskins, Mary Lou Good Haskins, and Margaret Helen Davis Good c. 1955. Eugene's work in the Air Force took him and his wife, Mary Lou, to numerous countries and states. After returning to Bristol, Eugene worked at Sperry Corporation and then King College for a number of years before he retired in 2000. (Courtesy of Eugene Haskins.)

An election notice from 1887 provides some interesting insight into the early voting procedure in Bristol. (Courtesy of Tim Buchanan.)

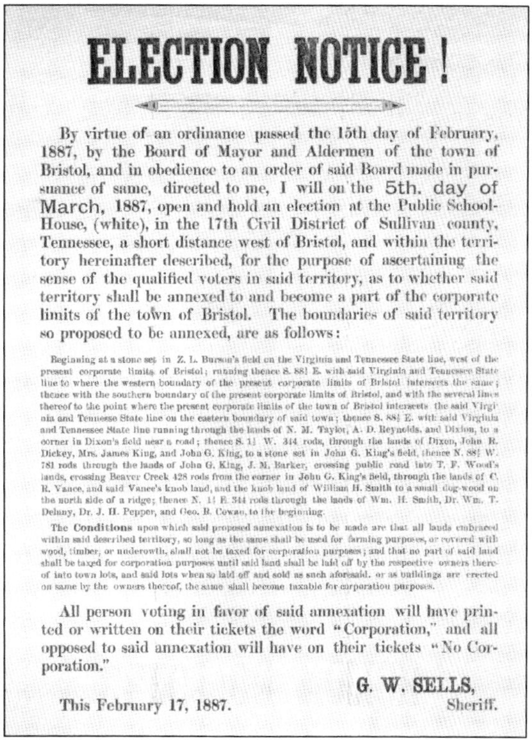

ELECTION NOTICE!

By virtue of an ordinance passed the 15th day of February, 1887, by the Board of Mayor and Aldermen of the town of Bristol, and in obedience to an order of said Board made in pursuance of same, directed to me, I will on the 5th. day of March, 1887, open and hold an election at the Public School-House, (white), in the 17th Civil District of Sullivan county, Tennessee, a short distance west of Bristol, and within the territory hereinafter described, for the purpose of ascertaining the sense of the qualified voters in said territory, as to whether said territory shall be annexed to and become a part of the corporate limits of the town of Bristol. The boundaries of said territory so proposed to be annexed, are as follows:

Beginning at a stone set in Z. L. Burson's field on the Virginia and Tennessee State line, west of the present corporate limits of Bristol; running thence S. 88½ E. with said Virginia and Tennessee State line to where the western boundary of the present corporate limits of Bristol intersects the same; thence with the southern boundary of the present corporate limits of Bristol, and with the several lines thereof to the point where the present corporate limits of the town of Bristol intersects the said Virginia and Tennesse State line on the eastern boundary of said town; thence S. 88½ E. with said Virginia and Tennessee State line running through the lands of N. M. Taylor, A. D. Reynolds, and Dixion, to a corner in Dixon's field near a road; thence S. 1½ W. 344 rods, through the lands of Dixon, John R. Dickey, Mrs. James King, and John G. King, to a stone set in John G. King's field, thence N. 88½ W. 781 rods through the lands of John G. King, J. M. Barker, crossing public road into T. F. Wood's lands, crossing Beaver Creek 428 rods from the corner in John G. King's field, through the lands of C. R. Vance, and said Vance's knob land, and the knob land of William H. Smith to a small dog-wood on the north side of a ridge; thence N. 1½ E. 344 rods through the lands of Wm. H. Smith, Dr. Wm. T. Delany, Dr. J. H. Pepper, and Geo. R. Cowan, to the beginning.

The **Conditions** upon which said proposed annexation is to be made are that all lands embraced within said described territory, so long as the same shall be used for farming purposes, or covered with wood, timber, or underowth, shall not be taxed for corporation purposes; and that no part of said land shall be taxed for corporation purposes until said land shall be laid off by the respective owners thereof into town lots, and said lots when so laid off and sold as such aforesaid, or as buildings are erected on same by the owners thereof, the same shall become taxable for corporation purposes.

All person voting in favor of said annexation will have printed or written on their tickets the word "Corporation," and all opposed to said annexation will have on their tickets "No Corporation."

G. W. SELLS,
Sheriff.

This February 17, 1887.

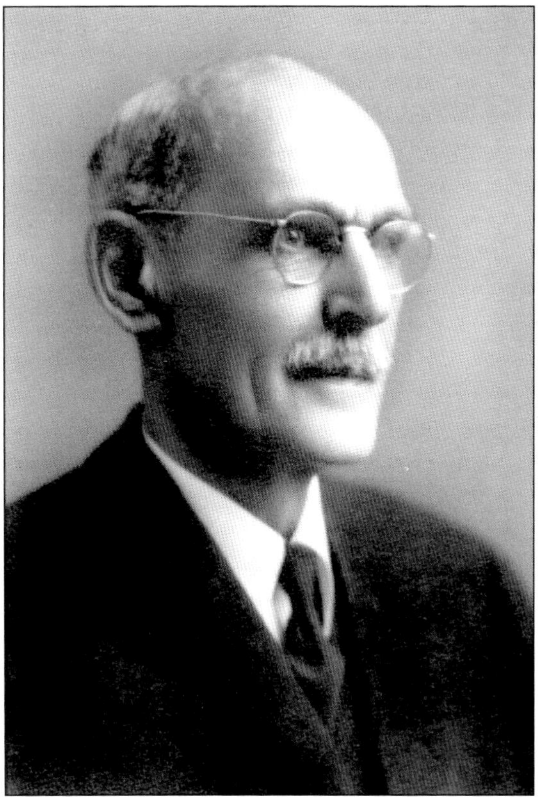

John S. Lipscomb was born on July 11, 1878. He served in the Spanish-American War and came to Bristol from Staunton, Virginia, in 1905. Lipscomb lived at 549 Alabama Street and organized what would become the Big Jack Overall Manufacturing Company, shown on page 47. He was a member of the First Baptist Church. Lipscomb died on January 9, 1946. (Courtesy of Mrs. Dick Easley.)

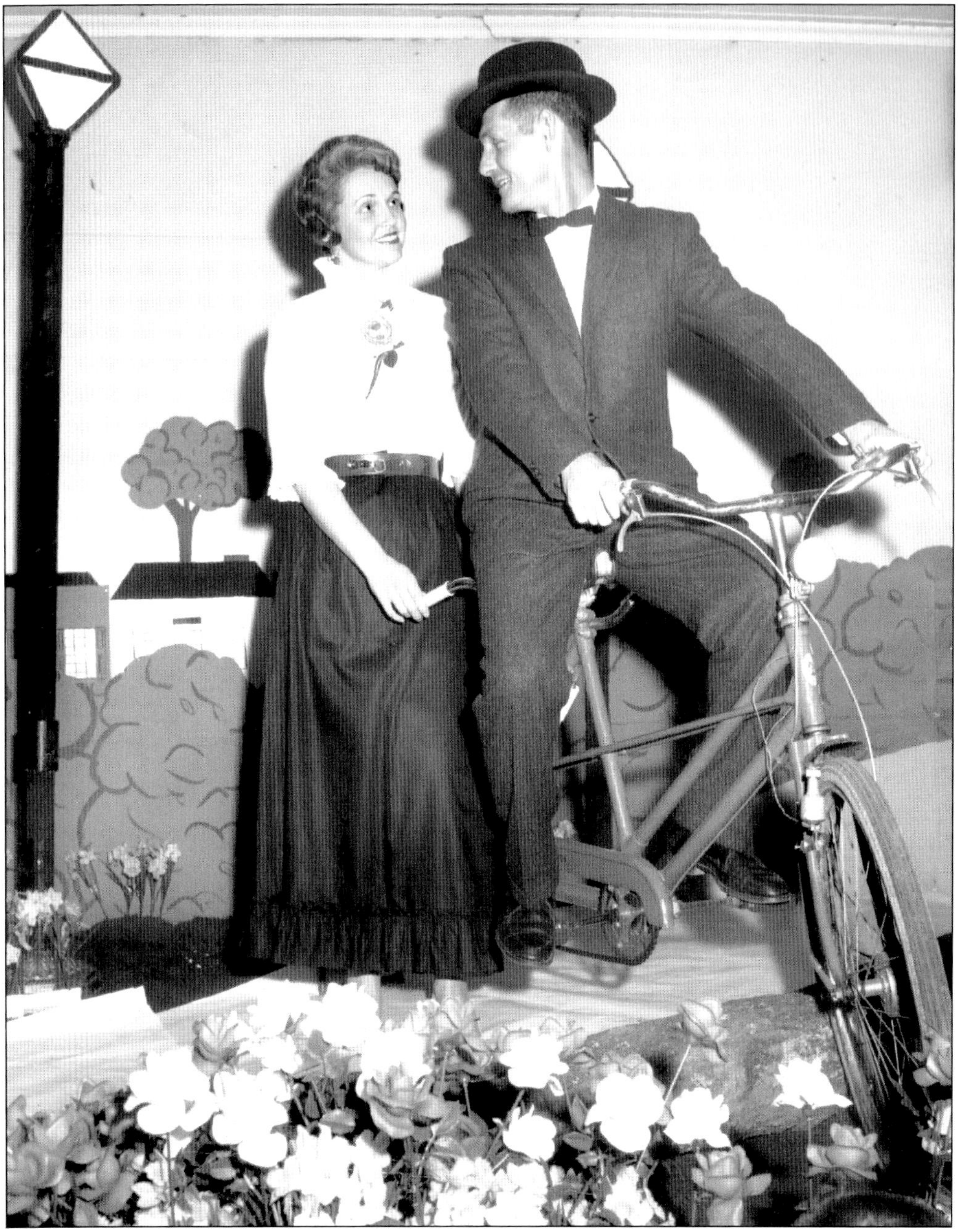

Genelle and Don Combs were married on March 29, 1940. They are shown here singing "Bicycle Built for Two" during a sweetheart banquet at Calvary Baptist Church *c.* 1947. Don and Genelle have passed on a firm Christian heritage to their children, grandchildren, and great-grandchildren and have been a wonderful example to others in the community as well. (Courtesy of Don and Genelle Combs.)

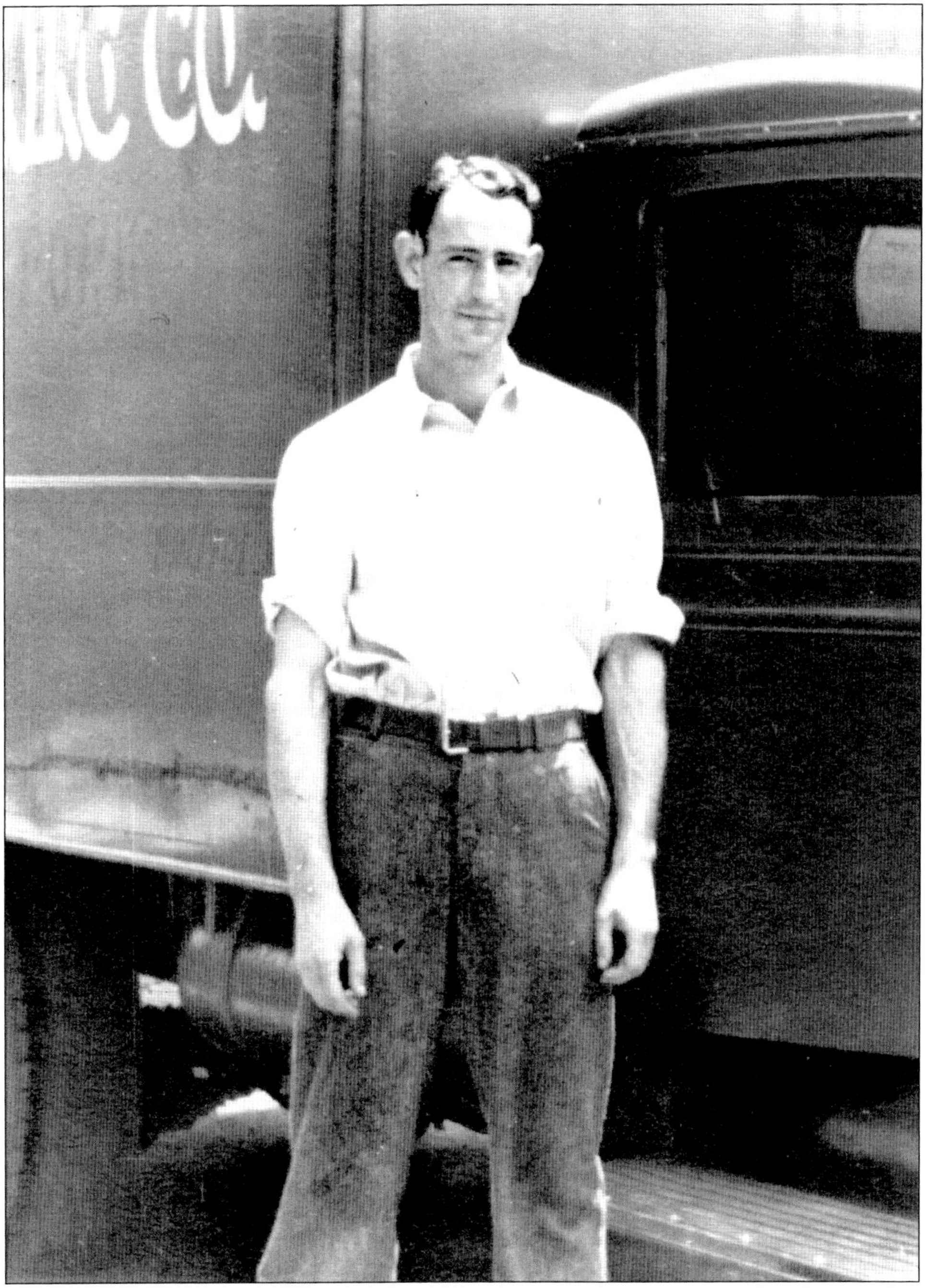

Charles H. (Billy) Aronhime stands in front of one of his father's trucks used at the Aronhime Packing Company c. 1940. Billy, a graduate of Bristol High School in Virginia and King College, worked at Aronhime Packing before entering the U.S. Air Force in February 1942 as a warrant officer. Aronhime, who was serving in Edmonton, Canada, was flying home on April 17, 1945, for his parents' 37th wedding anniversary when the Pennsylvania Central Airlines transport he and 20 others were riding crashed on a mountainside near Morgantown, West Virginia. Aronhime was 35 years old. (Courtesy of Tim Buchanan.)

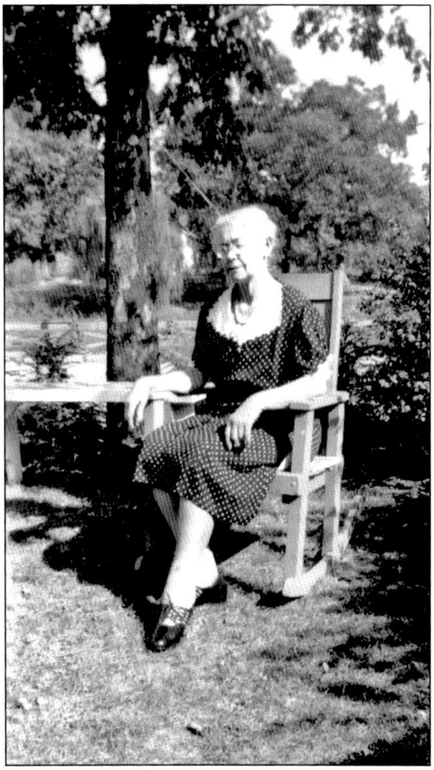

When the Bristol, Tennessee, Fire Department went from a horse-drawn engine to a red mechanized one, the firemen named the engine Huldah in honor of young Huldah Henninger's flaming red locks. Huldah (November 10, 1881–March 21, 1976) was also a Prohibition activist and remembered, at the age of 12, singing in a Prohibition program at the Harmeling Opera House. As an adult, Huldah married John B. Chambers. (Courtesy of King and Peggy Rogers.)

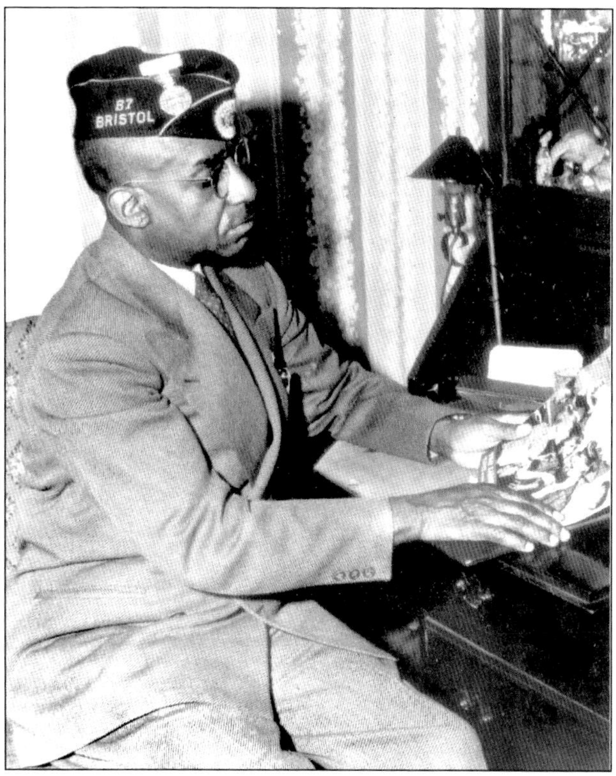

Hobart Shand served as district deputy commander of the VFW for the state of Tennessee, having the responsibility of visiting all the African American posts in Tennessee. Shand, shown here in 1954, served in the U.S. Army and worked in Bristol for Hotel Bristol and Hecht's Bakery. Shand also organized and coached the first football team at Douglass High School and was secretary of the Southern Little League. He died on February 5, 1955. (Courtesy of Bristol Historical Association.)

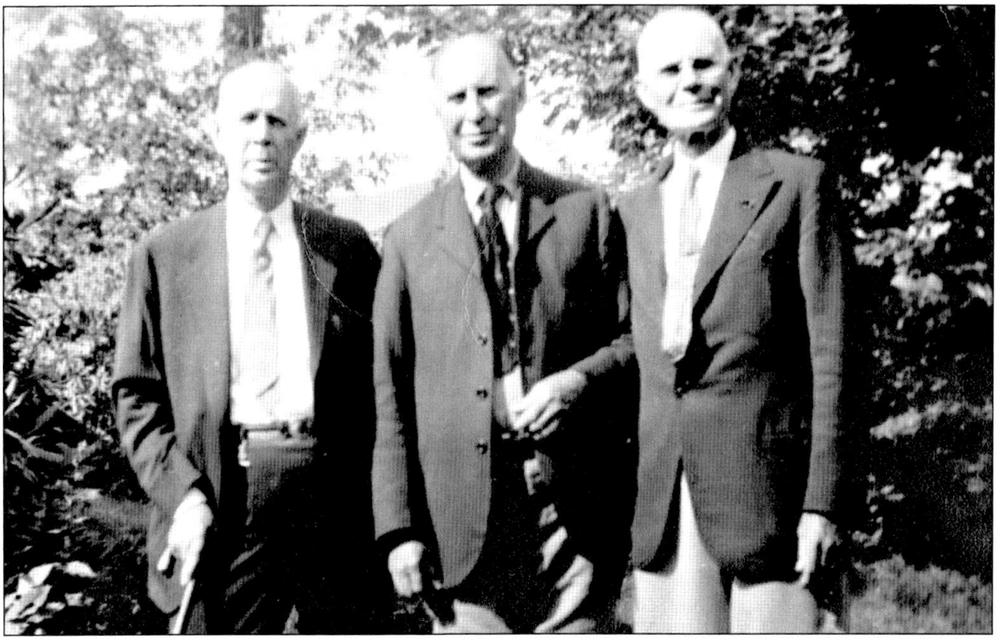

The three distinguished Vance brothers pictured here, from left to right, are Charles R. Vance (October 1, 1867–February 26, 1947), Dr. James I. Vance (September 25, 1862–November 24, 1939), and Dr. Joseph A. Vance (November 17, 1864–June 12, 1951). Charles was a lawyer and the other two brothers were ministers. (Courtesy of the Rocky Mount Historical Association.)

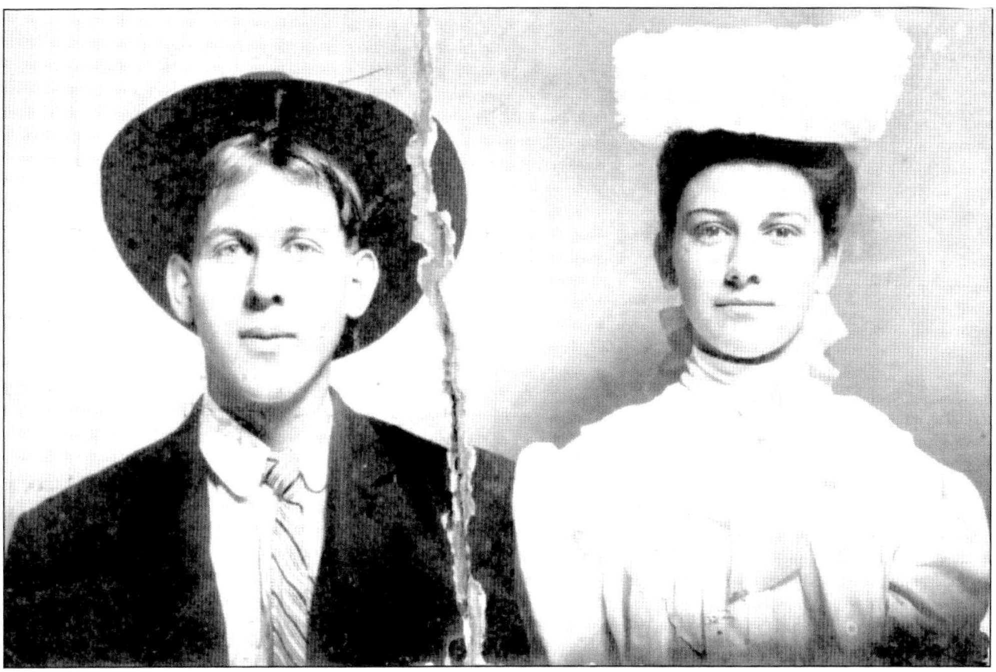

Joe Shankel (left) lived in the Three Springs community in Bristol, Virginia, from September 6, 1889, to August 19, 1934. Joe was a carpenter and a farmer. Maude (right) had the traditional homemaking duties of a loving wife and mother. The couple had four sons and one daughter. This photograph was taken c. 1912. (Courtesy of Kim Jones.)

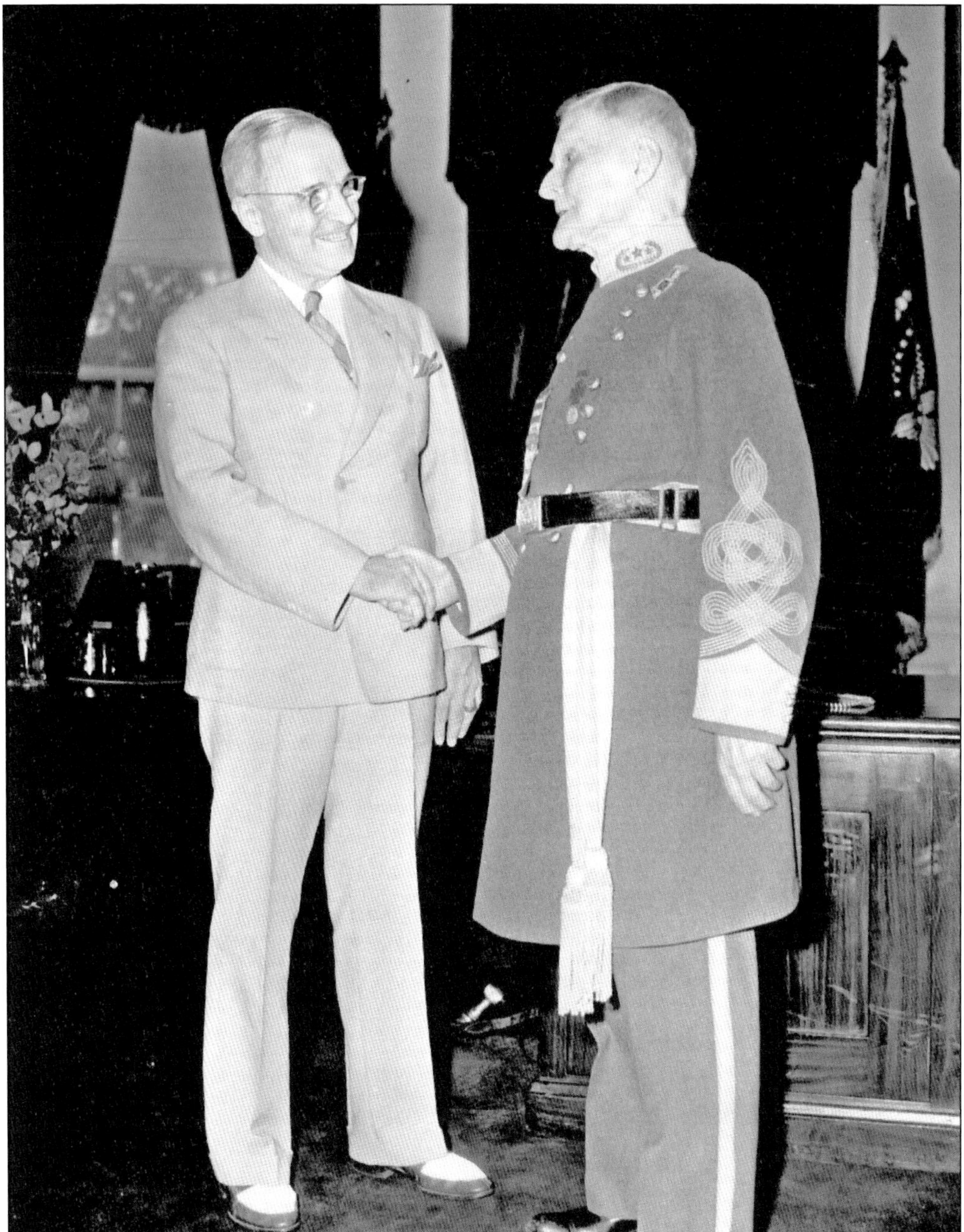

Julius Franklin Howell was born on January 17, 1846, in Nansemond County, Virginia. At age 16, he enlisted in the Confederate army and reached a rank of corporal, serving much of the time as a courier. After the war, he owned an insurance business in Bristol and served as president of Virginia Intermont College in 1901. On June 2, 1945, at age 99, Gen. Julius Franklin Howell traveled to Washington, D.C., to meet with Pres. Harry S. Truman, with whom he is shown here. "General" was an honorary title. Howell died on June 19, 1948, at his home on Moore Street. (Courtesy of Tony Marion.)

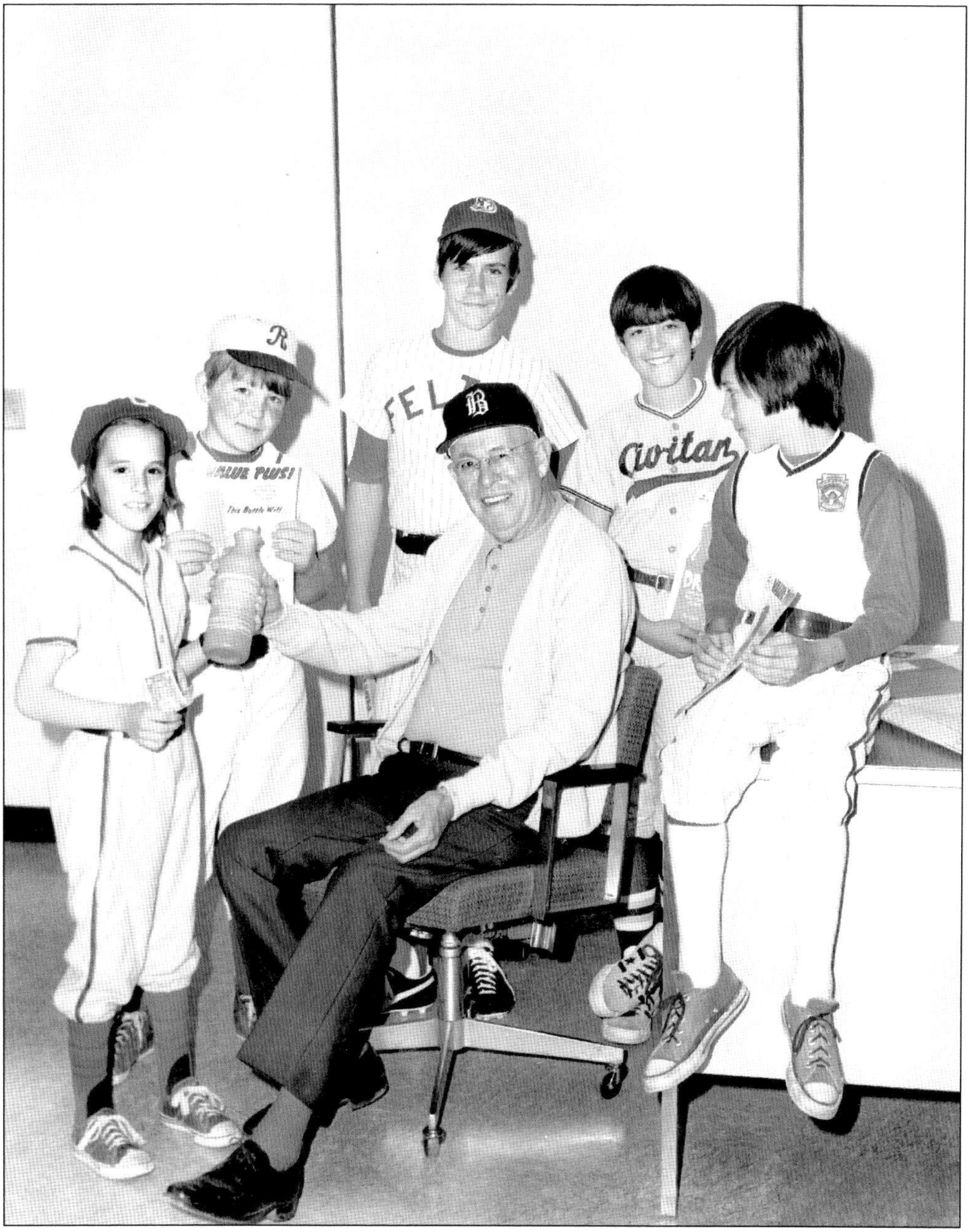

Gene "Pappy" Thompson is surrounded by young athletes c. 1970. Thompson graduated from Virginia High School, enrolled at Emory and Henry College, then transferred to King College, where he played basketball. In the late 1920s, Thompson became a part-time sports writer for the *Bristol Herald Courier* and later served as sports editor and executive sports editor. Even after his 1979 retirement, he continued to write his popular column "Looking at Sports." Thompson was elected to the Tennessee Sports Hall of Fame in 1982 and to the Virginia Sports Wall of Fame in 1987, a year before his death. (Courtesy of Jeanne Hurt.)

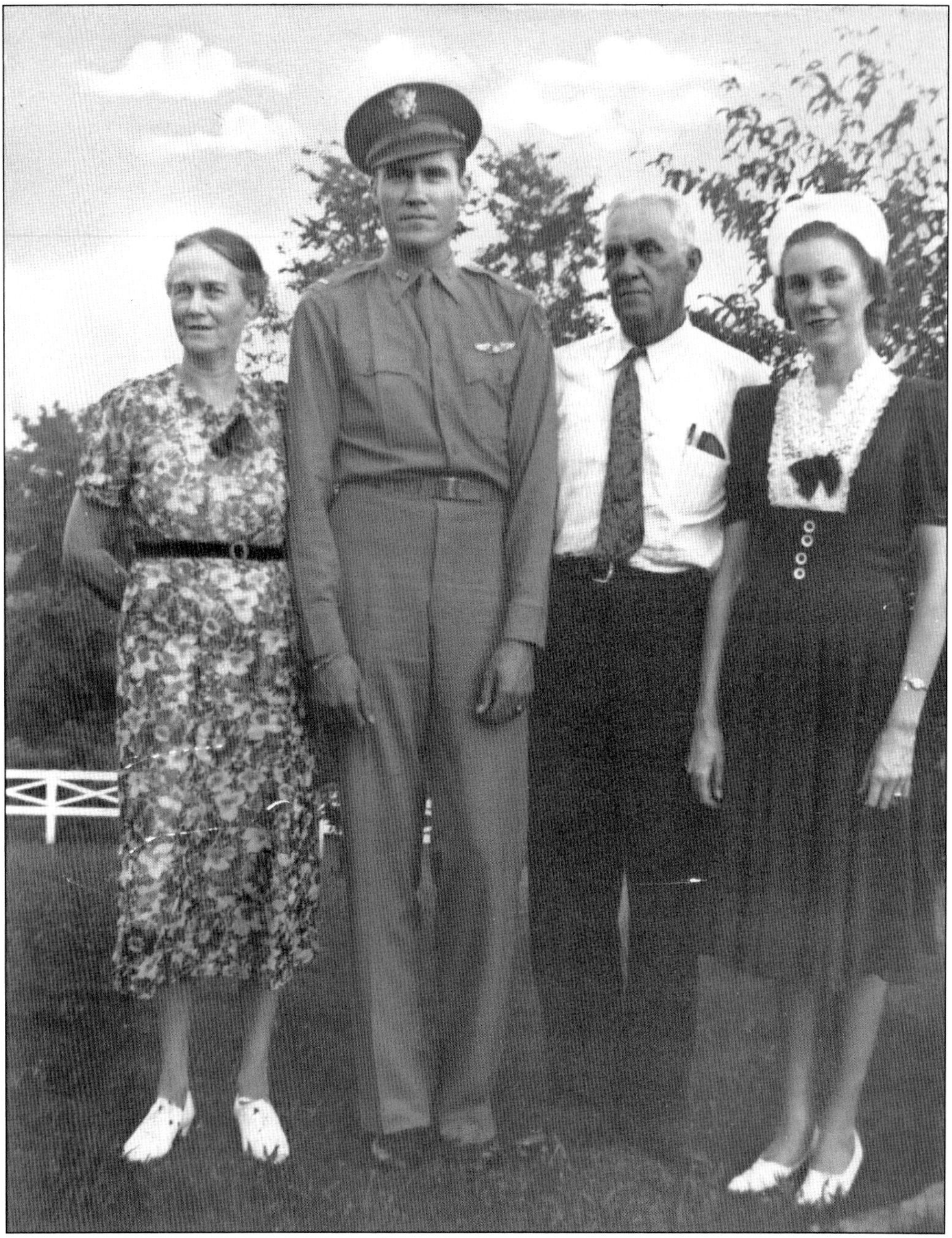

Members of the Crosswhite family gather for a photograph before Alfred leaves for duty in the U.S. Army Air Corps. Pictured from left to right are Lelia Crosswhite, Alfred Crosswhite, Worley Crosswhite, and Virginia Crosswhite. Alfred entered the corps on November 7, 1941, and was reported missing in action in the South Pacific on December 15, 1942, while piloting a B-25 Mitchell bomber on a routine flight from New Guinea to Australia. Wreckage of the plane was discovered a year later. The Patton-Crosswhite VFW Post in Bristol was named in his honor as he was Bristol, Virginia's first World War II casualty. (Courtesy of Lucretia Vance Gilmer.)

Two

BUILDINGS AND HOMES

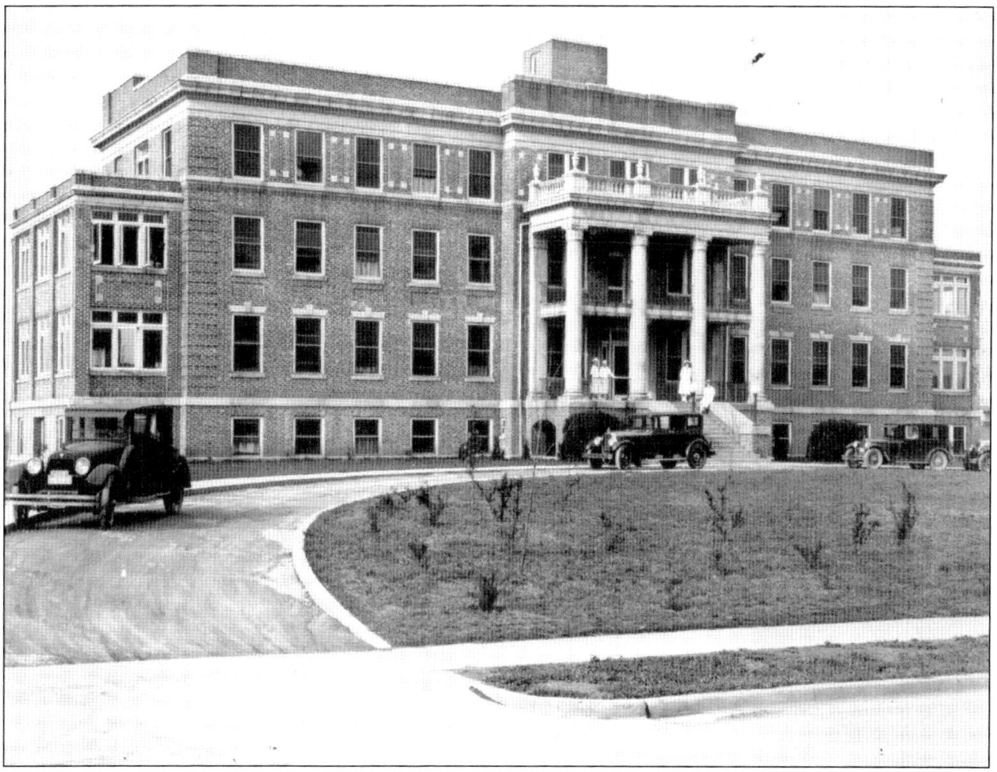

The King's Mountain Hospital, located on West State Street in Bristol, Virginia, opened on November 11, 1925, and a dormitory for the nurses opened in the 1940s. Doctors and nurses served sick people in the community at this 50-bed facility until the new 132-bed Bristol Memorial Hospital opened on January 18, 1953, and King's Mountain Hospital closed. (Courtesy of Sid Oakley.)

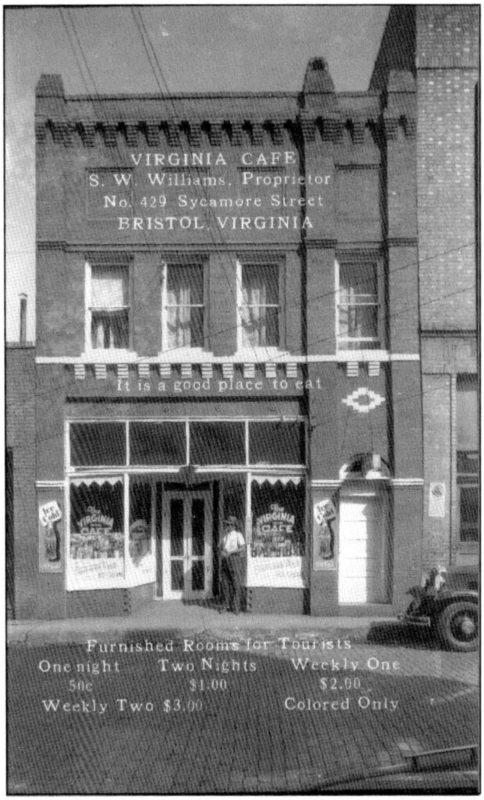

An advertisement for the Virginia Café, located at 429 Sycamore Street, lists prices for overnight accommodations for "colored only" tourists *c.* 1935. The price for one night in a furnished room was 50¢. Two nights cost $1, one week cost $2, and two weeks cost $3. The proprietor was S. W. Williams. (Courtesy of Walter Doane.)

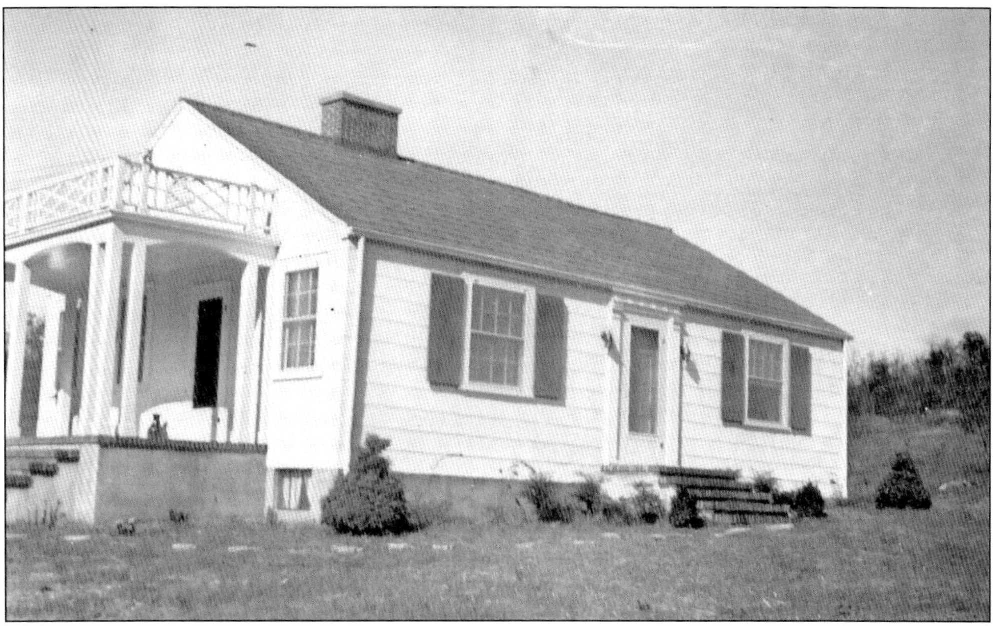

Architect Allen Dryden of Kingsport designed this Cape Cod home, which was built in 1938 for Doug Hale. Hale lived in the house with his wife and three daughters. He sold the home in 2001 to Scott and Katherine Thompson, who now live there with their children Alex and Nicholas. (Courtesy of Scott and Katherine Thompson.)

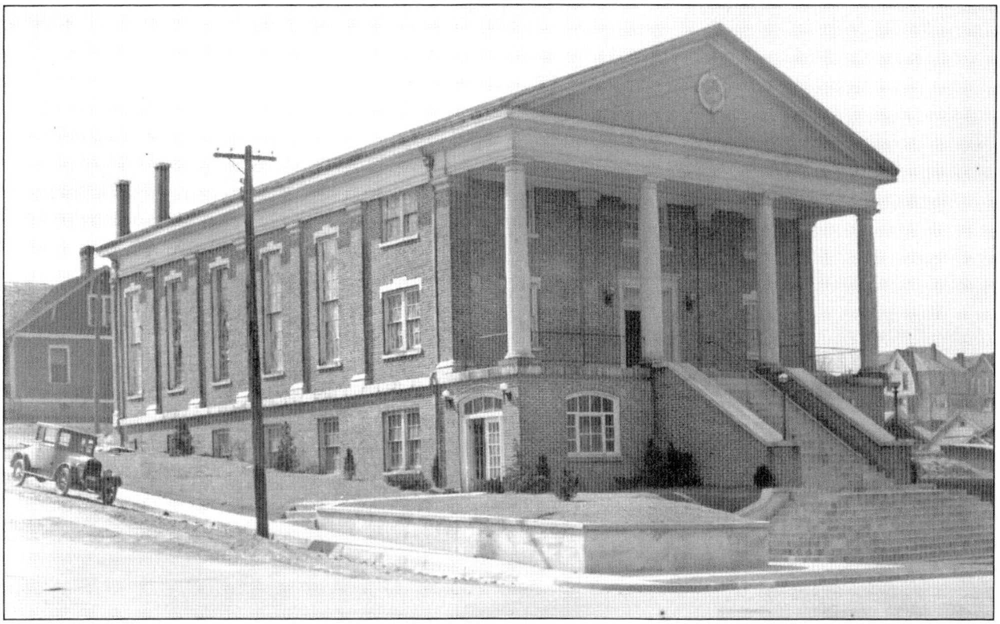

Euclid Avenue Baptist Church was first conceived by J. B. Denton and W. E. Glover, who had prayed for a church on the vacant lot at the Euclid Avenue and Park Street corner. The lot was purchased for $6,000, and permanent organization occurred on July 15, 1928, in the Virginia High auditorium. The first services were held in the basement of the present church in October 1928. (Courtesy of Euclid Avenue Baptist Church.)

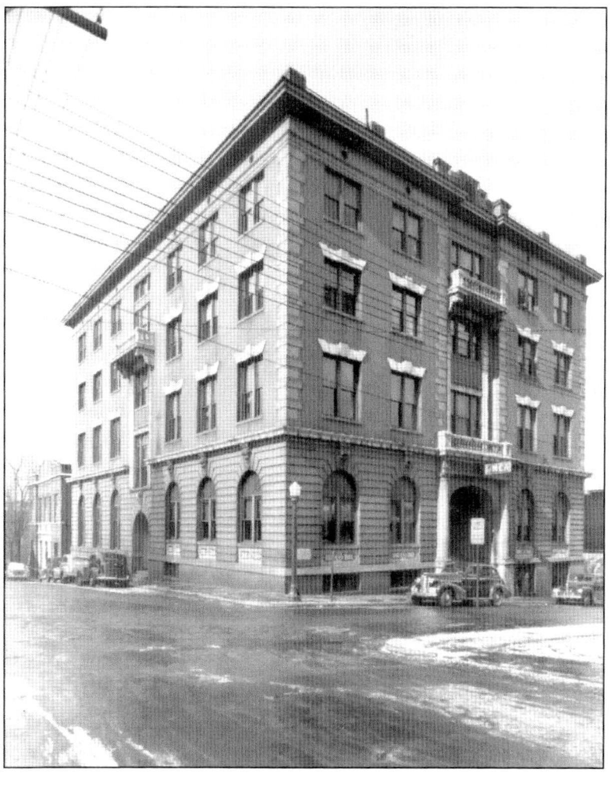

Bristol's YMCA was organized in 1884 in a small frame building on Fourth Street. In 1908, a four-story building with two bowling alleys, gymnasium, swimming pool, and 32 dorm rooms was constructed at the corner of Fifth and Shelby Streets. This YMCA building, now a Bristol landmark and office building, served the youth of Bristol until 1968, when the YMCA moved to a building on Edgemont Avenue. (Courtesy of Sid Oakley.)

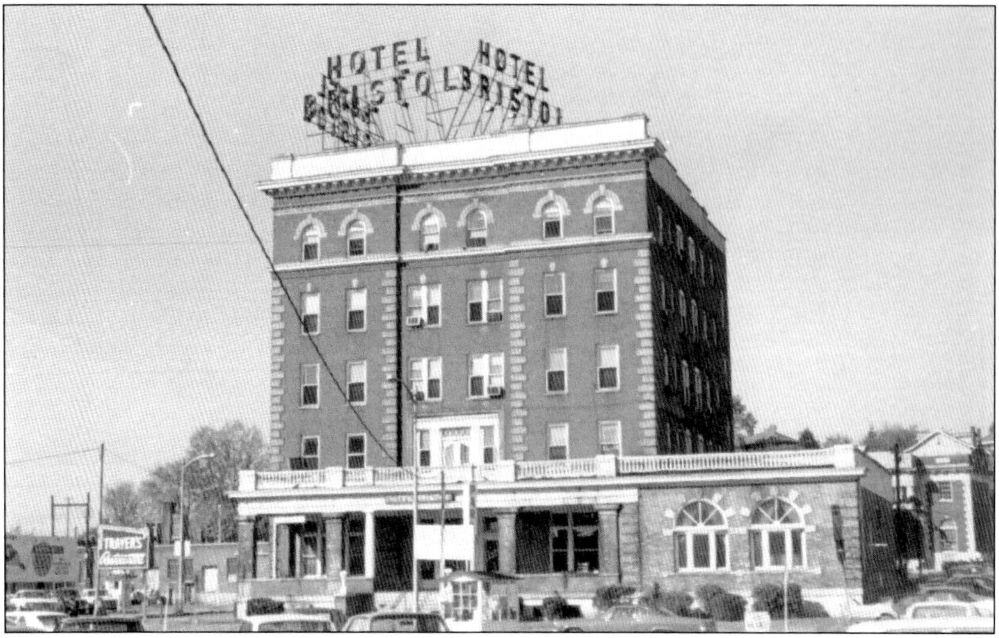

Hotel Bristol opened for business in 1907, and a long list of notable persons such as Pres. John F. Kennedy visited the five-story structure located on Moore Street in downtown Bristol. In the early 1970s, Hotel Bristol closed its doors. While plans were being made to tear down the old landmark, a fire turned the once fine hotel into rubble on May 19, 1973. (Courtesy of the authors' collection.)

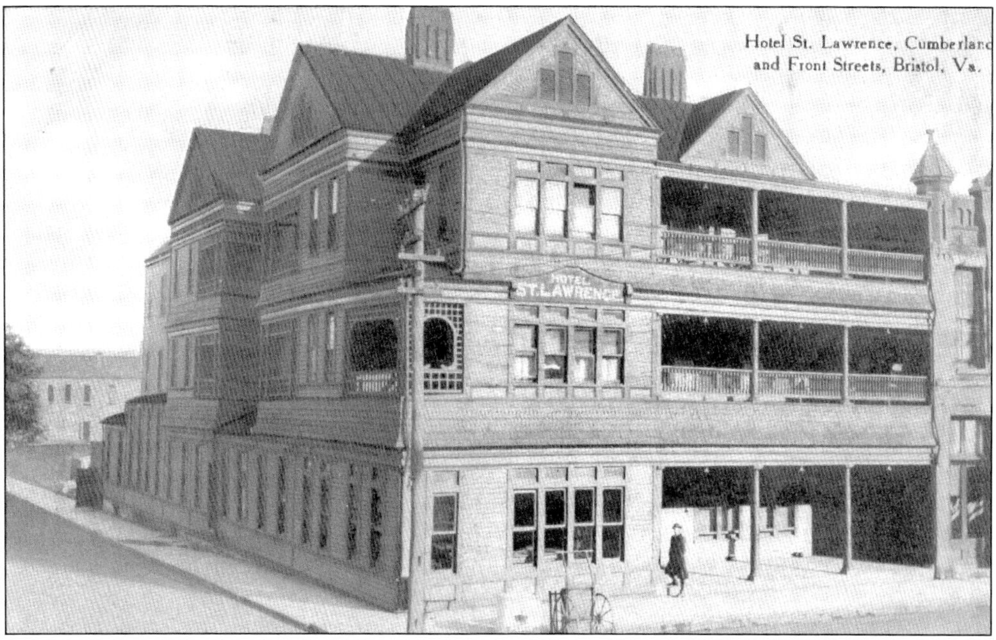

In the 1890s, when this hotel was known as The Palace, a tornado tore off the top floor. The floor was rebuilt, and in 1896, George S. Bunn changed this establishment to the Hotel St. Lawrence. In the 1900s, the Hotel St. Lawrence was torn down, and the General Shelby Hotel was built on the same site. This postcard was postmarked November 11, 1910. (Courtesy of Paul Stone Collection.)

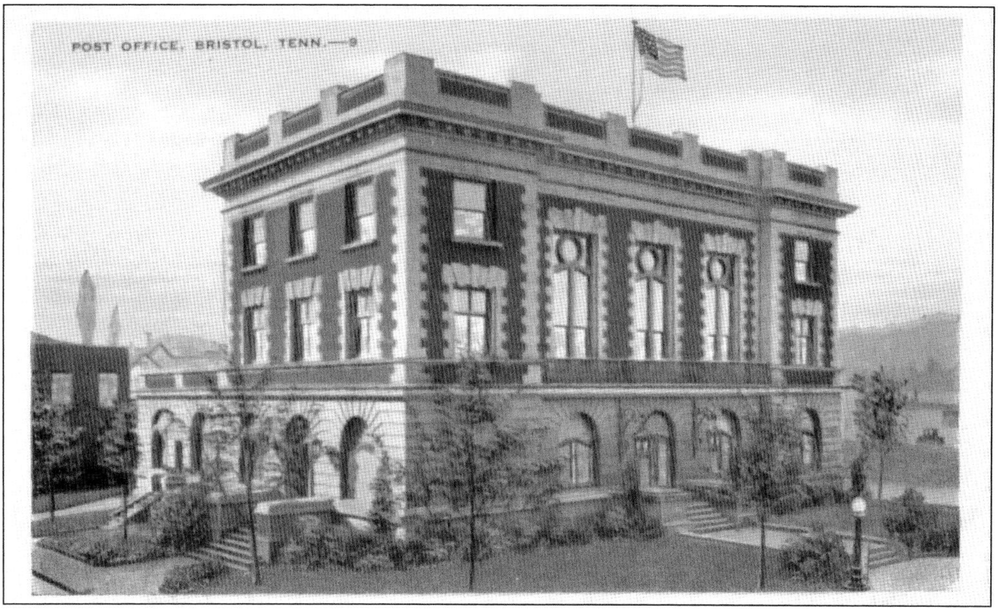

Residents of Sullivan County were accustomed to receiving postal mail in the late 1800s. Of course there were many small pick-up locations in general stores or homes throughout the county, and Blountville had been a major mail distributing point as early as 1802, but only three official post offices (Blountville, King's Port, and Paperville) existed in Sullivan County until 1850. (Courtesy of Paul Stone Collection.)

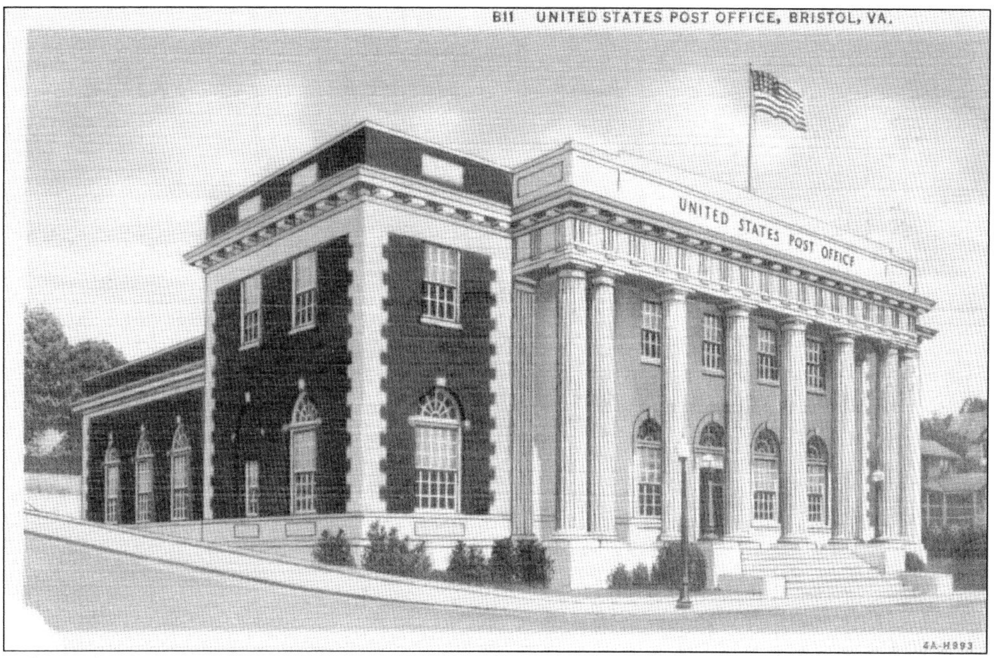

When it became obvious that Bristol was a growing city, it also became a major distributing point for mail. This postcard shows the Bristol, Virginia, post office, while the postcard at the top shows the Bristol, Tennessee, post office. (Courtesy of Paul Stone Collection.)

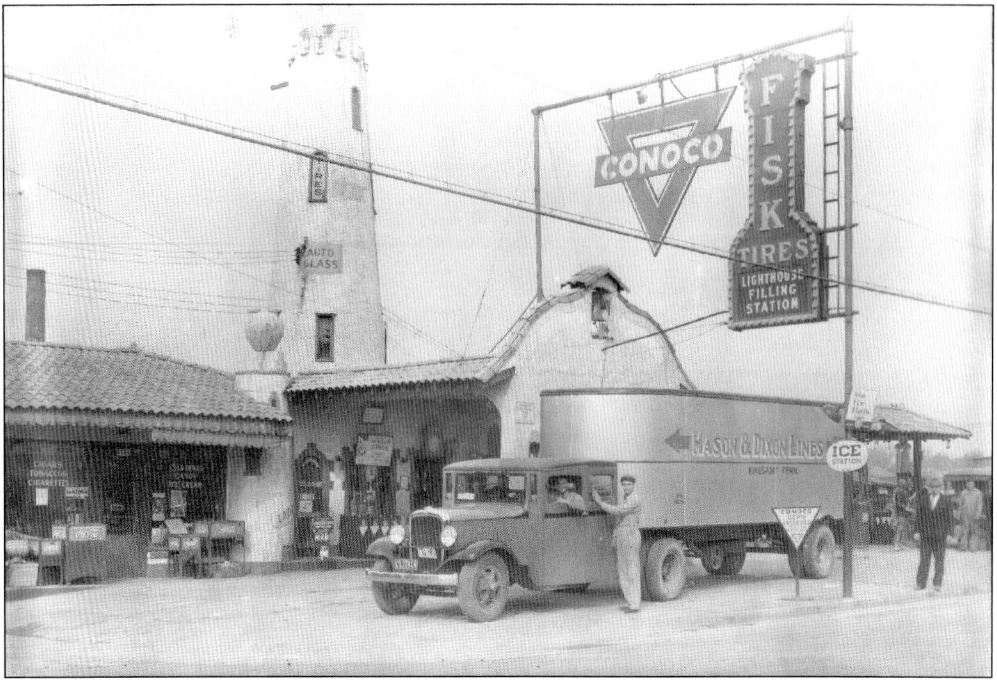

The Lighthouse Filling Station was located on the corner of State and Pierce Streets (now Morrison Boulevard). The station was one of three built by Ernest Rainero in the 1930s. (Courtesy of Bristol Historical Association.)

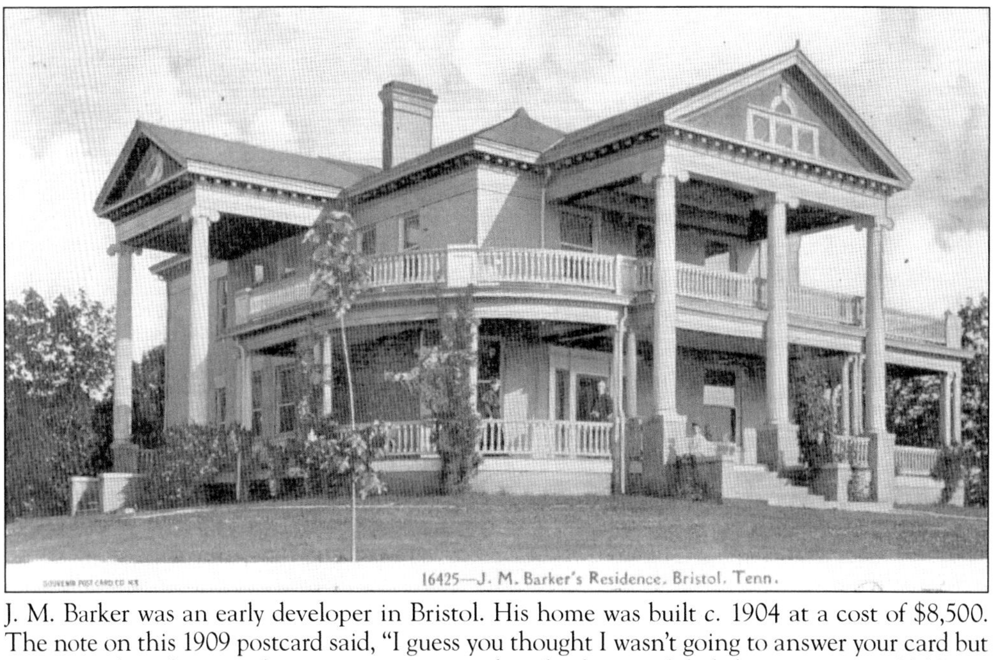

J. M. Barker was an early developer in Bristol. His home was built c. 1904 at a cost of $8,500. The note on this 1909 postcard said, "I guess you thought I wasn't going to answer your card but I am. . . . I have been working . . . on account of scarlet fever and diphtheria. . . . I would like to see you. . . . Your best friend, Myr." (Courtesy of Paul Stone Collection.)

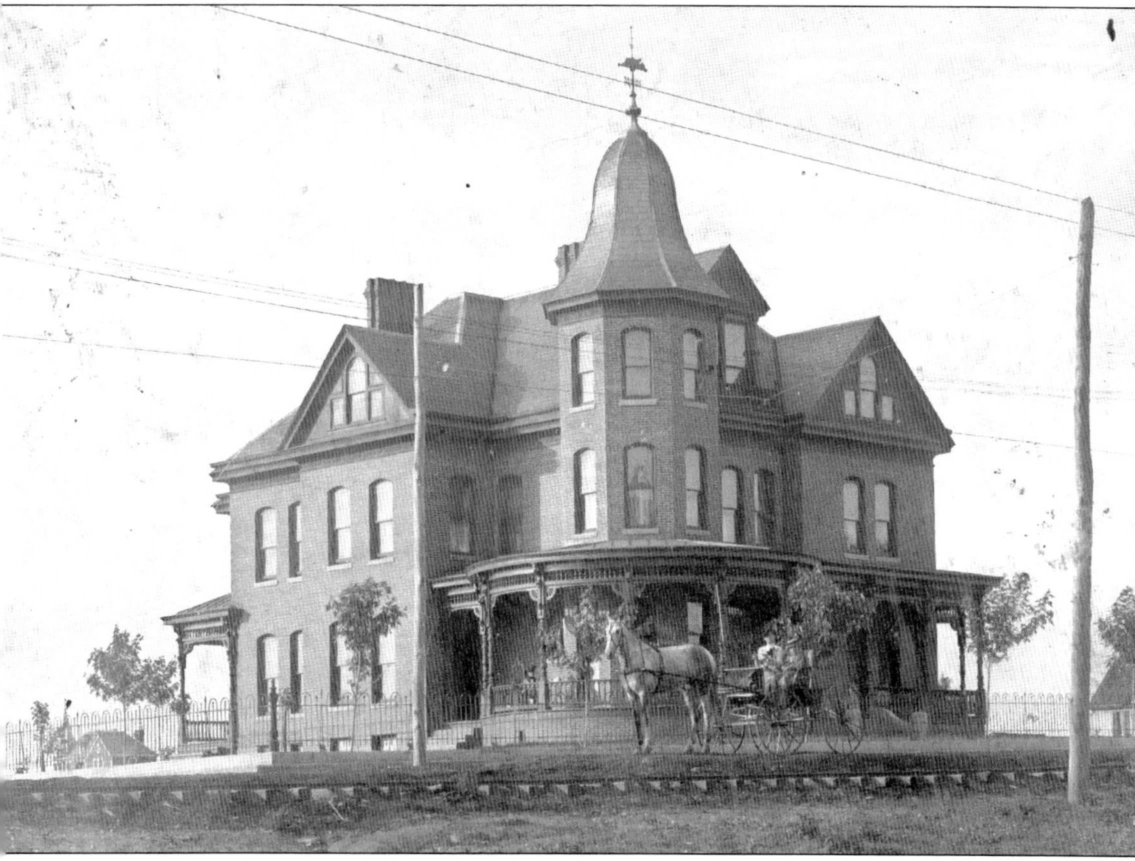

This was the home of Maj. A. D. Reynolds, a son of Hardin and Nancy Cox Reynolds. This photograph of the house was taken c. 1903. Reynolds built this fine home in the Fairmont section of town close to the end of his tobacco enterprise. This house was gutted by fire in the 1980s. There is a photograph of A. D. Reynolds on page 12 and his wife on page 13. (Courtesy of Bristol Historical Association.)

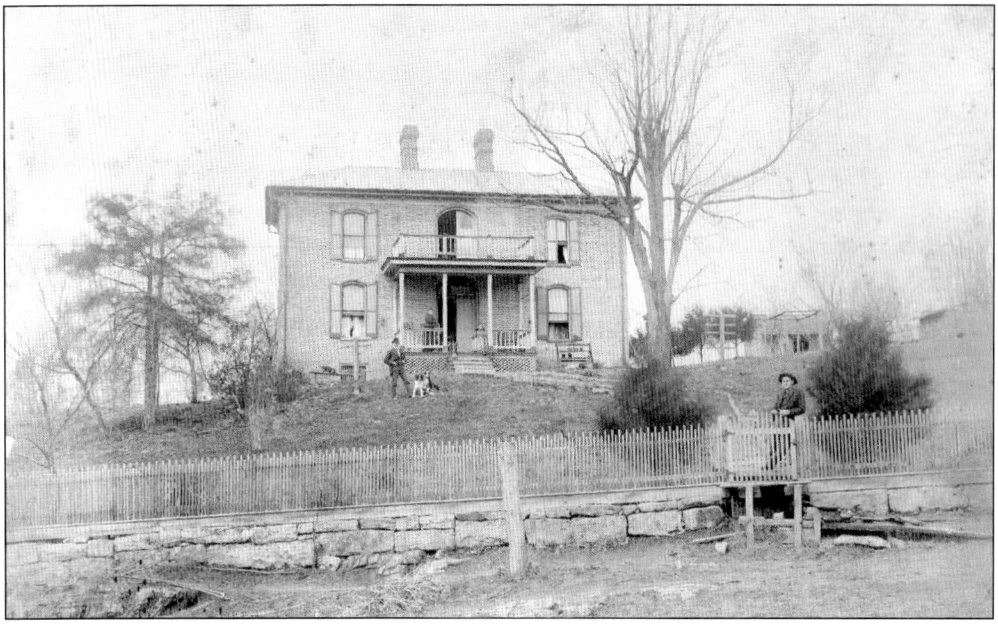

Jacob Susong Carmack built this house in 1884 on a farm located near the present site of King College. In this photograph, c. 1900, Jacob is standing in the yard beside his dogs. Jacob's wife, Jane Bushong Carmack, sits on the porch. Also on the porch is Ellen (Ella) Carmack, their first grandchild. Robert Carmack, who married Hattie Bushong, is standing by the gate. (Courtesy of Bud Phillips.)

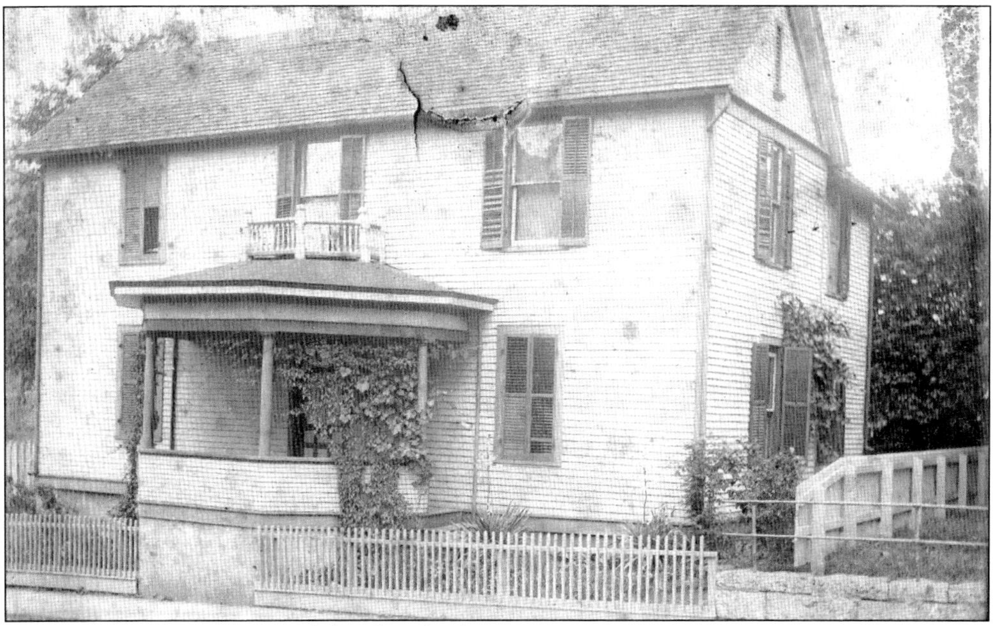

Joseph Lindsey Coleman Smith lived in this house on 15 Virginia Street. J. L. C. came to Bristol with the railroad in 1872 and married Martha Alice Hagy of Abingdon in 1878. Among other community activities, Smith served as the first chairman of the original Bristol Historical Society in 1908. His home was demolished in 1940 to make way for a Sunday school addition of First Baptist Church. (Courtesy of Tim Buchanan.)

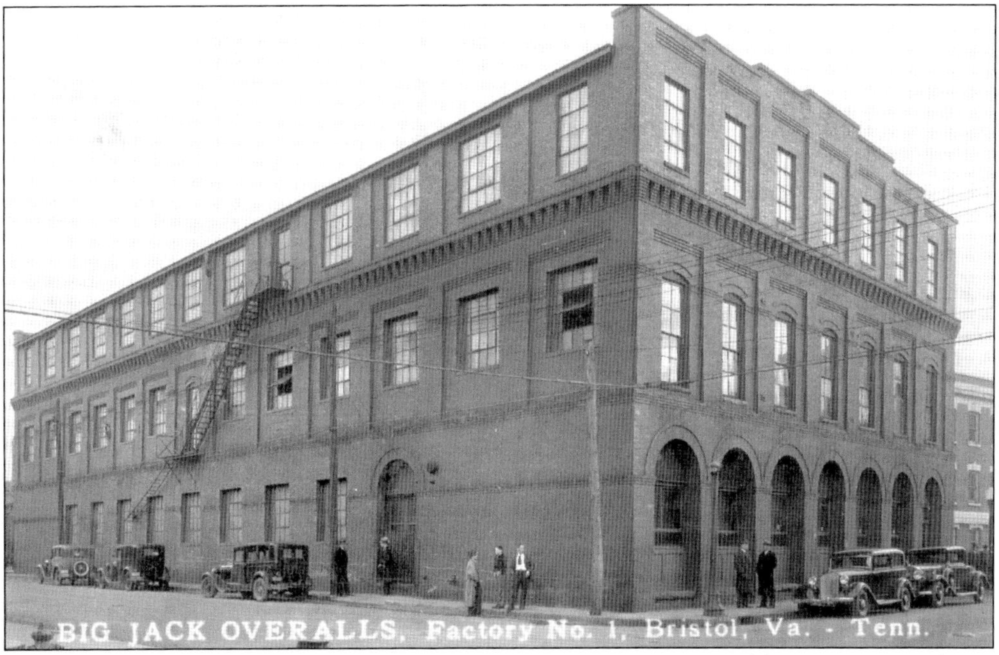

The Big Jack Overall Manufacturing Company was a mainstay in Bristol for many years. John S. Lipscomb organized the Mahoney-Lipscomb Overall Company in 1905. It later became known as the Head-Lipscomb-McCormick Overall Company and, in 1921, was reorganized under the name of the Big Jack Manufacturing Company. (Courtesy of Paul Stone Collection.)

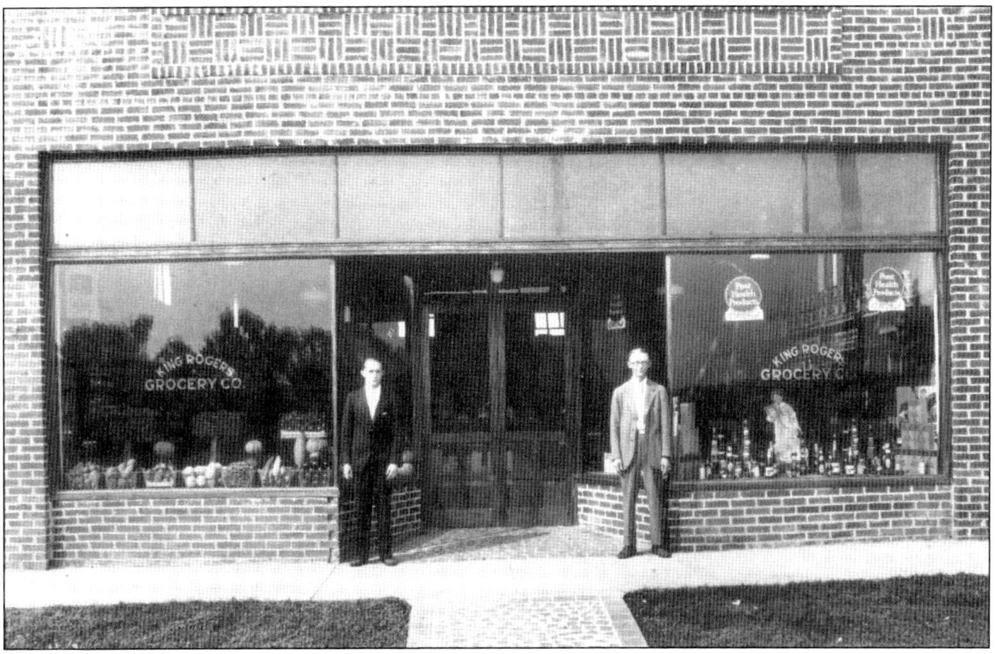

King Rogers Sr. (left) began the King Rogers Grocery Store with a small frame building on Fifth Street in 1923 at the age of 16 while still attending Bristol High School in Tennessee. William G. Rogers (right) helped his son in the store until his death on November 9, 1928. The store, shown here in 1926, had a slogan of "Heavenly Foods at Earthly Prices." (Courtesy of King Rogers Jr.)

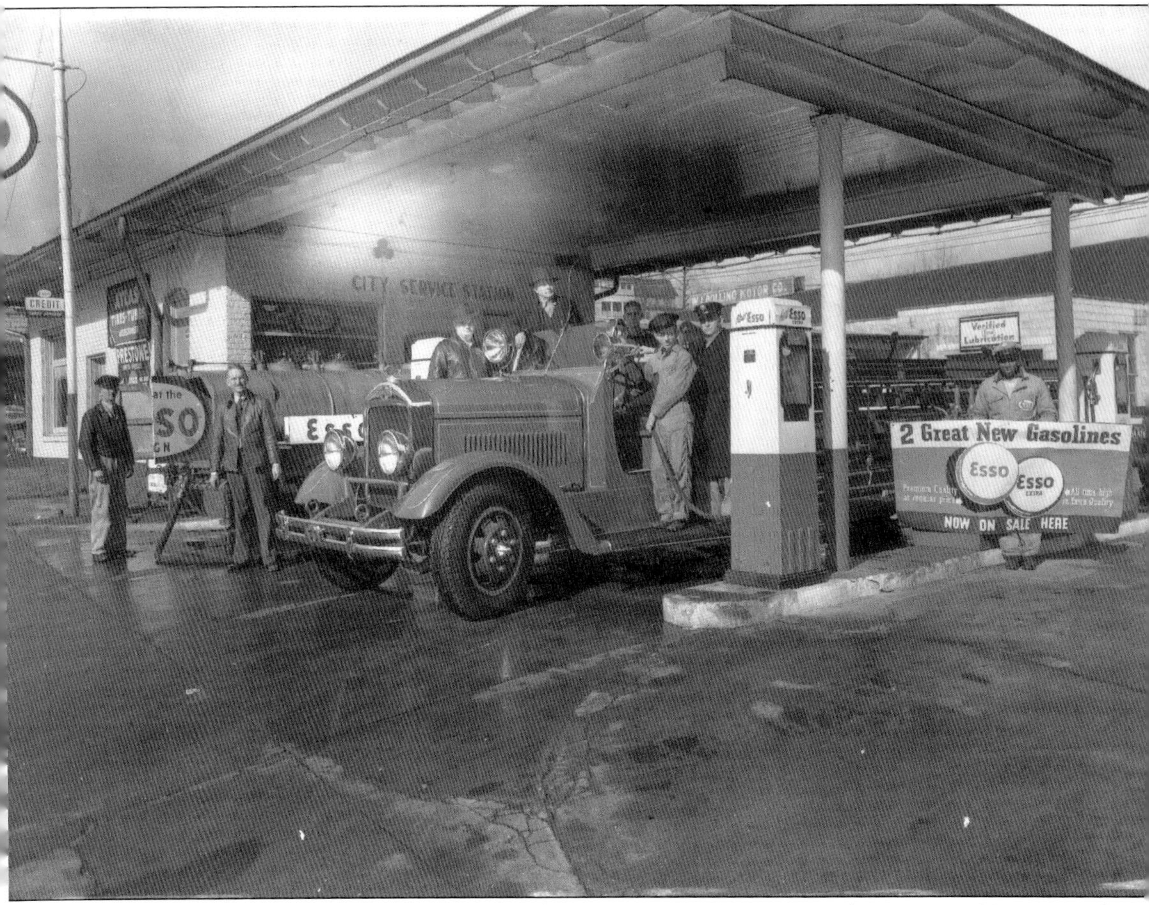

This photograph was taken *c.* 1936 at the City Service Station on the corner of Moore and Sycamore Streets. Vance Graham Sr. owned one Esso distributorship and two Esso service stations, including this one. On the far left is James Weaver, who drove the Esso tank truck. The man on the truck in a fireman's uniform is Hugh Worley, who would later serve as the Bristol, Virginia, Fire Department chief from 1945 to 1968. The truck is a ladder truck purchased for $9,550 in 1936 and is probably filling up for the first time. (Courtesy of Walter Doane.)

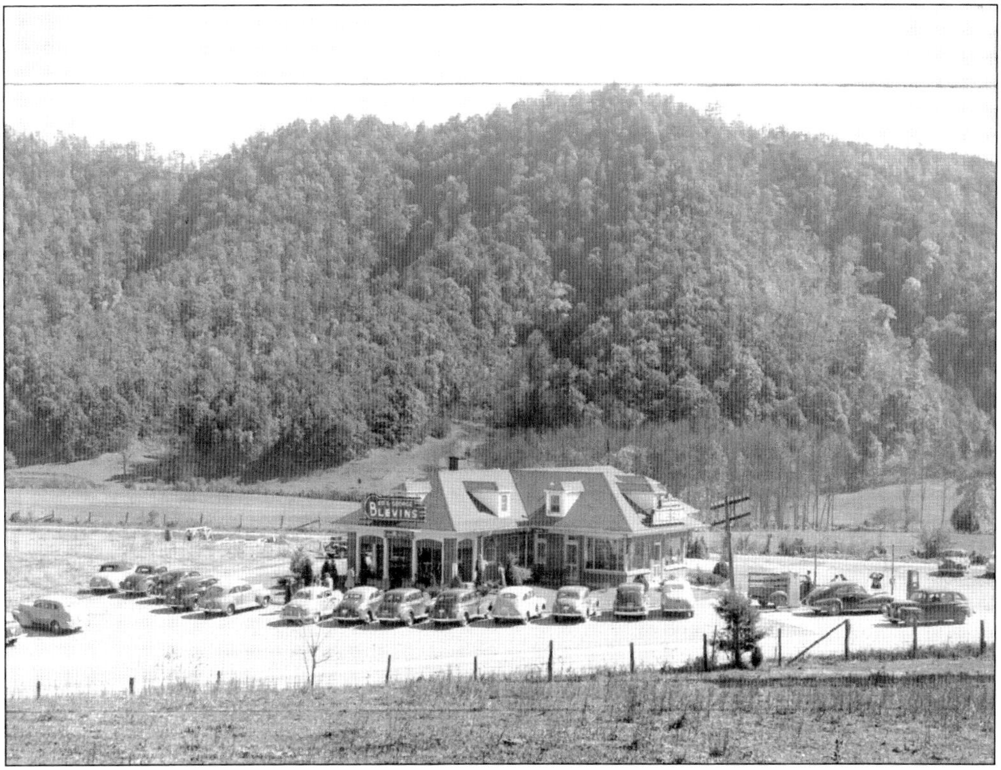

Ed and George Blevins's restaurant (top) operated in the 1950s and 1960s. The restaurant was located on Volunteer Parkway near the new Wal-Mart, where Oakley-Cook Funeral Home (bottom) is now located. If you look closely at these two photographs, you can see where Sid Oakley nicely incorporated the existing structure into the building plans for the funeral home, which opened in January 1982. (Courtesy of Sid Oakley.)

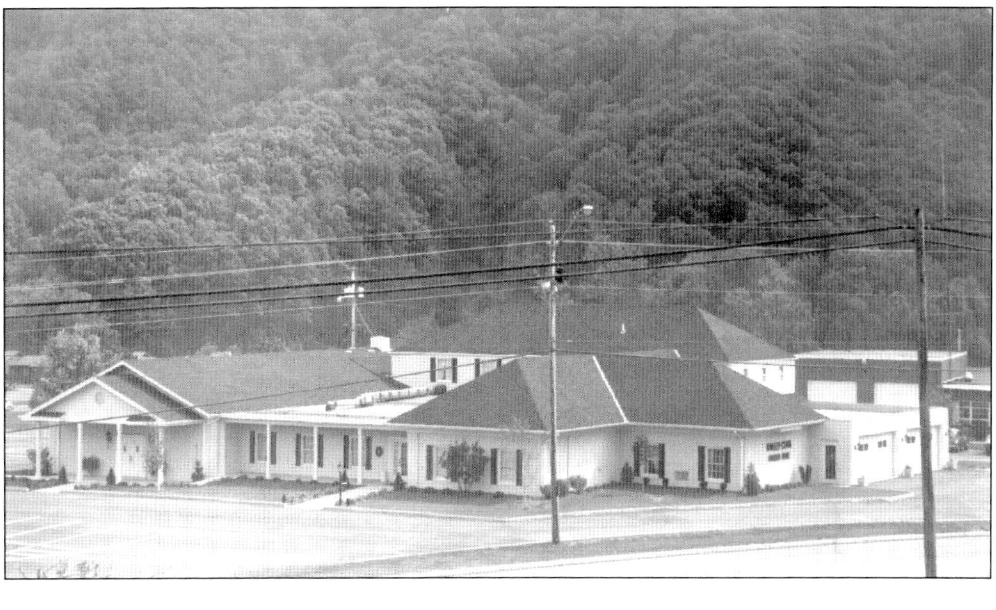

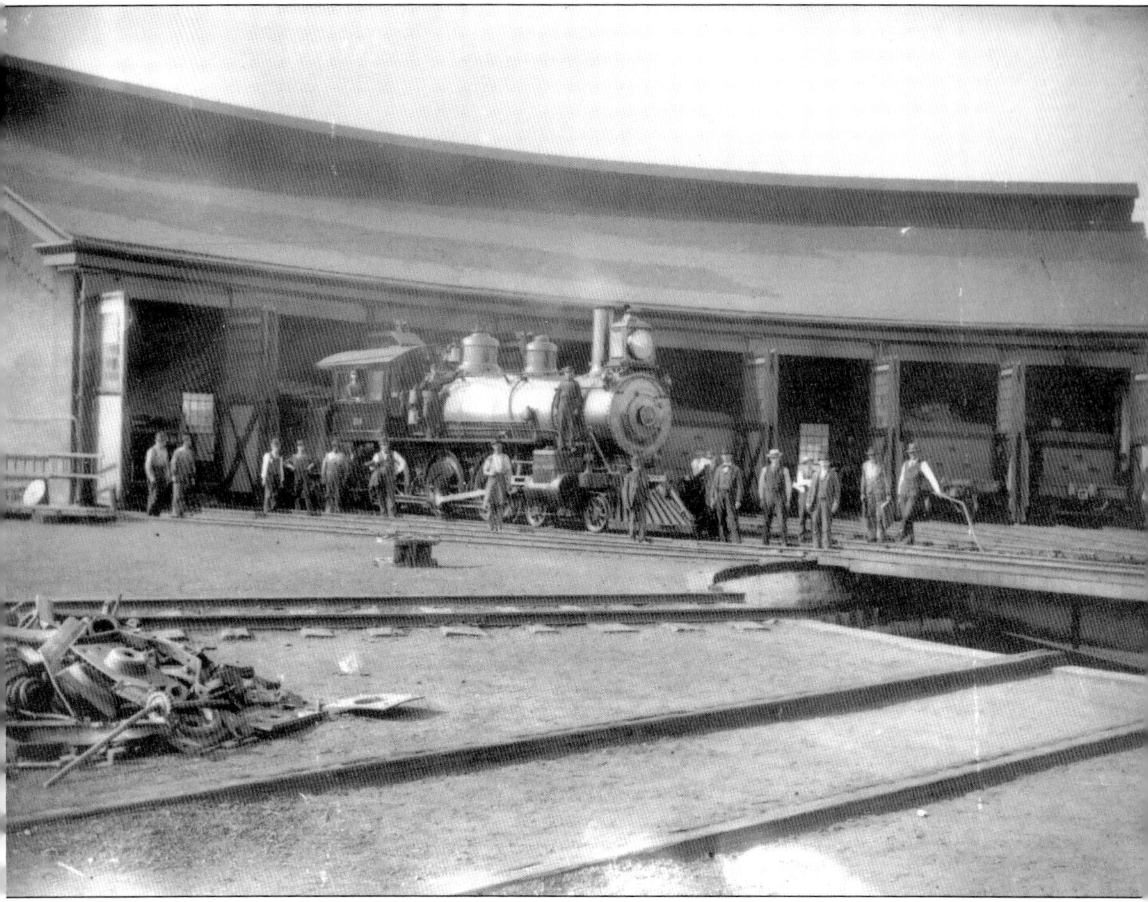

The roundhouse, a very instrumental part of every railroad, was used for basic maintenance of steam locomotives and other cars. A turntable that was used to reverse the direction of a locomotive can be seen in front of the roundhouse. The turntable also allowed engines to be moved into a particular stall. The roundhouse pictured here still exists, but it has changed a little in appearance. It is located at the end of Janie Hammit Drive in Bristol, Virginia. This photograph was taken by S. C. Hodges c. 1915. (Courtesy of Virginia Intermont College.)

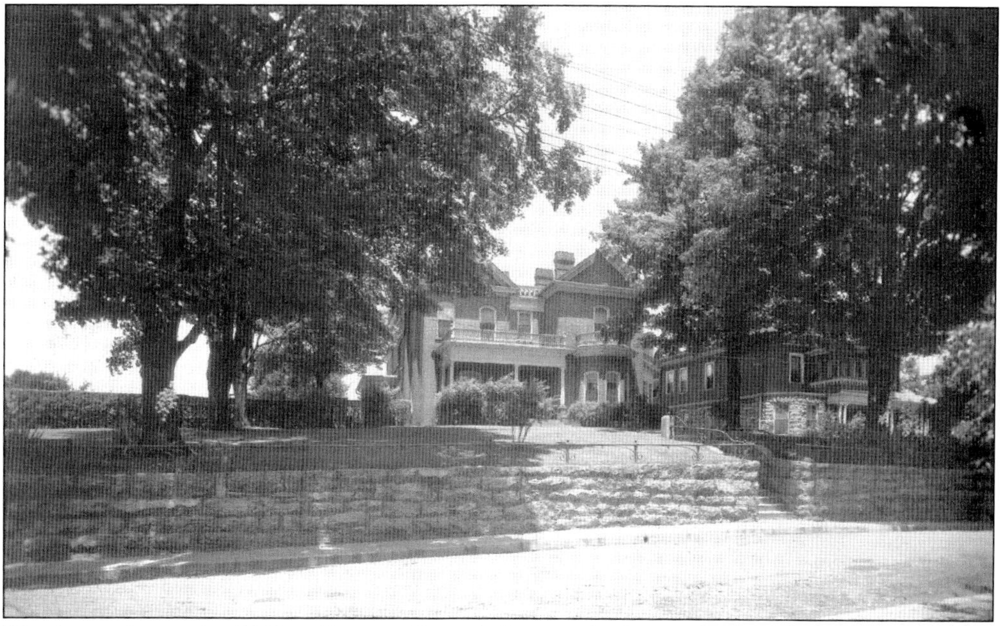

This house, located at 54 King Street in Bristol, Virginia, had several owners before J. D. Mitchell purchased it from H. E. McCoy in February 1899. The house stands where Rev. James King's house once stood, and two rooms of the original King house are still part of the present Mitchell house. J. D. Mitchell passed the home on to his daughter, Margaret, who lived there prior to her death. (Courtesy of Bristol Historical Association.)

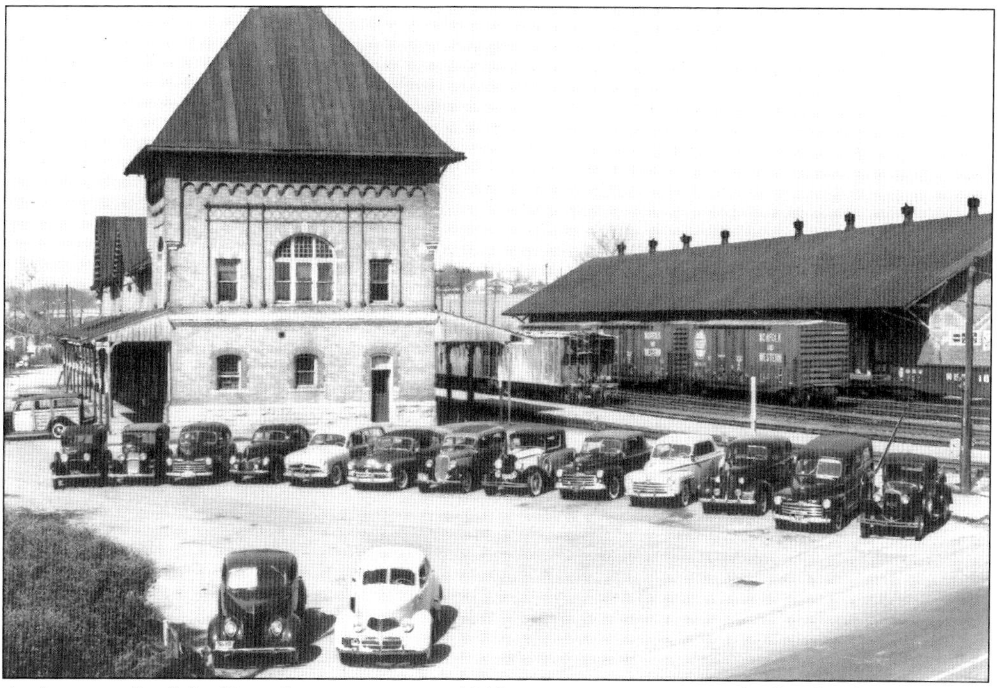

A photograph of the Bristol train station c. 1940 contains numerous vehicles that had come for a car show. These same sorts of car shows are still popular in the area today. (Courtesy of Bristol Virginia Police Department.)

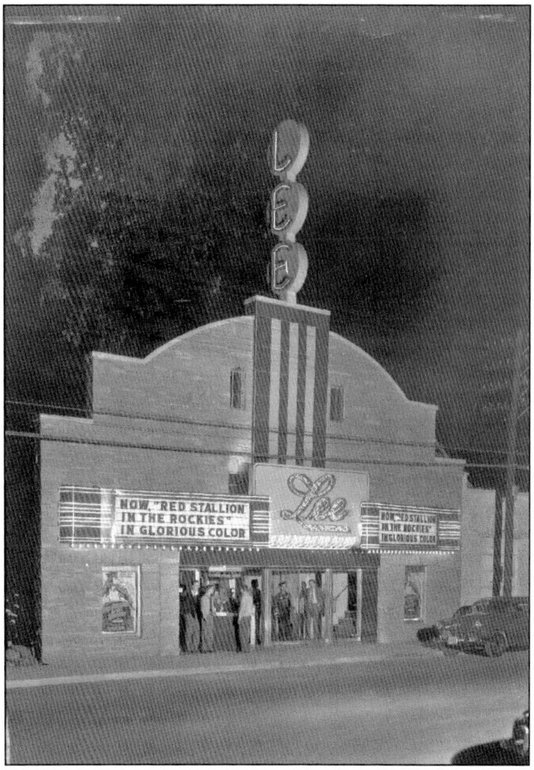

The Lee opened on West State Street Friday, April 15, 1949, with *Kiss in the Dark*, starring David Niven and Jane Wyman. The 800-seat theatre was packed on opening night. By the early 1950s, Lee was one of nine theatres in Bristol, including three drive-ins. As television became more popular, ticket sales plummeted, and in November 1956, the Lee closed. (Courtesy of Walter Doane.)

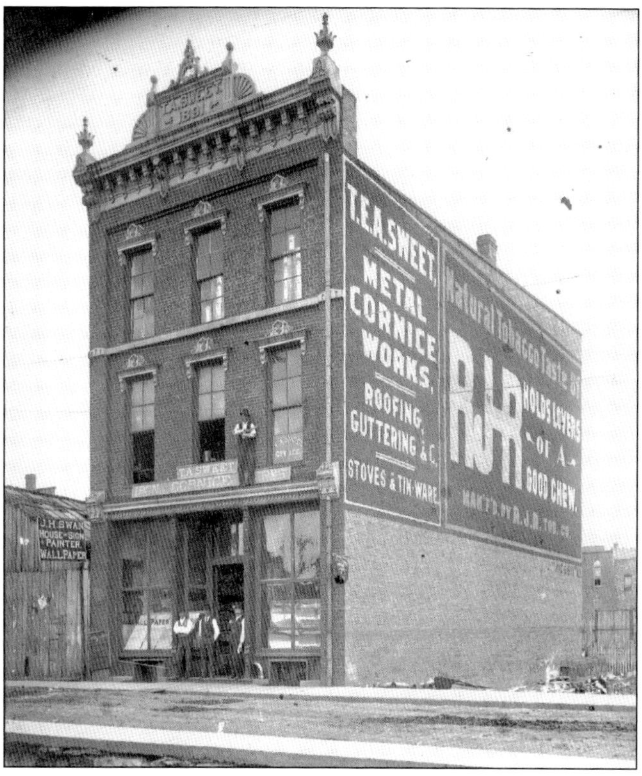

Thomas Sweet owned the T. E. A. Sweet Building located on Sixth Street. Sweet ran a manufacturing company that made tinning and roofing material. This photograph of the building was taken by S. C. Hodges in 1891. (Courtesy of Virginia Intermont College.)

Three
STREET SCENES

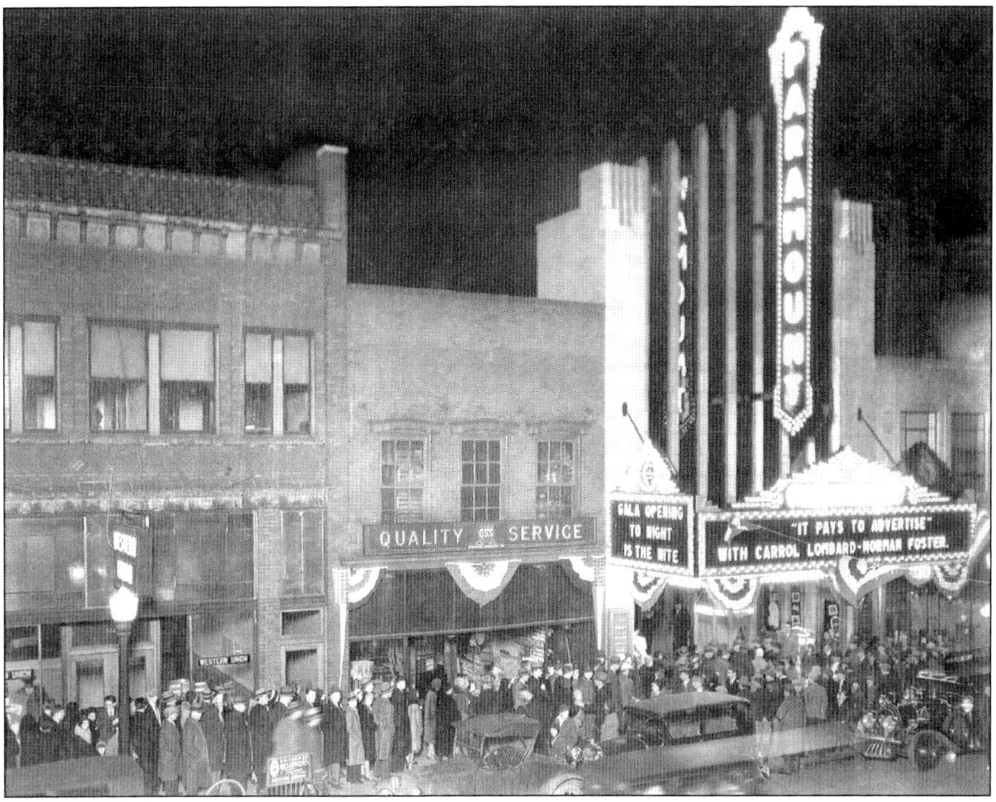

The Paramount Theatre opened its ticket booth in 1931 with the movie *It Pays to Advertise*. By 1979, the theatre had fallen into disrepair and sat empty for many years until it was restored and reopened in 1991, to the joy of many. Today the Paramount hosts concerts and other cultural activities and is the centerpiece of downtown Bristol. (Courtesy of Bill McKee.)

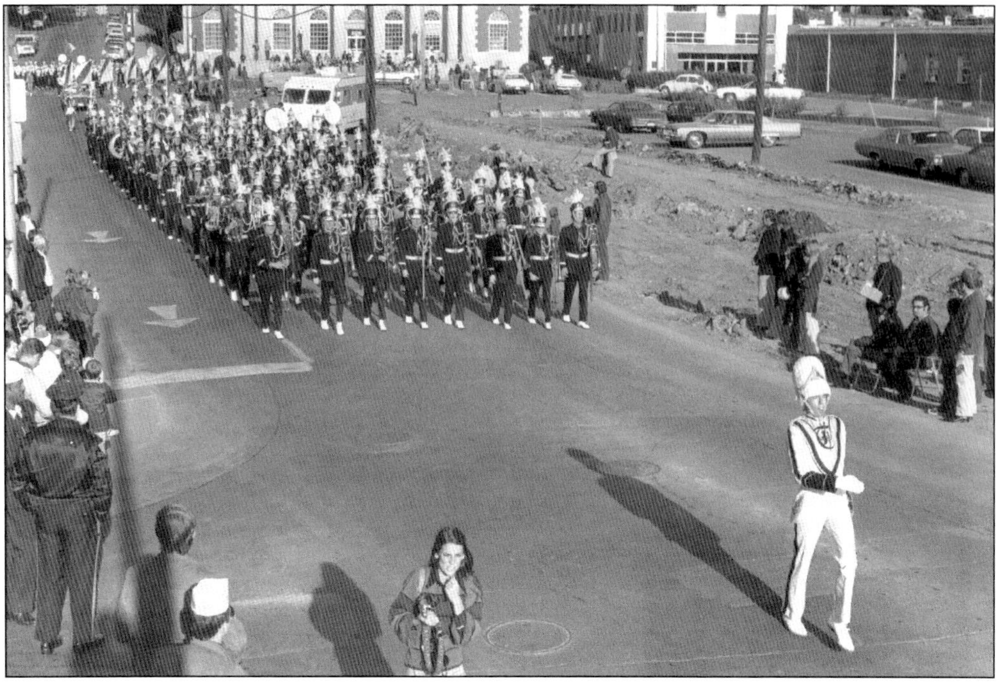

The Tennessee High School marching band heads down Cumberland Street as it participates in the 25th anniversary of the Southeastern Band Festival in 1975. The festival brought in high school bands from all over the Southeast for many years. (Courtesy of Bristol Historical Association.)

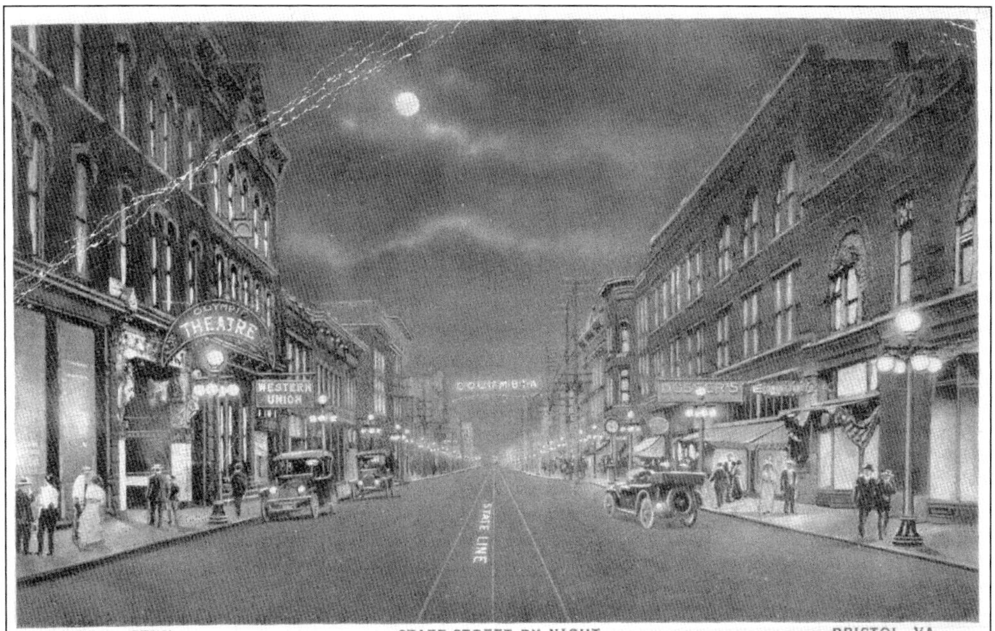

The back of this postcard that depicts State Street at night was addressed to a Mrs. A. D. Stone and postmarked July 7, 1924. The sender had written, "Dear Sister, Well, I didn't get to tell you good-bye. But 'twas the best we left when we did—as it never stopped raining from before 4 'til this a.m. . . . Make us that promised visit. Mary." (Courtesy of Paul Stone Collection.)

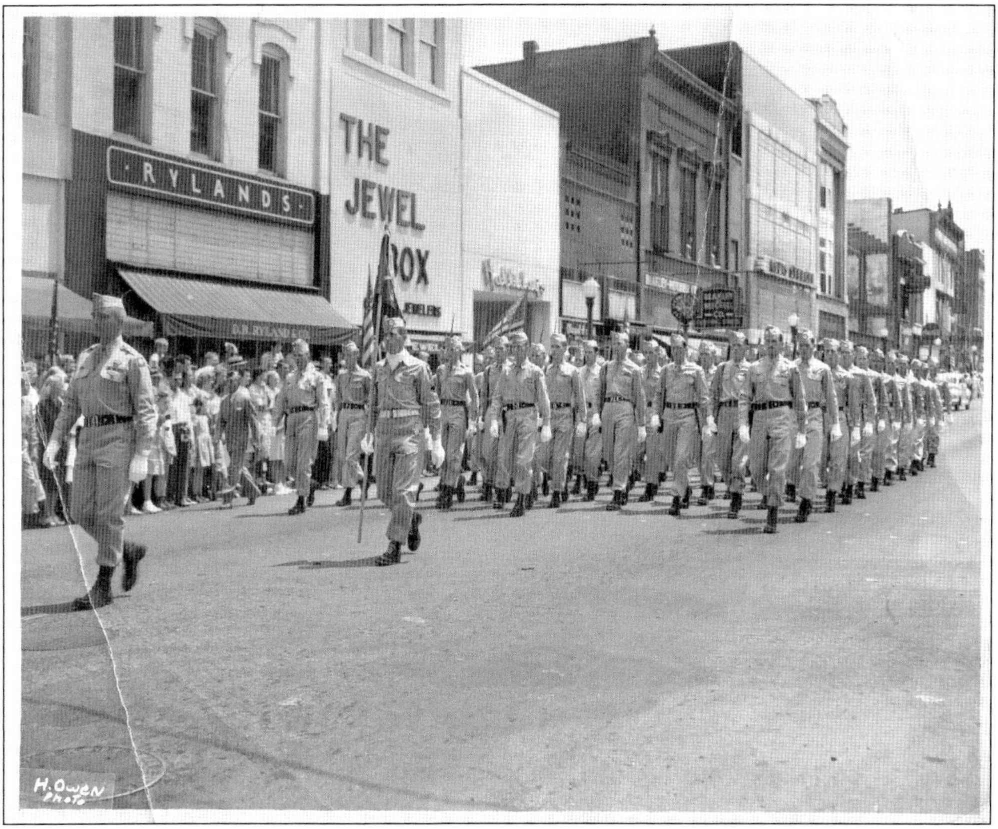

The 82nd Airborne Division marches down State Street past Rylands and the Jewel Box during the Fourth of July parade of 1947. The parade was sponsored by the Junior Chamber of Commerce. The photograph was taken by H. Owen. (Courtesy of Tim Buchanan.)

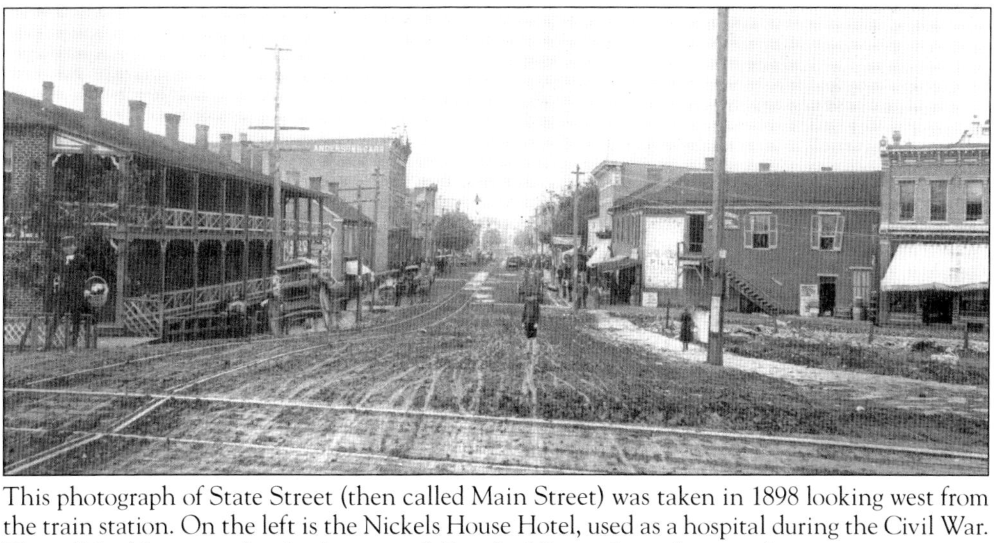

This photograph of State Street (then called Main Street) was taken in 1898 looking west from the train station. On the left is the Nickels House Hotel, used as a hospital during the Civil War. The tall building was the Anderson and Carr building, where the now famous country music recordings were made in 1927. In between those is the Joseph Anderson home. (Courtesy of Bristol Historical Association.)

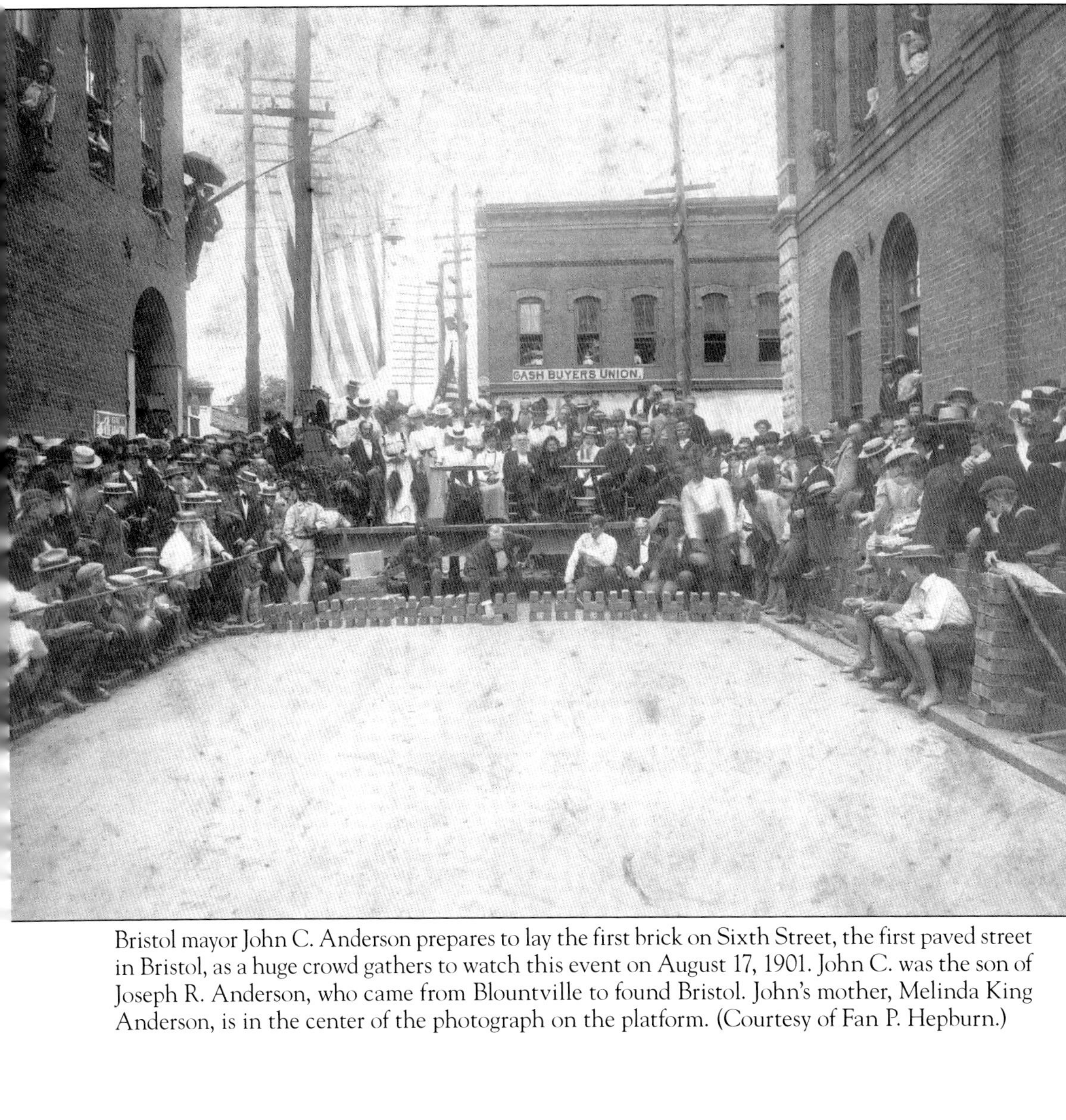

Bristol mayor John C. Anderson prepares to lay the first brick on Sixth Street, the first paved street in Bristol, as a huge crowd gathers to watch this event on August 17, 1901. John C. was the son of Joseph R. Anderson, who came from Blountville to found Bristol. John's mother, Melinda King Anderson, is in the center of the photograph on the platform. (Courtesy of Fan P. Hepburn.)

Four

Children

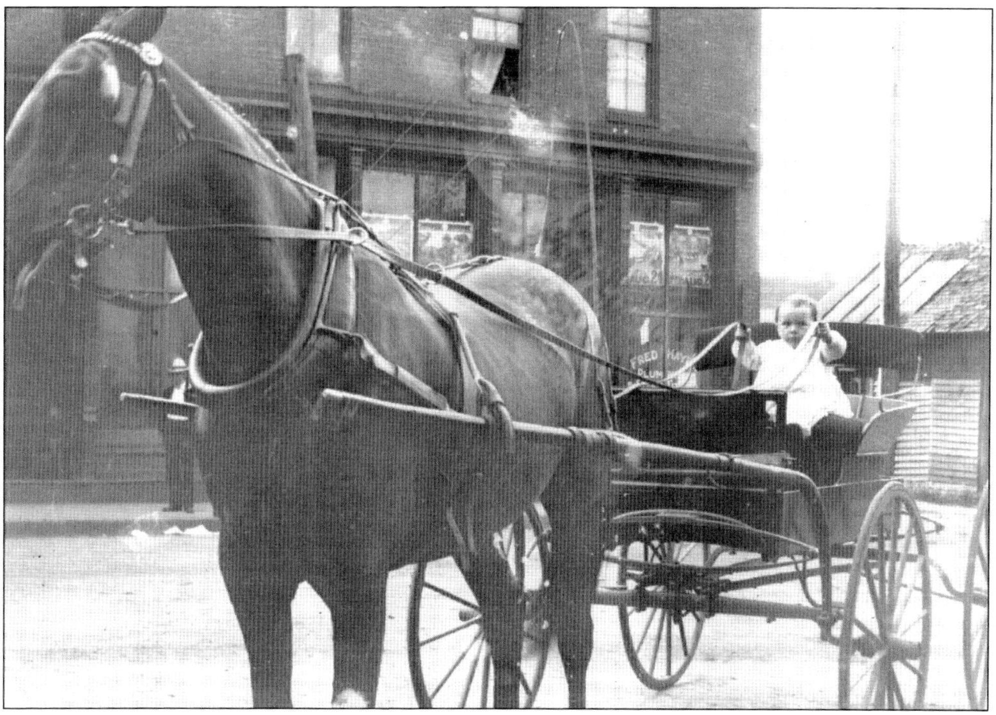

Though children of the 19th and early 20th centuries were trained and expected to be proficient at using household and farm equipment much earlier than youngsters today, the infant son of J. L. C. Smith, mayor of Bristol, Virginia, is trying his hands at the reins a bit early. (Courtesy of Tim Buchanan.)

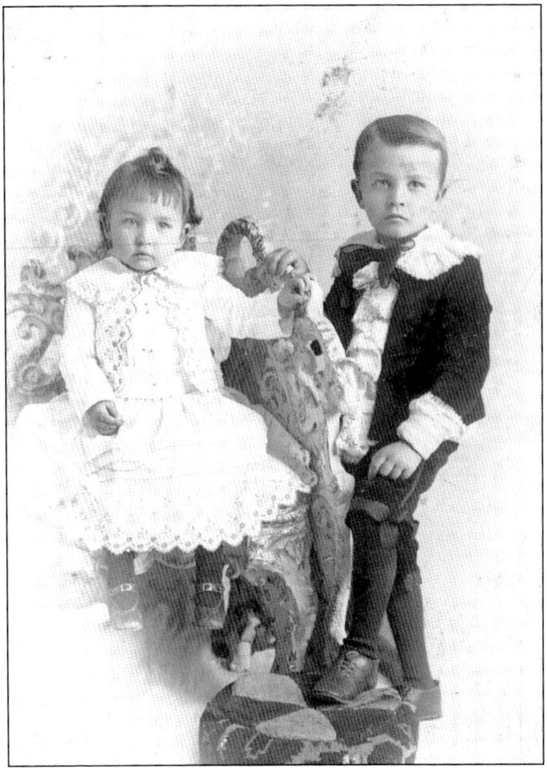

Will and Clarence Reynolds were sons of Maj. A. D. Reynolds. Will died while in his 20s, about a month after his marriage. Clarence was born in 1890 and long lived in Bristol in the house now occupied by William King on Holston Avenue. He was one of three brothers (Abram, Richard, and Clarence) that founded the U.S. Foil Company, later named Reynolds Metals. (Courtesy of Bristol Historical Association.)

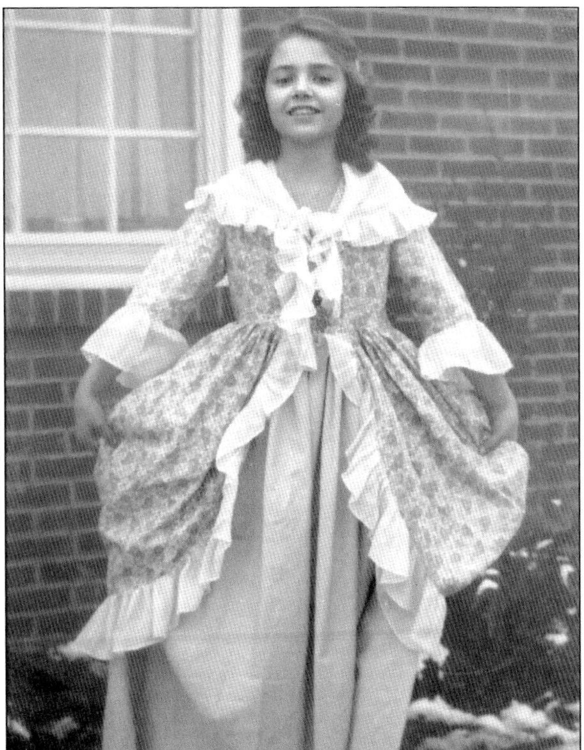

Jane Helton was in the sixth grade at Haynesfield Elementary School c. 1953 when her class performed a skit about the Colonial days. (Courtesy of Barbara Jane Maust.)

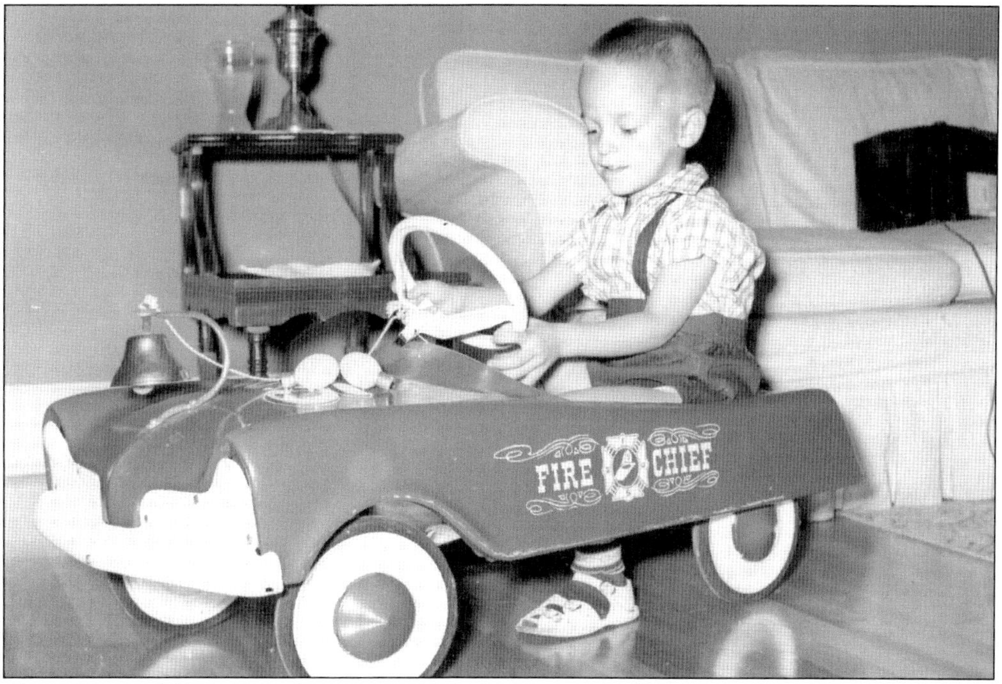

Though it would be quite a few more years before two-year-old Gary Haskins was ready to drive a real vehicle, he is shown here enjoying a child's fire chief car c. 1959. Gary is the son of Eugene and Mary Lou Haskins. (Courtesy of Eugene Haskins.)

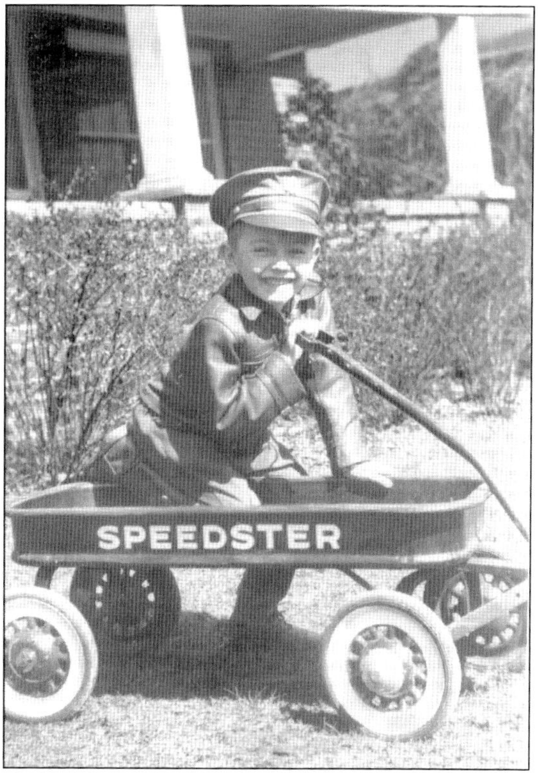

Robert Cawood Helton, shown here c. 1941, is the son of Rue and Ethel Helton. Robert attended Tennessee High School, graduated from King College, and owned the Bristol Racquet and Fitness Club for a while. He is also a local tennis pro who continues to succeed. In 2004, Robert ranked number one in the country for U.S.T.A. men's 65 singles and number seven in the world. (Courtesy of Barbara Jane Maust.)

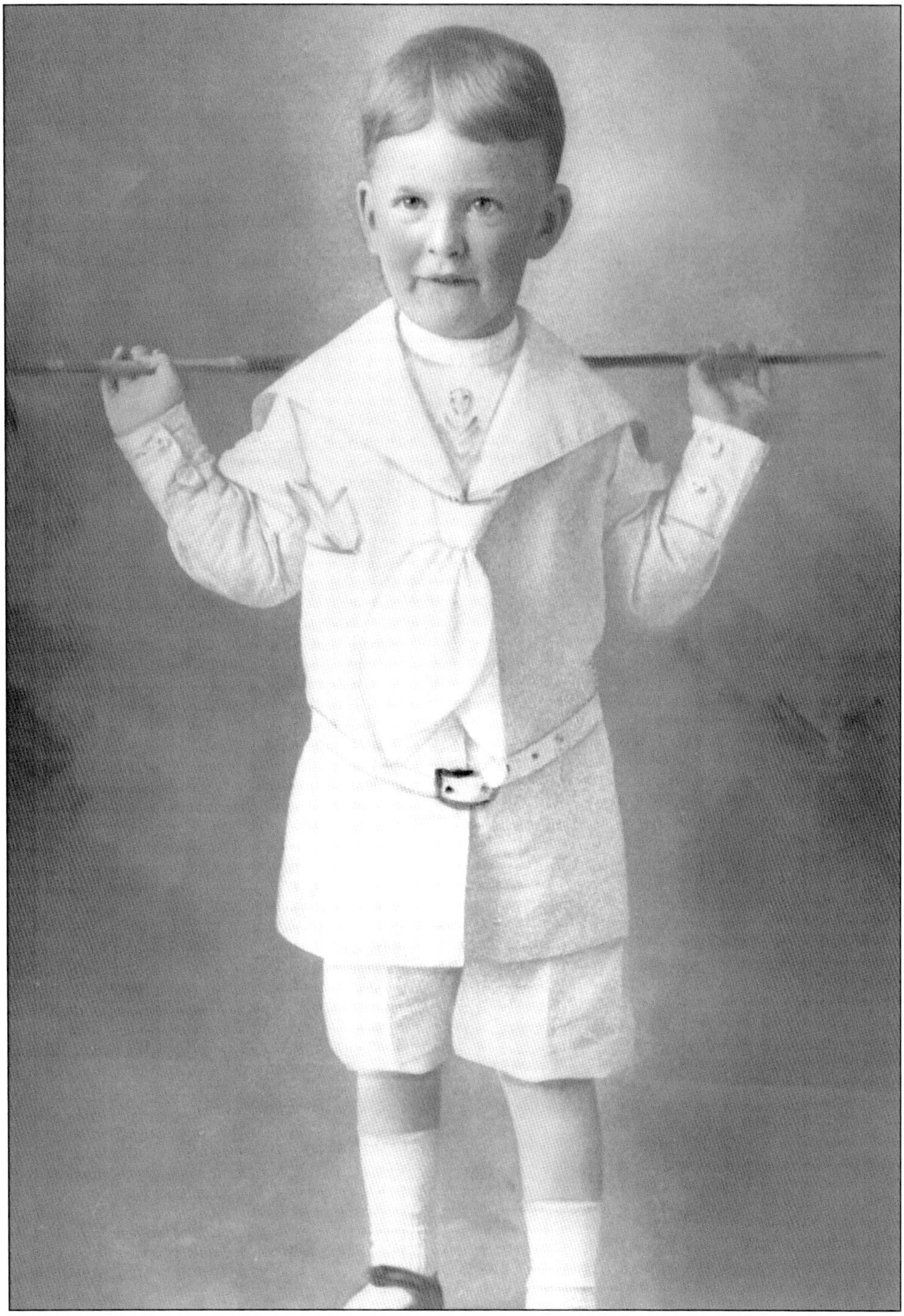

Joseph Downman Mitchell, Jr. was born June 30, 1900. He was a lifelong resident of Bristol and a member of Emmanuel Episcopal Church, where he served as treasurer and trustee. Downman, as he was called, graduated from Princeton University, was a president of the Men's Club, was a member of the Bristol Country Club and was an active member of the YMCA until his death on March 18, 1987. (Courtesy of Bristol Historical Association.)

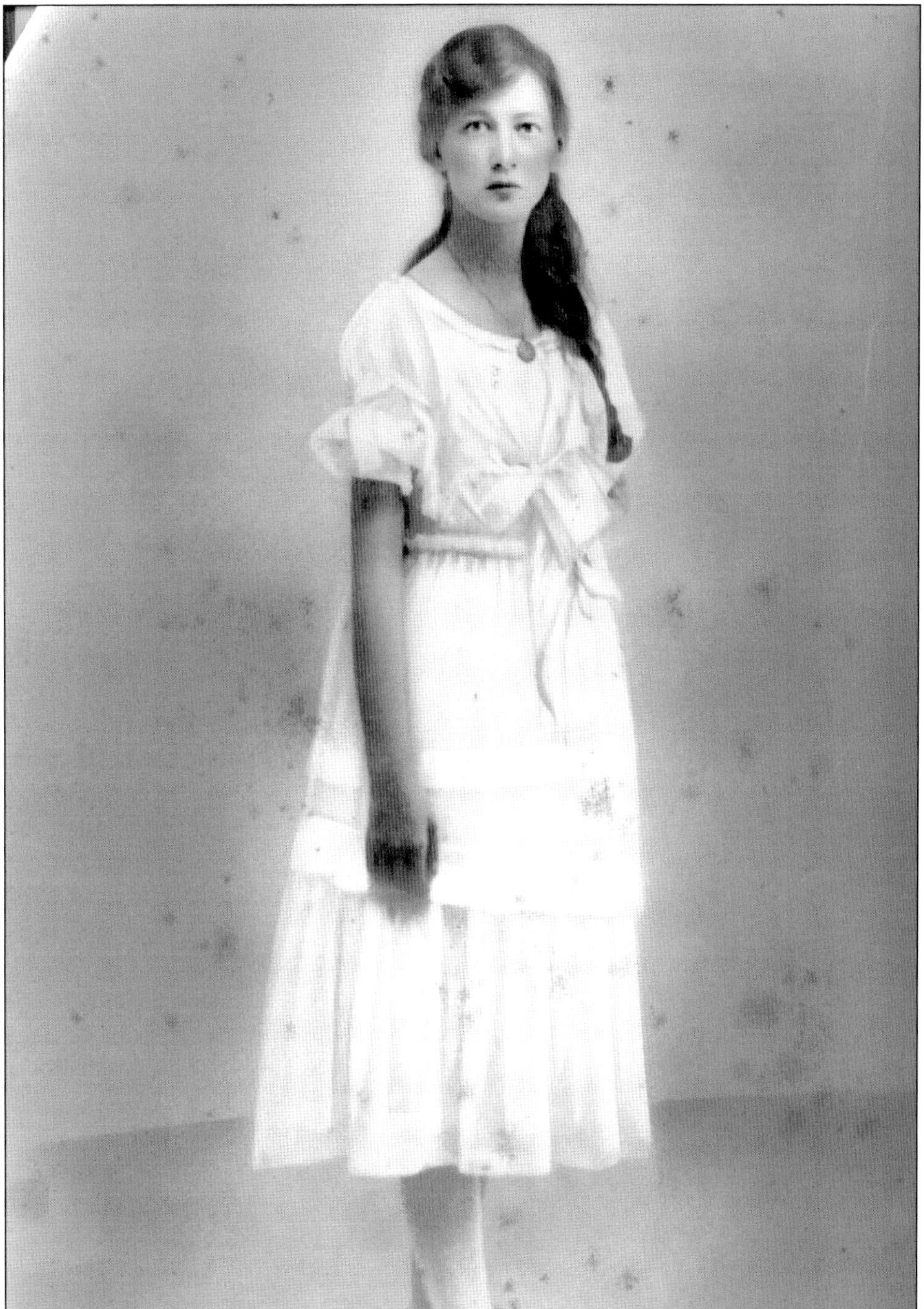

Margaret Mitchell was born on August 13, 1901, to Joseph and Louise Mitchell. Margaret graduated from Virginia High School in 1916 and is shown here at age 16 as she prepares to enter Baldwin School in Bryn Mawr, Pennsylvania. She graduated from Baldwin in 1920 and graduated from Wellesley College in 1924. She played a vital role in establishing the Bristol Chapter of the Humane Society and was a 77-year member of the Daughters of the American Revolution. Margaret died on December 31, 2003. (Courtesy of Bristol Historical Association.)

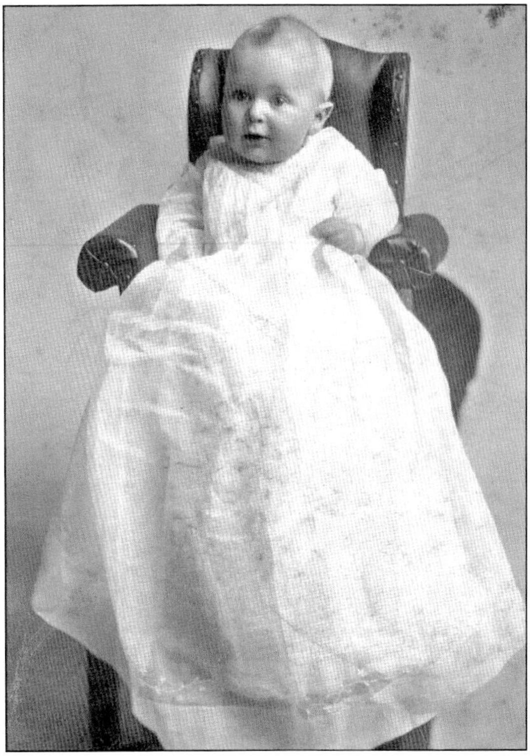

Austin Mitchell Jr., just six months and nine days old in this 1908 portrait, is propped up in a tiny chair perfect for helping capture this moment of childhood forever. (Courtesy of Bristol Historical Association.)

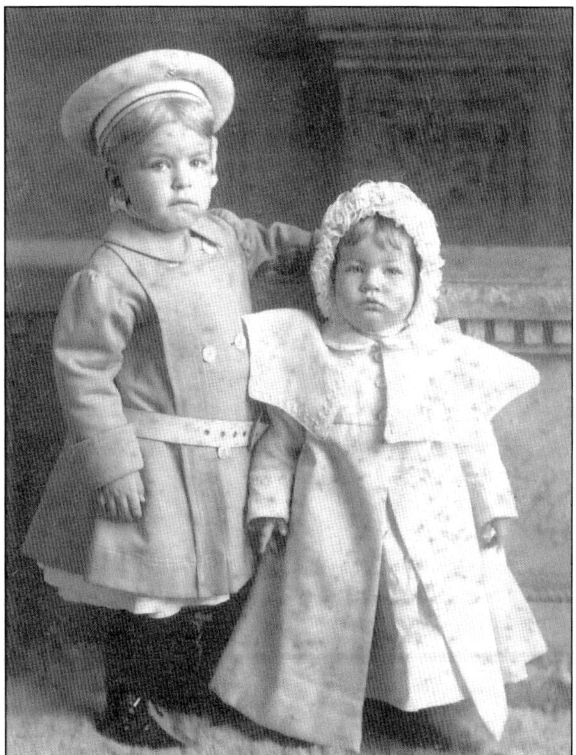

Downman (left) and Margaret Mitchell hold a serious pose for the camera in this portrait c. 1903. Like other children of upper-class families in the early 20th century, Margaret and Downman would have been expected to do well in school and learn the social skills of the privileged. (Courtesy of Bristol Historical Association.)

Clarence K. Reynolds strikes a handsome pose in this turn-of-the-century photograph taken at Hodges Photography in Bristol, Tennessee. Clarence was a son of Maj. A. D. Reynolds. (Courtesy of Bristol Historical Association.)

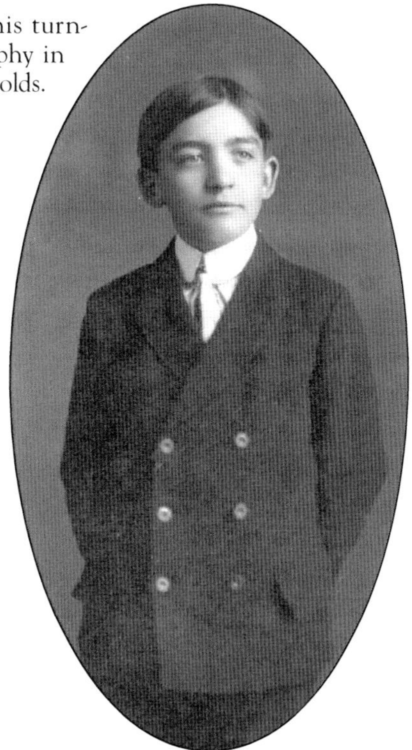

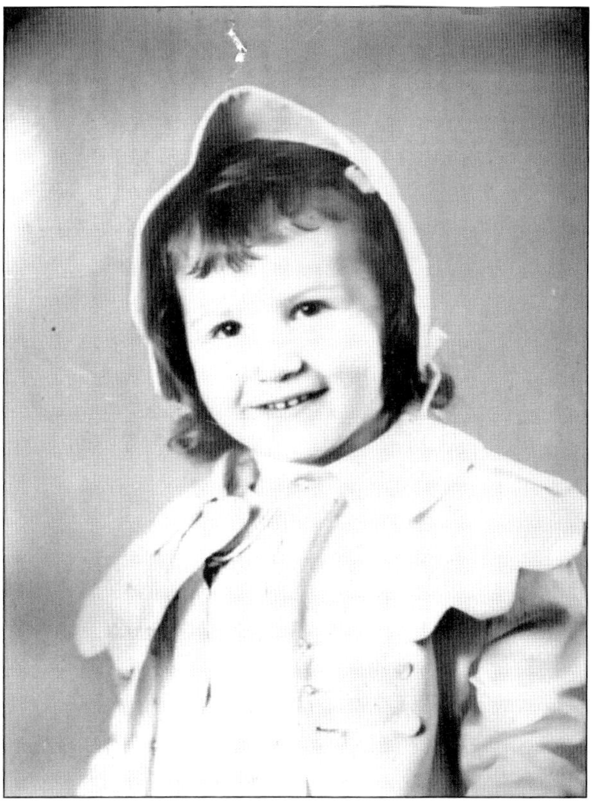

Betty Lee Honaker, shown here c. 1960, was the daughter of Raymond and Cassie Honaker. When she grew up, Betty married Zane Gray and had one child, David. Betty received a master's degree in education from East Tennessee State University in 1984. She passed away in 2003. (Courtesy of David and Angela Gray.)

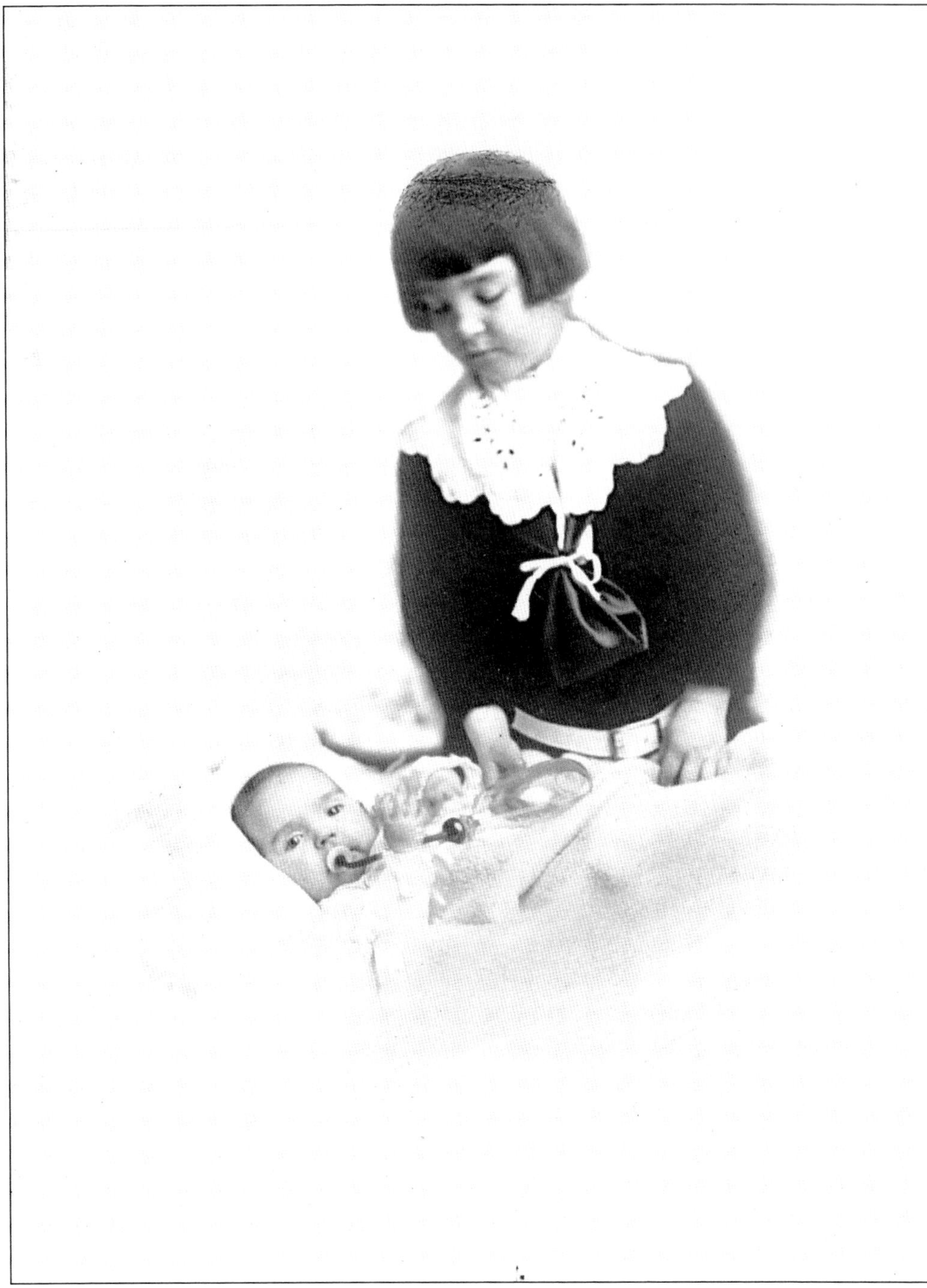

Thomas Franklin Staley Jr. had wanted a little sister for several years. His wish came true on August 7, 1908, when Senah Reynolds Staley was born. The children's mother, Sue Reynolds Staley, stated in memoirs written for her son that he was devastated when Senah died on April 28, 1909, at eight months of age. One of the youngster's statements was, "I don't want any little sister unless I can have my same one back; I am so glad she didn't die as quick as she came; she was the sweetest little thing." (Courtesy of Bristol Historical Association.)

The lovely young girls posing for this portrait c. 1885, from left to right, are Sue Mason (Easley), Sue Reynolds (Staley), and Sarah Mason (Angel). Their married names are noted in parentheses. (Courtesy of Bristol Historical Association.)

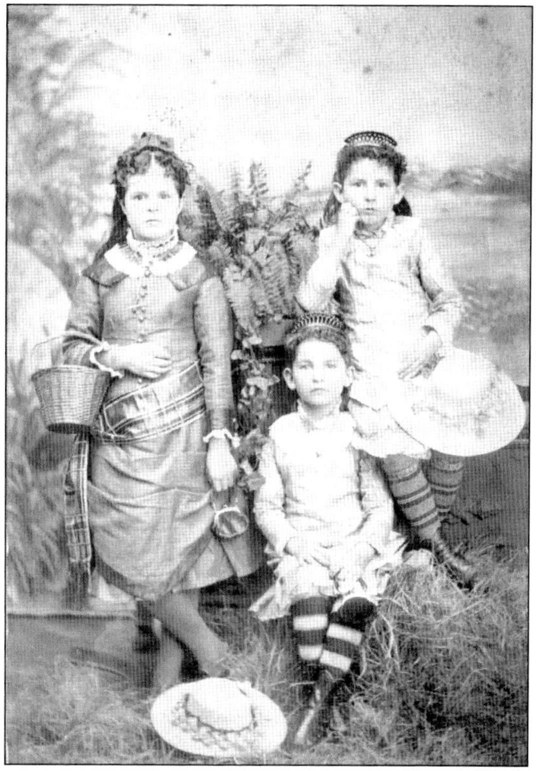

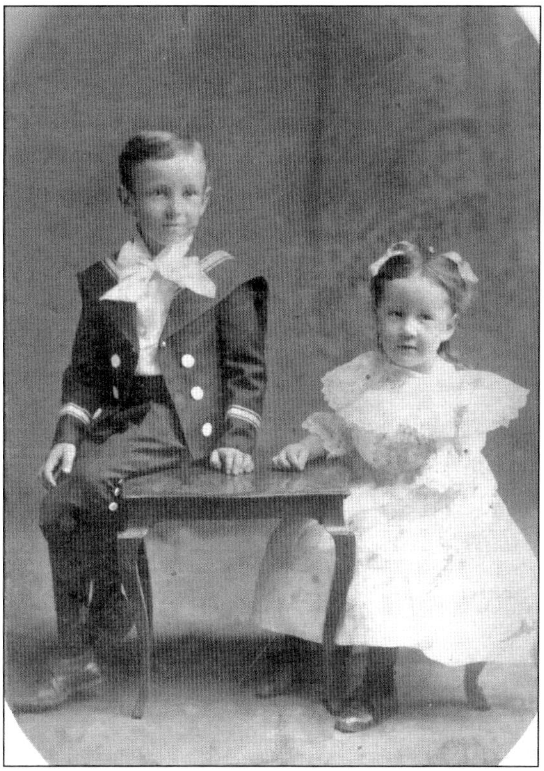

William Earl and Martha E. Good, the children of William David and Emma Johnson Good, were descendants of Pres. Andrew Johnson. This endearing image of the children was made c. 1900. As an adult, William worked for both the Bristol and Johnson City power boards. He had a minor stroke and died of a thrombosis in 1954. (Courtesy of Eugene Haskins.)

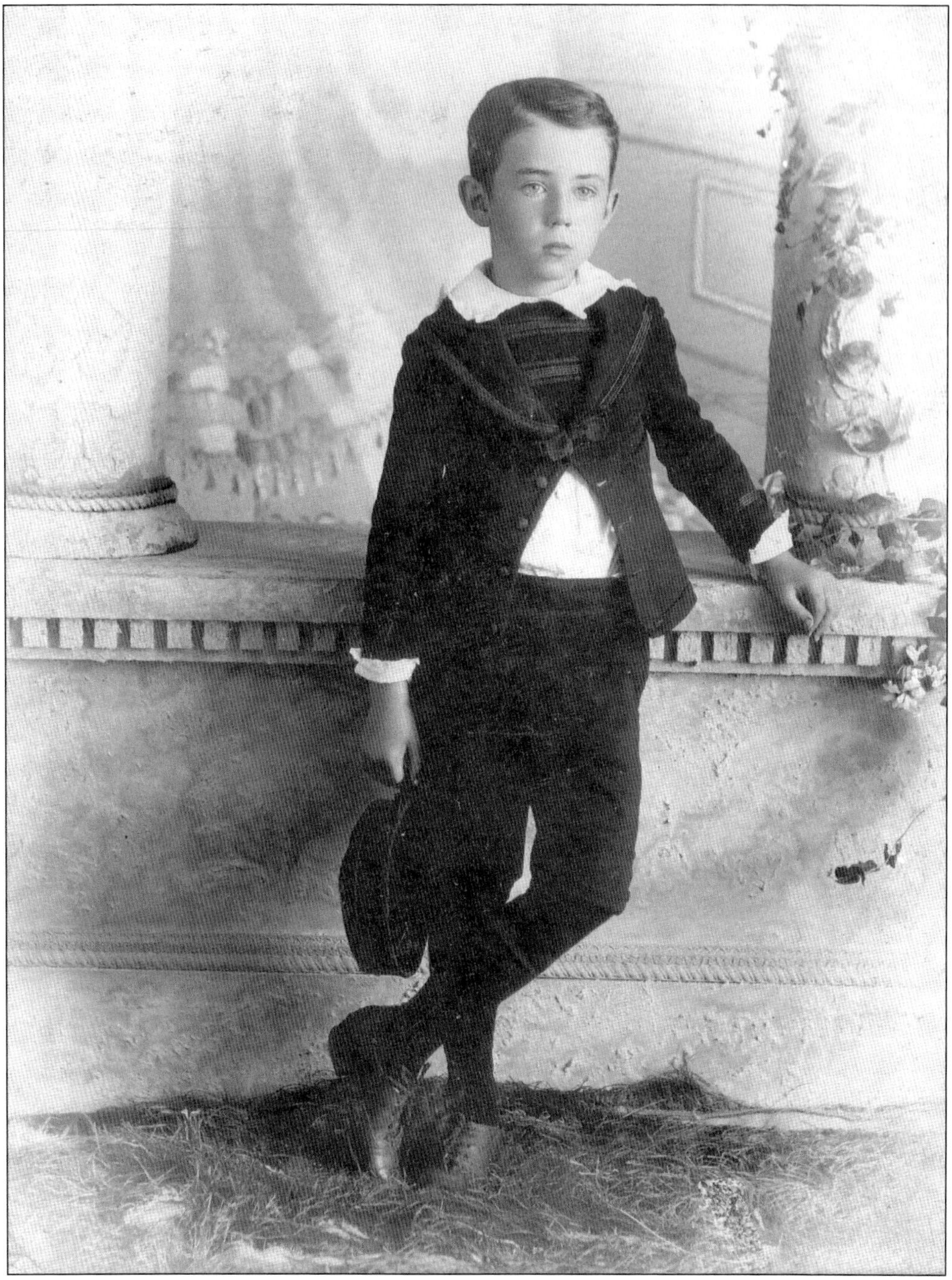

Joseph Anderson Caldwell, son of John H. Caldwell and Margaret Anderson Caldwell, was born December 28, 1884. Joseph was the grandson of Bristol's founder, J. R. Anderson. As an adult, Joseph served as juvenile judge in Bristol and then county judge in Blountville. He married Isabel Hawley on January 3, 1912. She died in 1931, and Joseph later married Virginia Byars Koontz. In 1940, the couple bought the old Deery Inn in Blountville. Joseph Anderson Caldwell died on May 23, 1963. This attractive portrait was taken by Hodges Photography Studio c. 1890. (Courtesy of Bud Phillips.)

Phipps King was the son of Col. Samuel L. and Annie Phipps King of Bristol. He was born May 16, 1899, and was given his mother's maiden name. Sadly, Phipps did not reach his fourth birthday as he died in 1902. He was survived by three siblings, Samuel Lee King Jr., John Goodson King, and Charles L. King. (Courtesy of Tim Buchanan.)

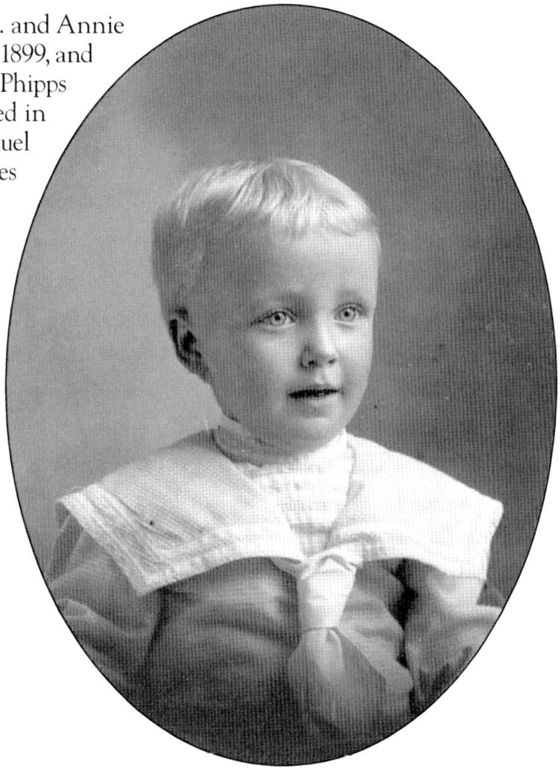

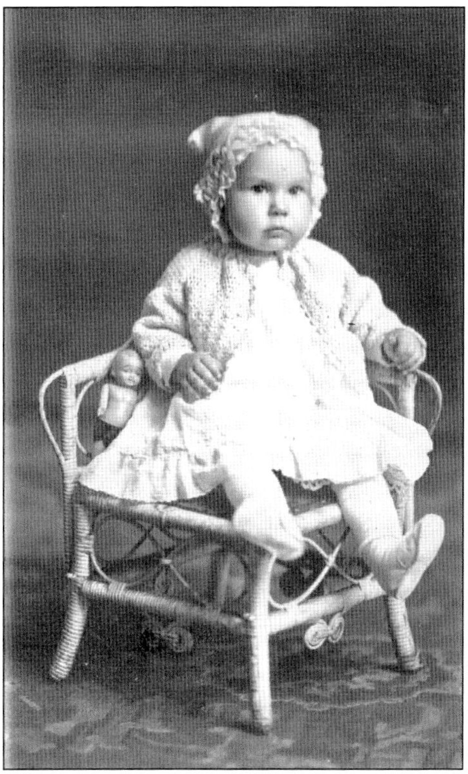

Alma Simmons was born September 12, 1921. When she grew up, Alma married Stacy Jennings Grayson. The couple raised three daughters in Bristol, where Stacy (shown on page 69) served as mayor for a time and Alma was a homemaker. (Courtesy of Beth Grayson Taylor and Patt Grayson Phipps.)

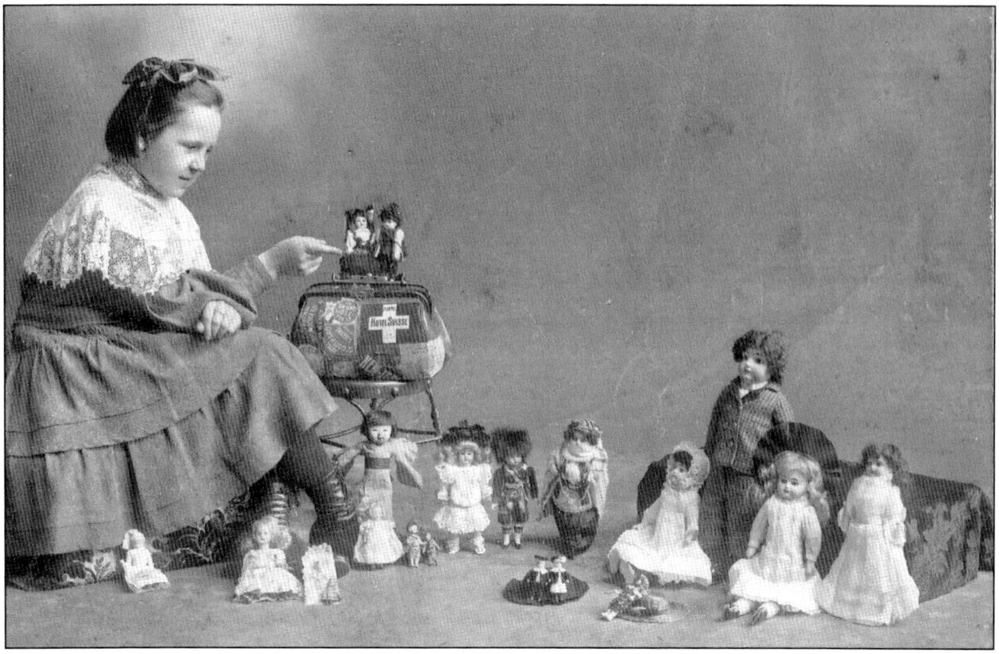

Playing with dolls has been a favorite pastime of little girls across cultures and through time. Shown in this adorable photograph is Nannie Lin Anderson *c.* 1904 with her doll collection from foreign lands. Nannie was nine years old when this was taken. (Courtesy of Fan Hepburn.)

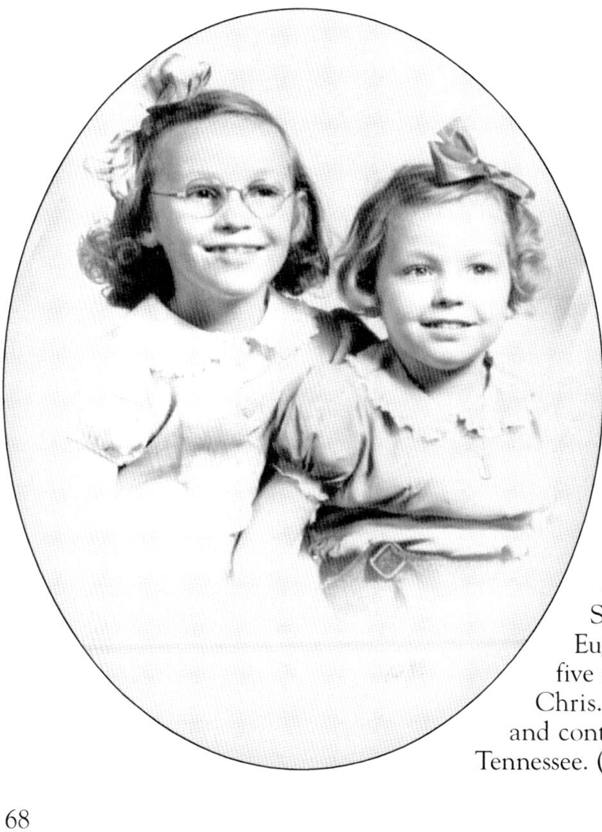

Mary Lou (left) and Linda Good, daughters of William and Helen Good, are pictured here *c.* 1942. Mary Lou was born August 29, 1935, and died January 25, 2003, of colon cancer. She married her teenage sweetheart, Eugene Haskins, and together they had five children: Gary, Kerry, Jeff, Amy, and Chris. Linda was born February 20, 1940, and continues to enjoy her home in Bristol, Tennessee. (Courtesy of Eugene Haskins.)

Stacy Jennings Grayson was born March 21, 1916. His family moved to Bristol by wagon while he was still a young boy. Stacy served as mayor of Bristol, Tennessee, from 1960 until 1964. (Courtesy of Beth Grayson Taylor and Patt Grayson Phipps.)

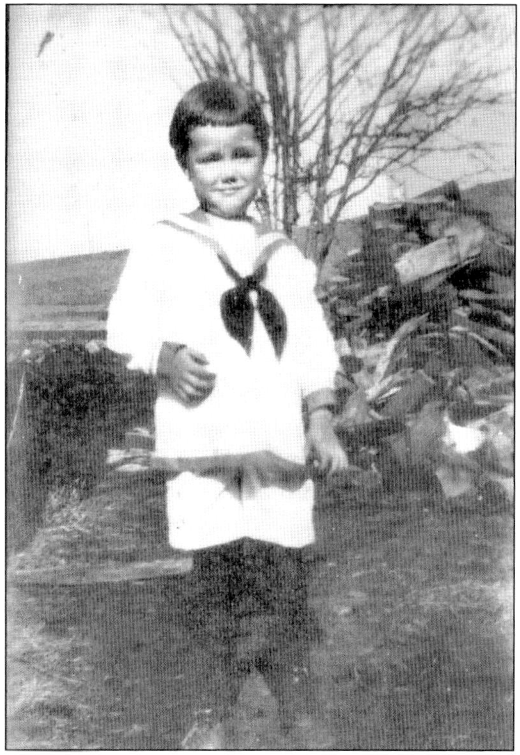

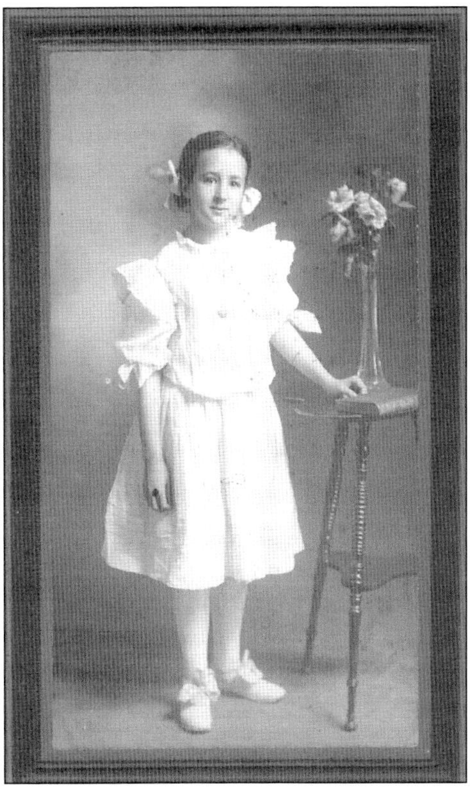

Ida Lorene Smith was born October 3, 1895, in Bristol, Virginia. She married Glen Simmons on April 3, 1926, and had two children, Martha and Peggy. Ida's father, J. L. C. Smith, was elected Bristol, Virginia, treasurer in 1890 and later president of the city council. Ida lived a gracious life and died on May 12, 1969. She is buried in East Hill Cemetery beside her husband. (Courtesy of Tim Buchanan.)

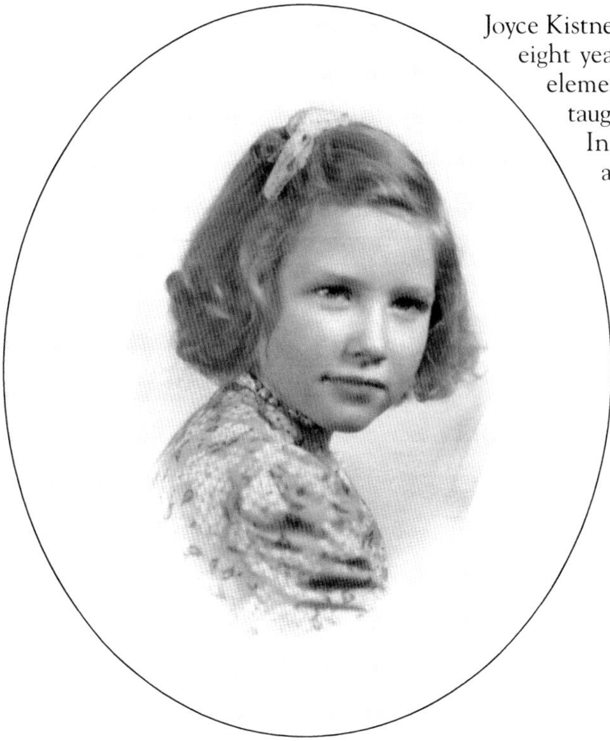

Joyce Kistner, shown here in 1946 when she was eight years old, retired as a Bristol, Virginia, elementary school teacher in 1991. Joyce taught at several local elementary schools. In 1979, Joyce made a decision that affected all future Bristolians and Bristol visitors, including everyone enjoying this book. At that time, she chartered the Bristol Historical Association, which is still going strong. (Courtesy of Joyce Kistner.)

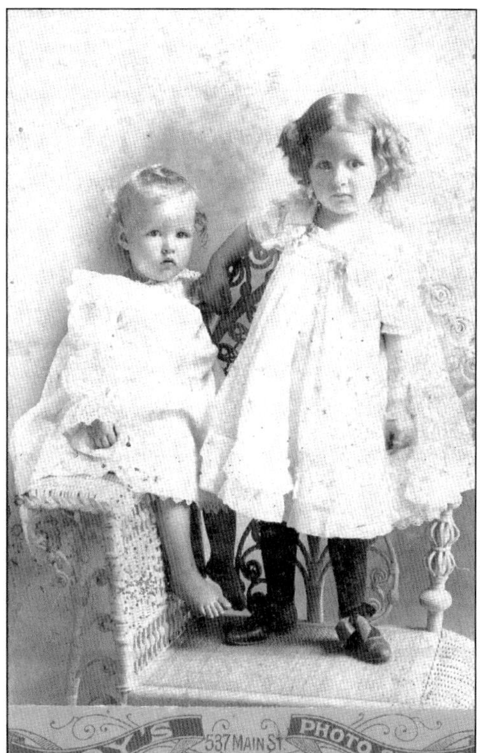

Robert Myron ("Slim") Easley and his sister Eva, the children of John and Margaret Easley, pose in this 1899 Boy's Photo Studio portrait. Slim, as he was called, founded Easley Insurance Agency and was treasurer of Twin City Federal and Loan Association. Eva was born in 1896 and never married. She worked for Norfolk & Western Railroad and passed away in 1986. Slim died in 1963. (Courtesy of Mrs. Dick Easley.)

Christopher Jay Haskins posed for this adorable photograph c. 1972 while his father was stationed in Japan with the Air Force. The family moved back to the States shortly after his father took this picture. Chris graduated from King College in 1991 and currently serves as the computer network manager at Milligan College. He lives in Jonesborough, Tennessee, with his wife, Sonya, and their children. (Courtesy of Eugene Haskins.)

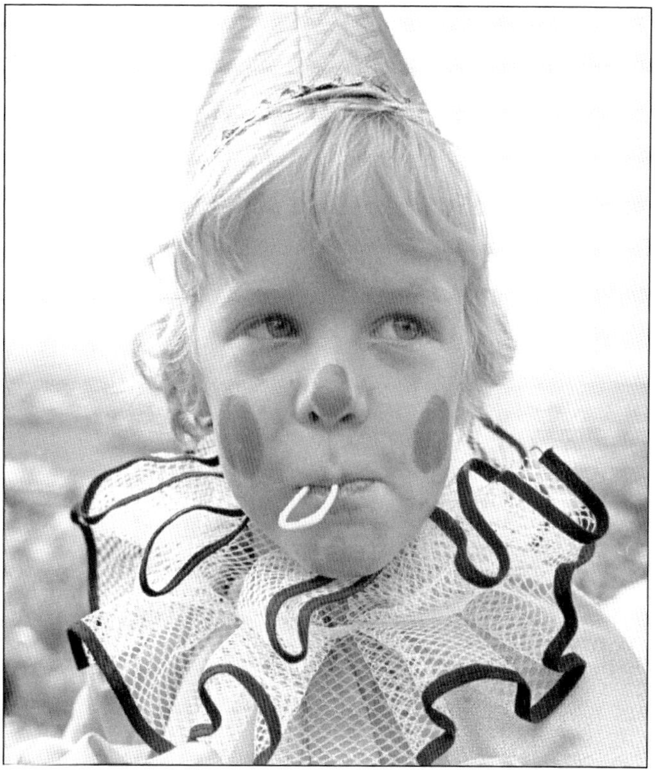

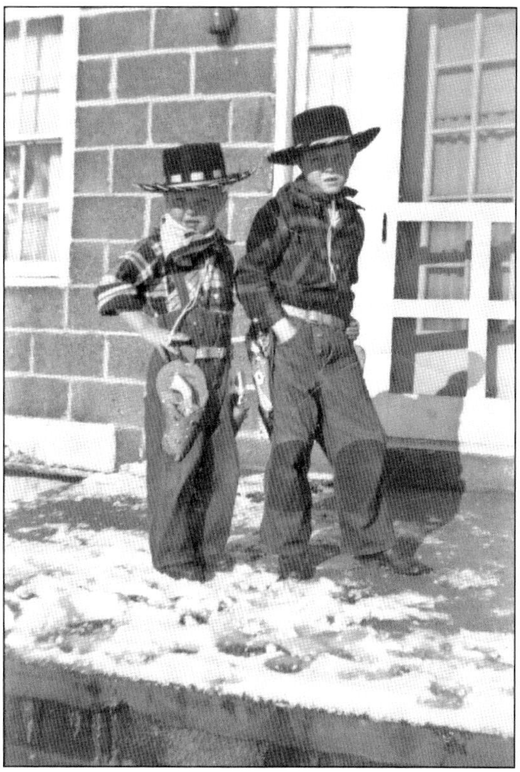

Jeff and Tom Combs show off their new cowboy attire c. 1950 at their home on the Gate City Highway in Bristol, Virginia. Tom now serves as a data or catastrophe control specialist in Garner, North Carolina, and Jeff is an Allstate insurance agent in Bristol, Virginia. (Courtesy of Don and Genelle Combs.)

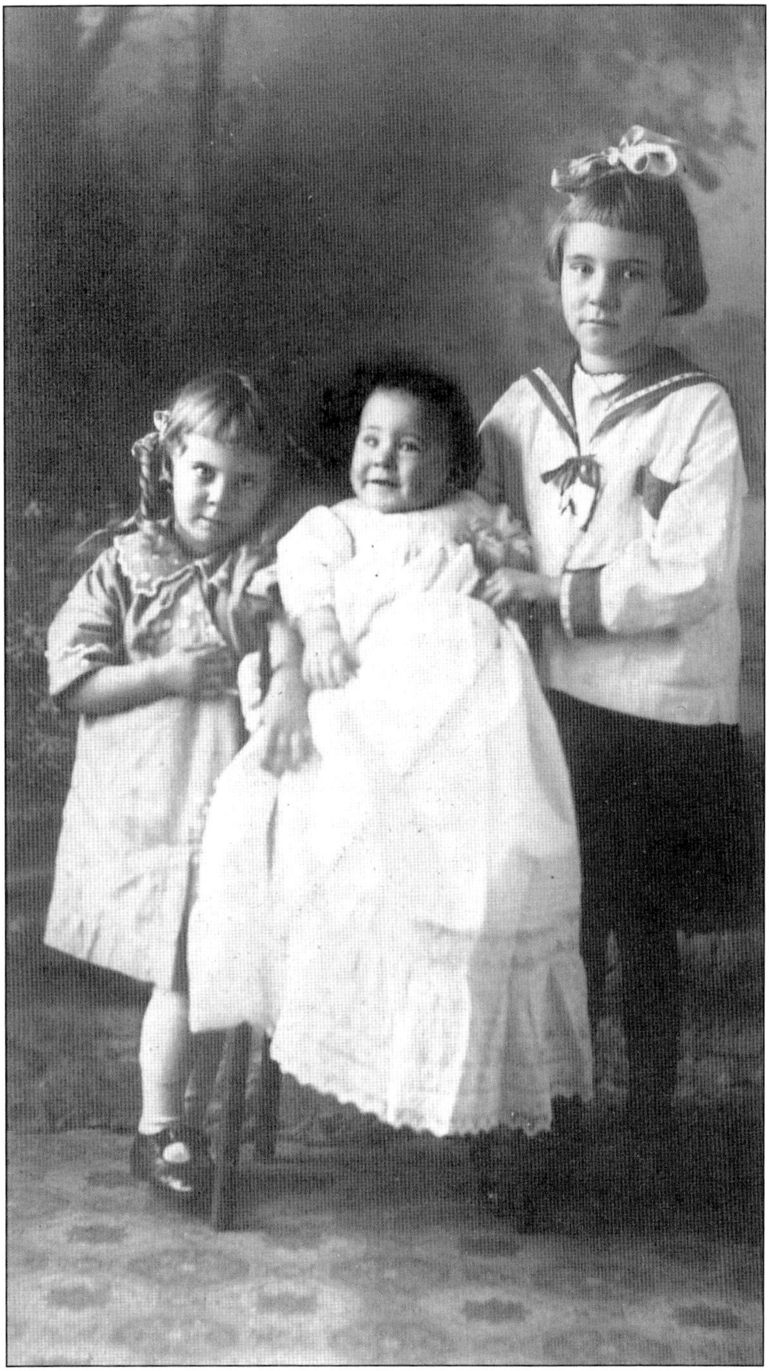

Pictured from left to right are Hazel Clay Crosswhite, Alfred Parks Crosswhite, and Virginia Lee Crosswhite in 1917. Their parents, Lelia and Worley Crosswhite (shown on page 38), had a total of five children. Tragically, only Virginia Lee outlived them. Hazel died at the age of 11 during physical education class at the Jefferson School gymnasium in 1926. Alfred died during a routine mission in the U.S. Army Air Corps. Worley Jr. died of whooping cough at only 19 days of age, and Warren was electrocuted at the age of 7 while flying a kite. (Courtesy of Lucretia Vance Gilmer.)

Five

EDUCATION

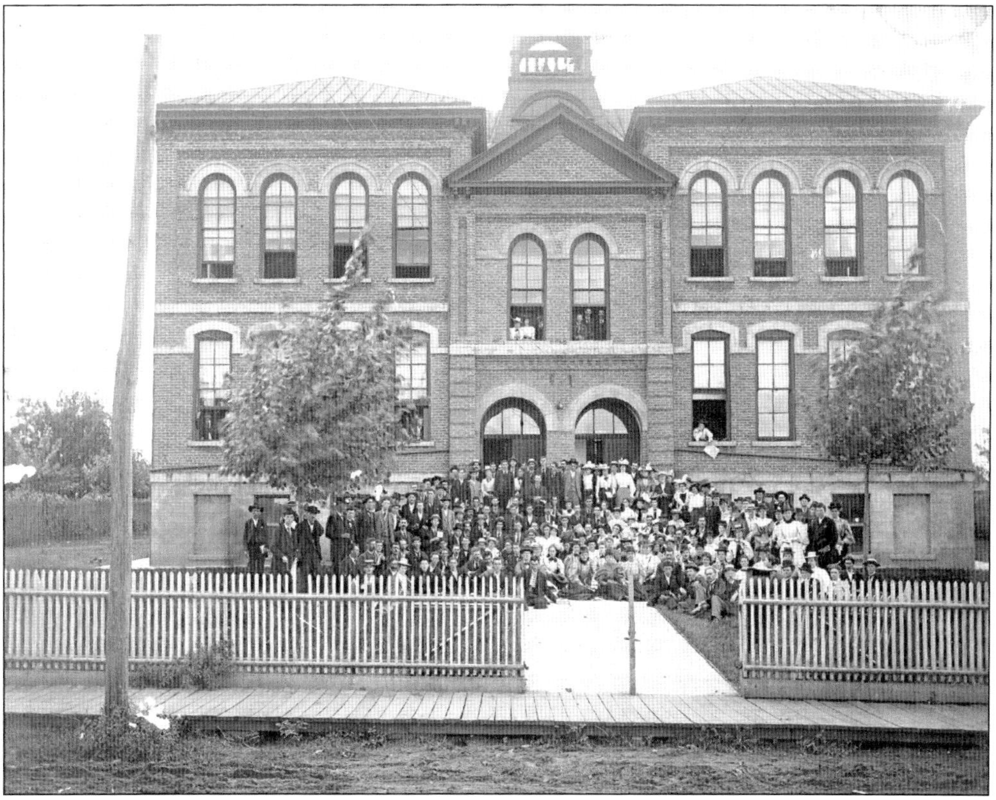

The Central School opened on September 5, 1892, as the first high school in Bristol, Virginia. In 1915, grades 9 through 11 moved to the newly built Virginia High School on Piedmont. The Central School later became known as Thomas Jefferson Elementary. (Courtesy of Bristol Historical Association.)

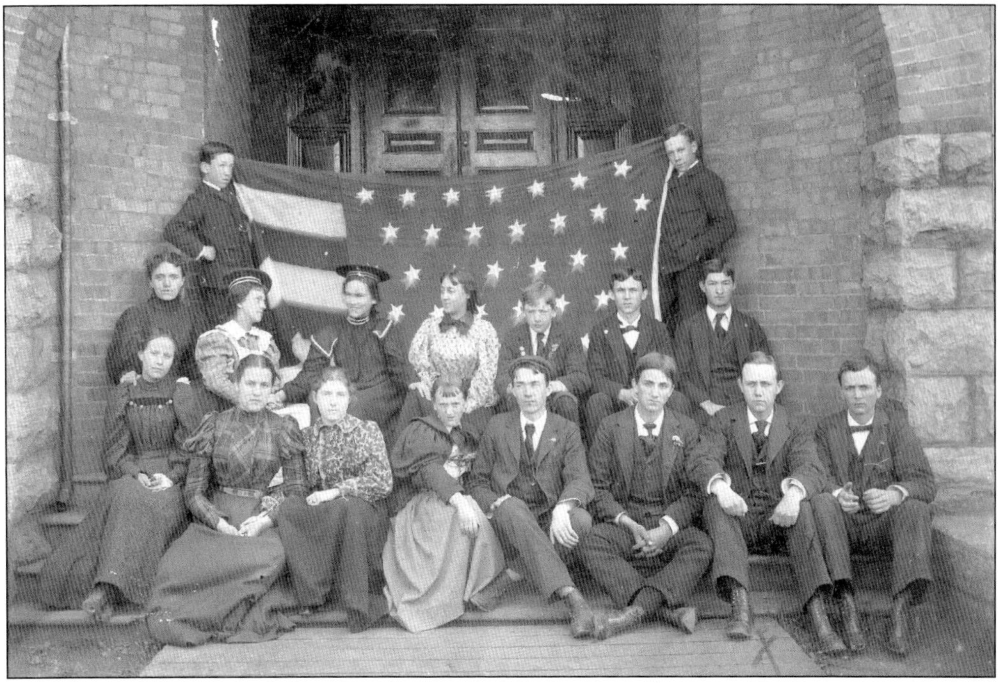

The Fifth Street School stood on the corner of Fifth and Ashe Streets in Bristol, Tennessee. The school was torn down in the 1950s when S. E. Massengill Company expanded its facilities. Shown here is the eighth-grade class of 1896–1897. King Anderson is located in the first row, second from right. Anderson was the son of former Bristol mayor John C. Anderson. (Courtesy of Fan Hepburn.)

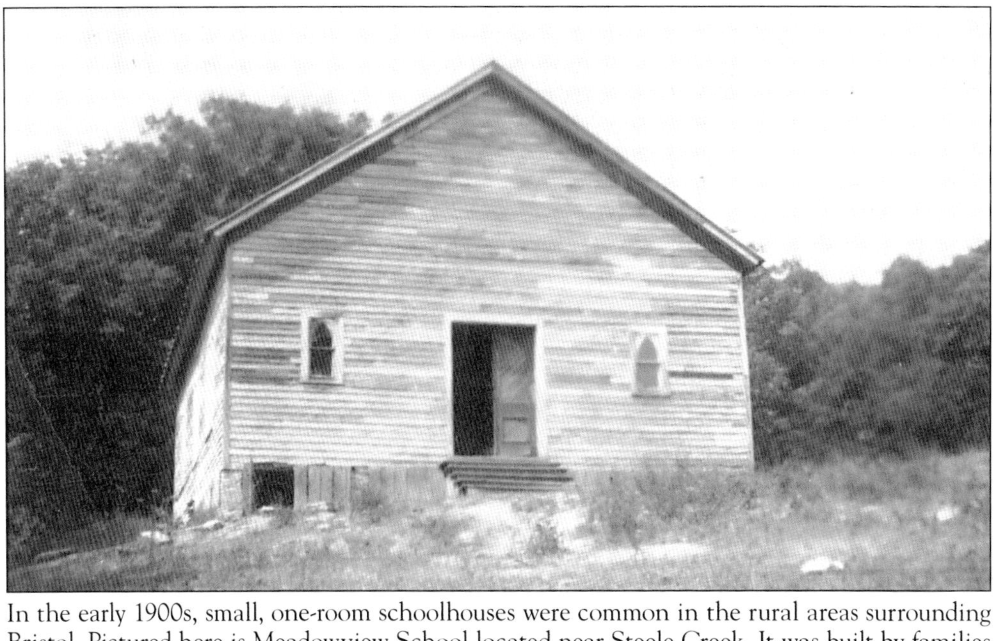

In the early 1900s, small, one-room schoolhouses were common in the rural areas surrounding Bristol. Pictured here is Meadowview School located near Steele Creek. It was built by families in the area just before the turn of the 20th century and remained a vital part of the community until it closed in 1934. (Courtesy of Paul Stone Collection.)

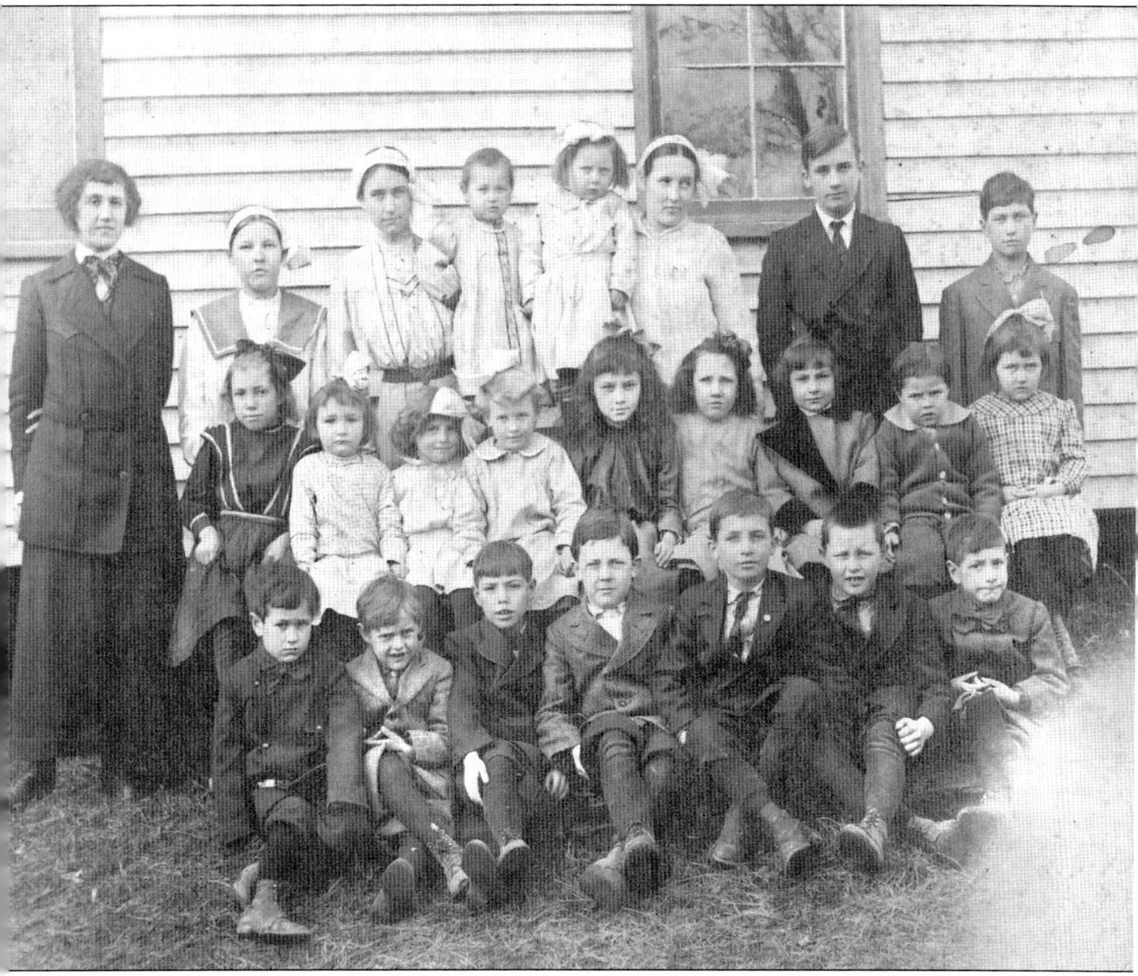

Daisy Harr is shown here with her students in 1912 at Meadowview School. One teacher handled all the duties for various aged students in the one-room schoolhouses customary in the late 1800s and early 1900s. Pictured here, from left to right, are: (first row) Edgar Clark, Oscar Reed, unidentified, Basil Moore, and three unidentified children; (second row) ? Reed, Joanna Miller, Virginia Goodman, Clara Goodman, Annette Clark, Clarice Moore, Frances Shankle, Benny Booher, and Jewell Booher; (third row) Daisy Harr, Lula Moore, Ellen Clark, James Clark, Eva Moore, Ada Moore, ? Goodman, and George Clark. (Courtesy of John Stone.)

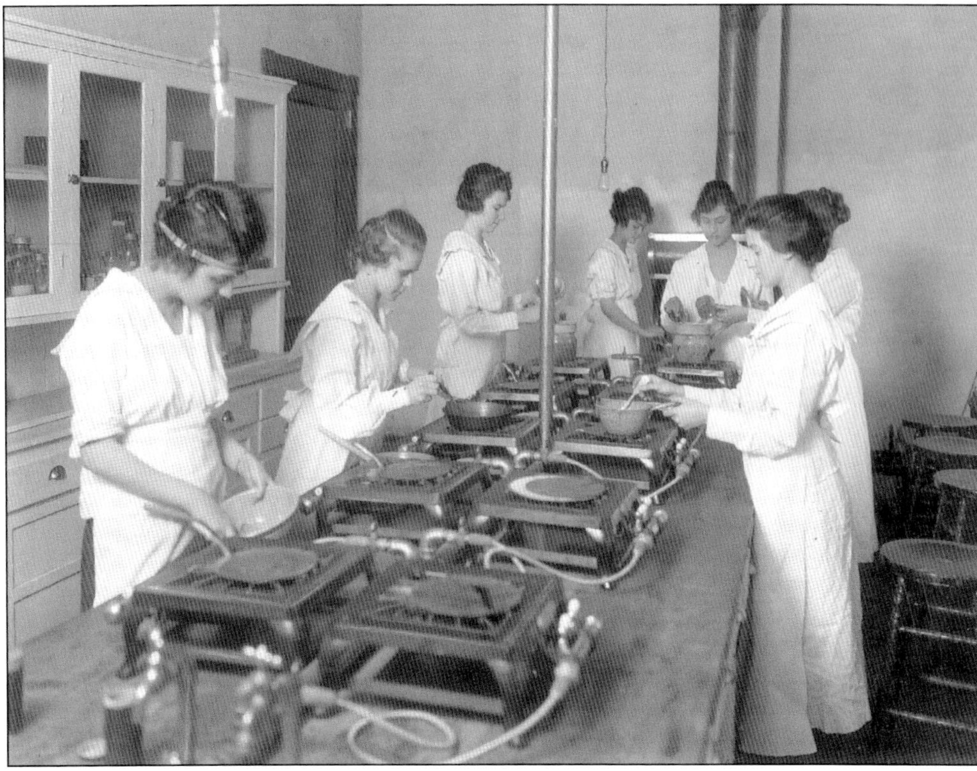

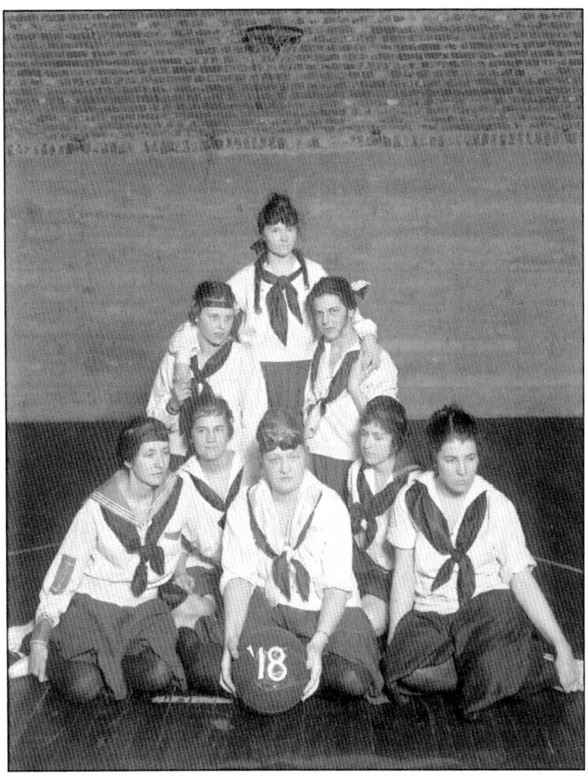

Founded in 1870 and named for Rev. David Sullins, its first president, Sullins College included a grammar school and high school curriculum in addition to the college curriculum until 1915. During the 1915 Christmas vacation, the school burned. It reopened in 1917 as a two-year liberal arts college for young women that closed in 1977. Shown here are a Sullins College cooking class and basketball team. (Courtesy of Bristol Historical Association.)

Rev. James Doak Tadlock was the first president of King College. King began classes on August 5, 1867, and Doak served as president until 1885. Doak died in Bristol on August 26, 1899. (Courtesy of King College.)

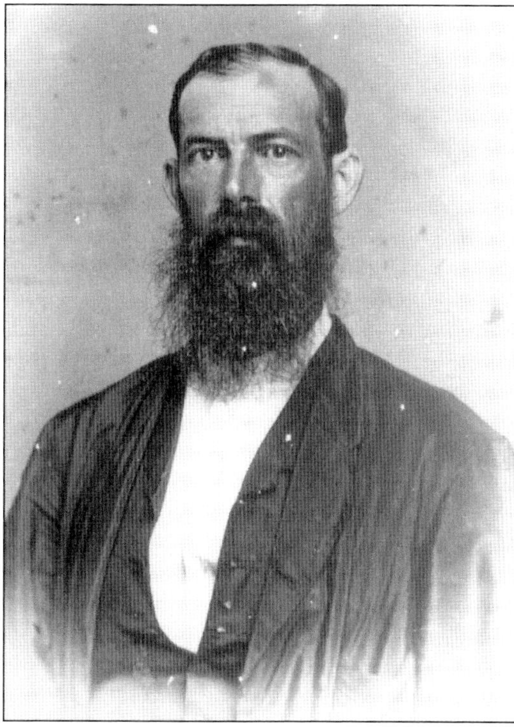

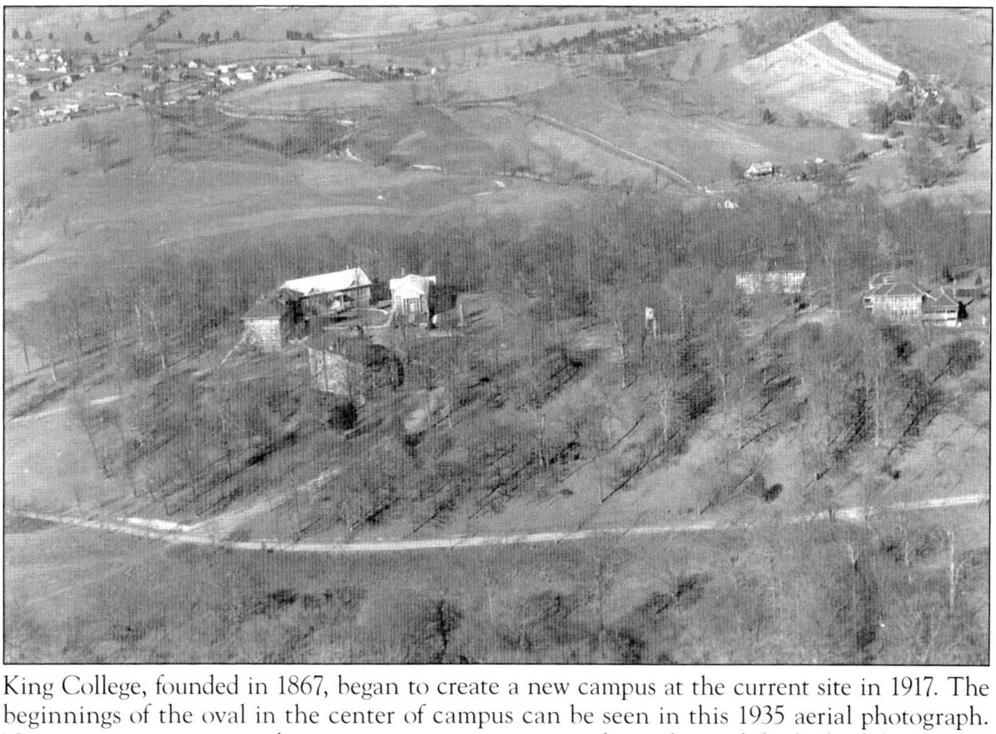

King College, founded in 1867, began to create a new campus at the current site in 1917. The beginnings of the oval in the center of campus can be seen in this 1935 aerial photograph. Numerous renovations and improvements in recent years have changed the look of the campus dramatically, but the oval remains a permanent feature of the Christian, liberal arts college. (Courtesy of Bristol Historical Association.)

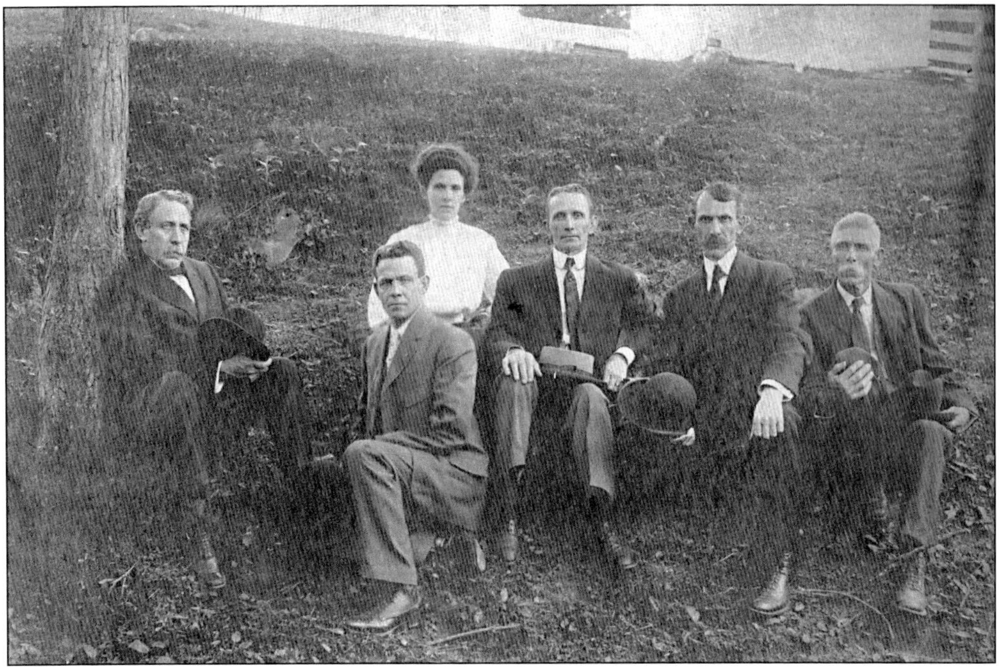

Some of the King family took time out to pose for this photograph that was taken sometime around 1930. Pictured from left to right are siblings E. W. (1852–1945), Rutledge (1866–1957), Sarah Josephine (1855–1937), Anson (1860–1954), Henry Preston or H. P. (1862–1944), and James (1851–1931). Some of Bristol's most prominent businesses are credited to this family. (Courtesy of King College.)

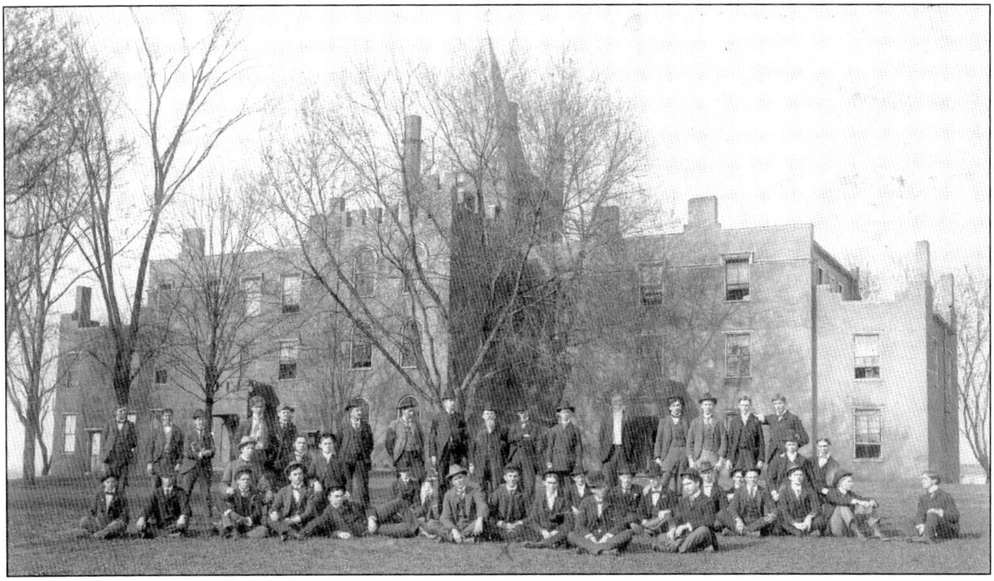

King started in a residence on August 5, 1867, and later moved to this building, which was eventually used for S. E. Massengill Pharmaceutical Company. There was a faculty of 3 with 48 students. As the school and student body grew, plans were made to build a new campus, and in September 1917, the campus on Fifth Street was closed. This photograph was taken c. 1900. (Courtesy of King College.)

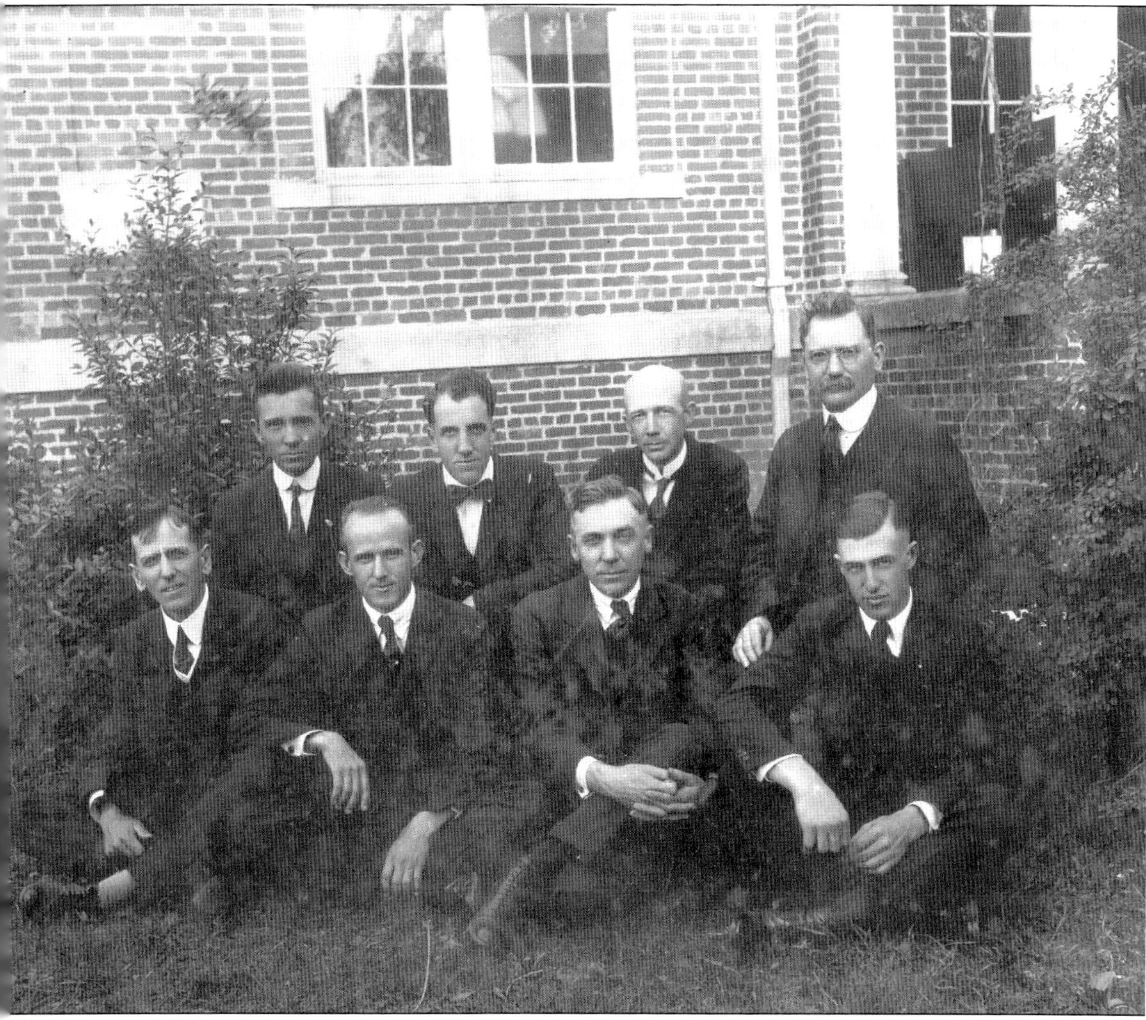

The King College faculty, shown from left to right, in 1921–1922 was comprised of the following professors: (first row) King A. Hagy (Latin), O. R. Post (English and Greek), Frank W. DeFriece Sr. (history, economics, and business), and A. B. Spahr (chemistry lab assistant and assistant commandant); (second row) Tilden Scherer (president of King College), Austin Vanderhoff (mathematics and physical training), Anton Verhulst (Bible and philosophy), and W. A. Garrison (biology and chemistry). (Courtesy of King College.)

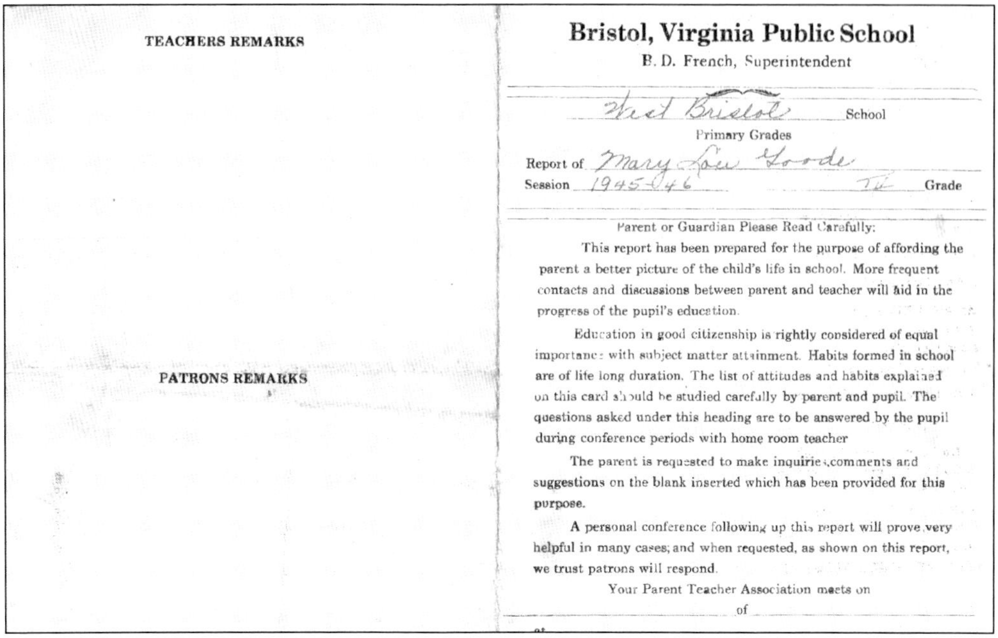

TEACHERS REMARKS

PATRONS REMARKS

Bristol, Virginia Public School

B. D. French, Superintendent

West Bristol School

Primary Grades

Report of Mary Lou Goode

Session 1945-46 IV Grade

Parent or Guardian Please Read Carefully:

This report has been prepared for the purpose of affording the parent a better picture of the child's life in school. More frequent contacts and discussions between parent and teacher will aid in the progress of the pupil's education.

Education in good citizenship is rightly considered of equal importance with subject matter attainment. Habits formed in school are of life long duration. The list of attitudes and habits explained on this card should be studied carefully by parent and pupil. The questions asked under this heading are to be answered by the pupil during conference periods with home room teacher

The parent is requested to make inquiries, comments and suggestions on the blank inserted which has been provided for this purpose.

A personal conference following up this report will prove very helpful in many cases; and when requested, as shown on this report, we trust patrons will respond.

Your Parent Teacher Association meets on

of

On the front of this 1945–1946 fourth-grade report card is a note for parents stating, "Education in good citizenship is rightly considered of equal importance with subject matter attainment. Habits formed in school are of life long duration." Mary Lou Good (incorrectly spelled on the report card with an "e") attended West Bristol School with W. Wolfe as principal and A. Ridge as her teacher. In addition to doing well in her academic subjects, Mary Lou did learn good citizenship. (Courtesy of Eugene Haskins.)

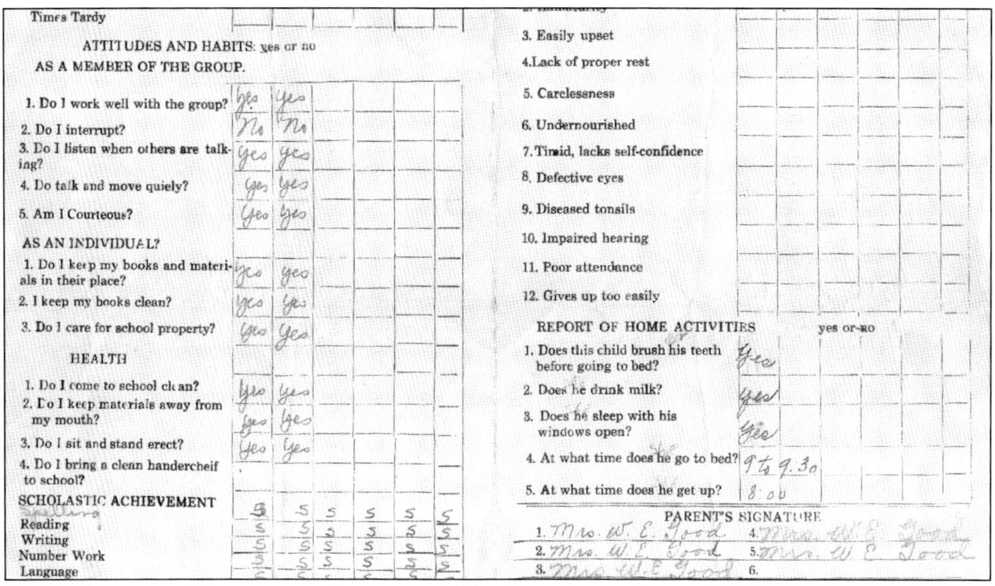

Times Tardy

ATTITUDES AND HABITS: yes or no
AS A MEMBER OF THE GROUP.

1. Do I work well with the group?	yes	yes
2. Do I interrupt?	No	No
3. Do I listen when others are talking?	yes	yes
4. Do talk and move quiely?	yes	yes
5. Am I Courteous?	yes	yes
AS AN INDIVIDUAL?		
1. Do I keep my books and materials in their place?	yes	yes
2. I keep my books clean?	yes	yes
3. Do I care for school property?	yes	yes
HEALTH		
1. Do I come to school clean?	yes	yes
2. Do I keep materials away from my mouth?	yes	yes
3. Do I sit and stand erect?	yes	yes
4. Do I bring a clean handercheif to school?		

SCHOLASTIC ACHIEVEMENT

Spelling	S	S	S	S	S	S
Reading	S	S	S	S	S	S
Writing	S	S	S	S	S	S
Number Work	S	S	S	S	S	S
Language	S	S	S	S	S	S

3. Easily upset
4. Lack of proper rest
5. Carelessness
6. Undernourished
7. Timid, lacks self-confidence
8. Defective eyes
9. Diseased tonsils
10. Impaired hearing
11. Poor attendance
12. Gives up too easily

REPORT OF HOME ACTIVITIES yes or no

1. Does this child brush his teeth before going to bed?	yes
2. Does he drink milk?	yes
3. Does he sleep with his windows open?	yes
4. At what time does he go to bed?	9 to 9.30
5. At what time does he get up?	8:00

PARENT'S SIGNATURE

1. Mrs. W. E. Good
2. Mrs. W. E. Good
3. Mrs. W. E. Good
4. Mrs. W. E. Good
5. Mrs. W. E. Good
6.

Notice that most of the space on the report card has been devoted to attitude and social development. The small amount of space allotted for scholastic achievement almost indicates that it was expected that the student would perform well in these areas. This particular report card also has an area for parents to report home activities. Note that this child doesn't have to get up until 8:00 each morning. (Courtesy of Eugene Haskins.)

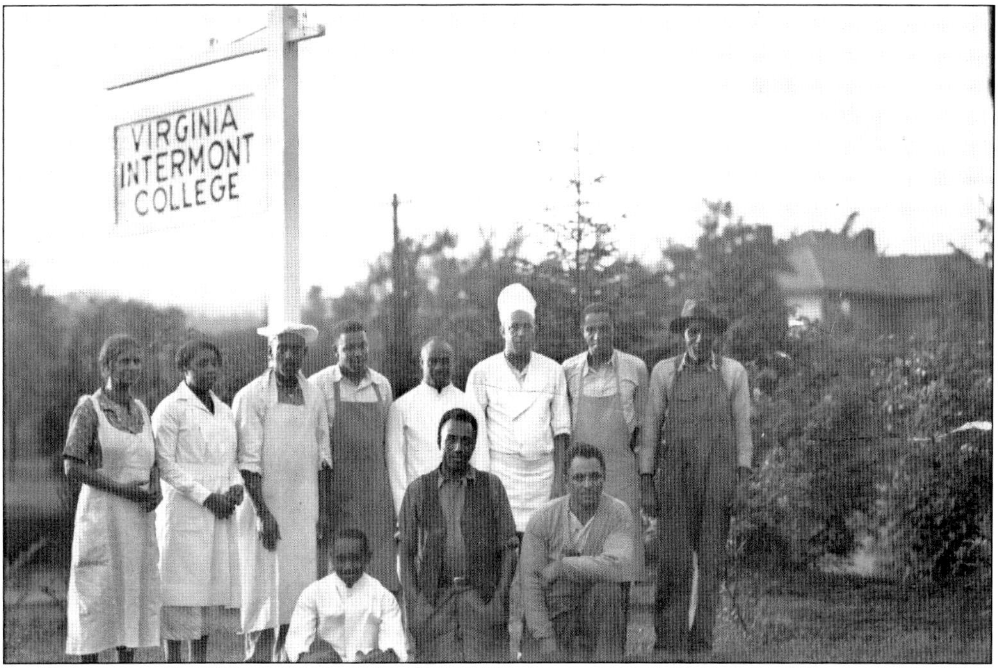

This photograph, taken around 1930, shows those at Virginia Intermont College who did the cooking, cleaning, and general maintenance. Rev. J. R. Harrison founded the school in 1884 as Southwest Virginia Institute located in Glade Spring, Virginia. In 1891, the move was made to Moore Street in Bristol. Once an all-girls school, the college became co-ed in 1972. (Courtesy of Virginia Intermont College.)

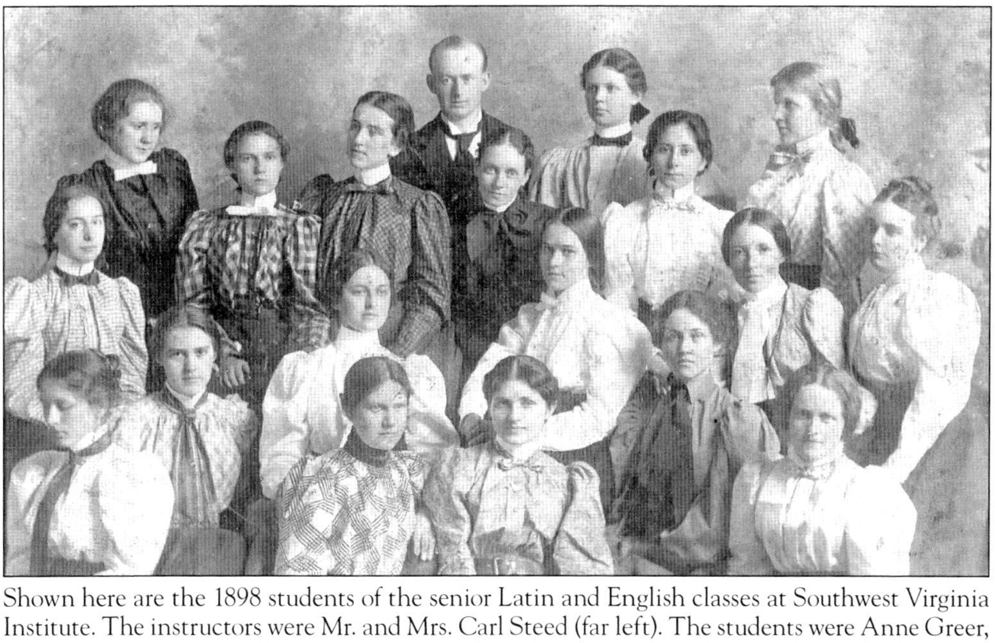

Shown here are the 1898 students of the senior Latin and English classes at Southwest Virginia Institute. The instructors were Mr. and Mrs. Carl Steed (far left). The students were Anne Greer, Dora Susong, Vivien Coffey, Bodie Bidgood, Toler Moore, Lucy Dickinson, Bessie Taylor, Flora Pendleton, Alice Seward, Helen Wainright, Ida Eastland, Olive Dungan, Francis Acree, Mary Minor, Addie Huff, and Josie St. John. (Courtesy of Virginia Intermont College.)

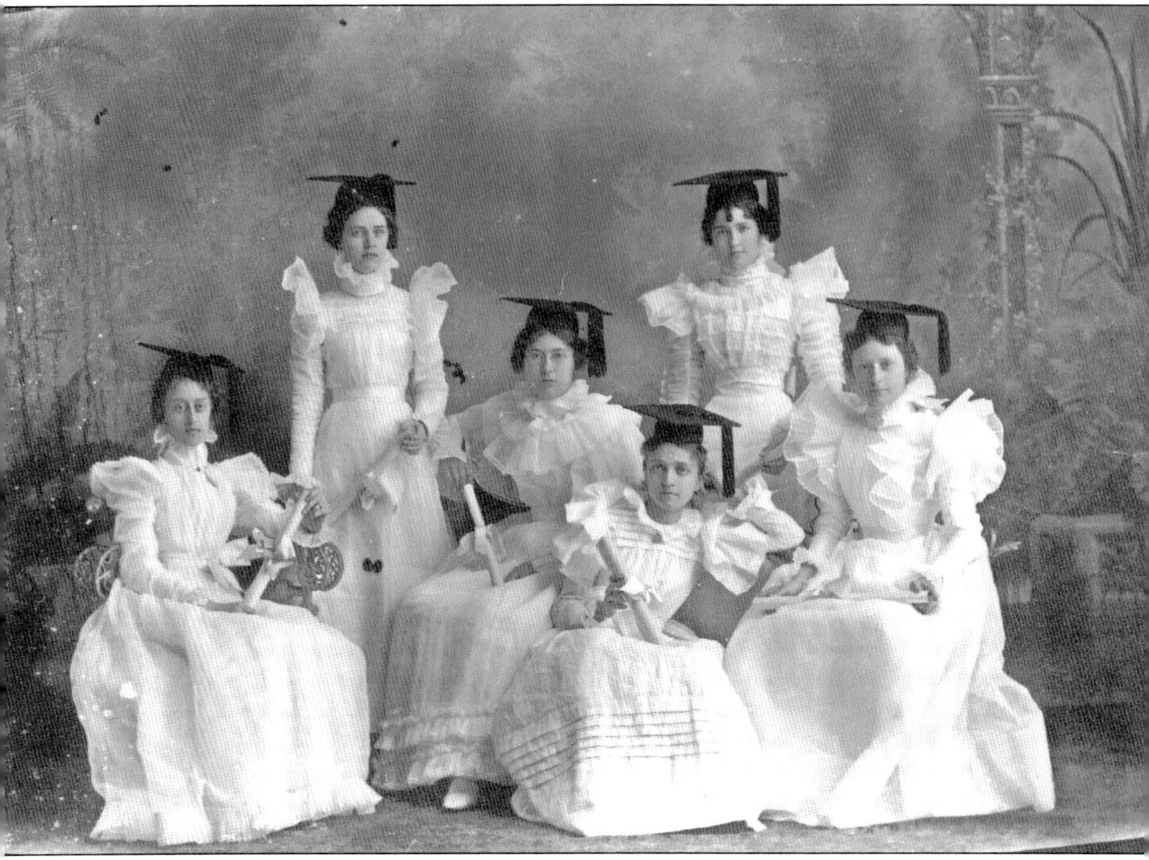

This Southwest Virginia Institute (now Virginia Intermont) photograph shows the 1910 graduates who were from Bristol. Pictured from left to right are Roberta Good, Sarah Martin, unidentified, Elizabeth McChesney, Annie Aaron, and Margaret Roller. The photograph was taken by Hodges Photography Studio. (Courtesy of Virginia Intermont College.)

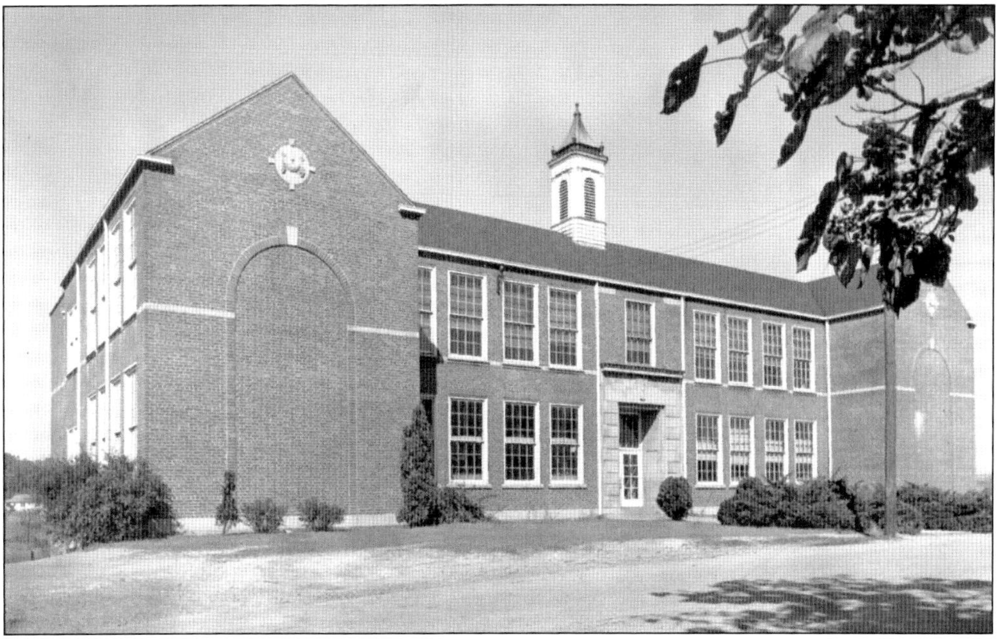

Rosemont Elementary School was located on Broad Street in Bristol, Tennessee. Tri-Cities Christian School purchased the building from the City of Bristol on May 9, 1984. Tri-Cities Christian School provides "a Christ-centered, Biblically directed education" and serves children in nursery through sixth grade at the Broad Street location. The school averages about 200 students per year. (Courtesy of Bristol Historical Association.)

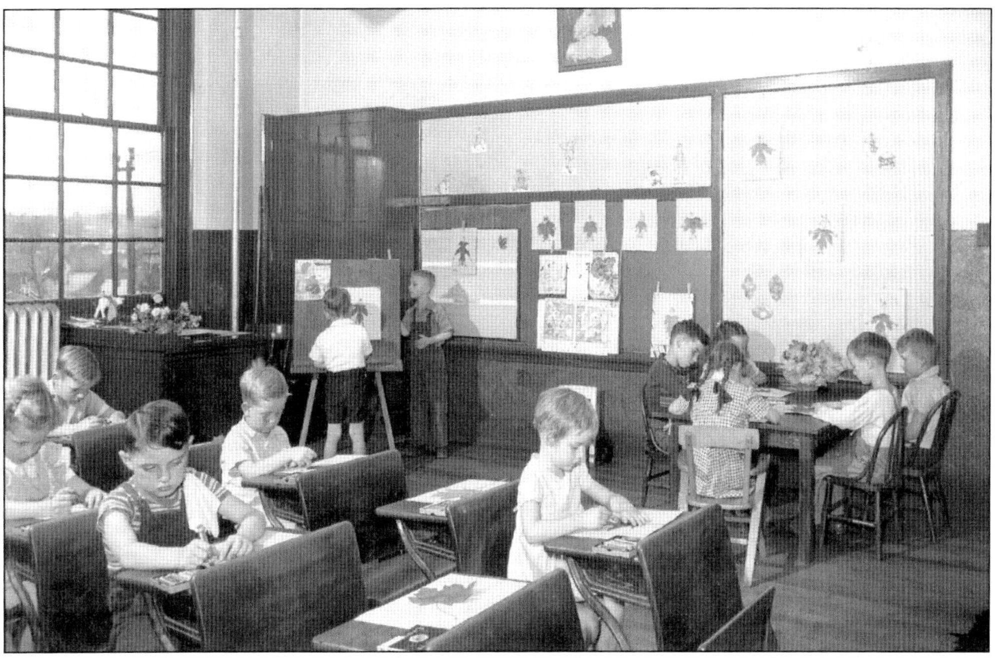

These young students at Rosemont Elementary School are busy turning leaves into art forms. Some of their finished projects, little leaf people, are displayed on the bulletin board in the right side of the picture, which was taken c. 1930. (Courtesy of Bristol Historical Association.)

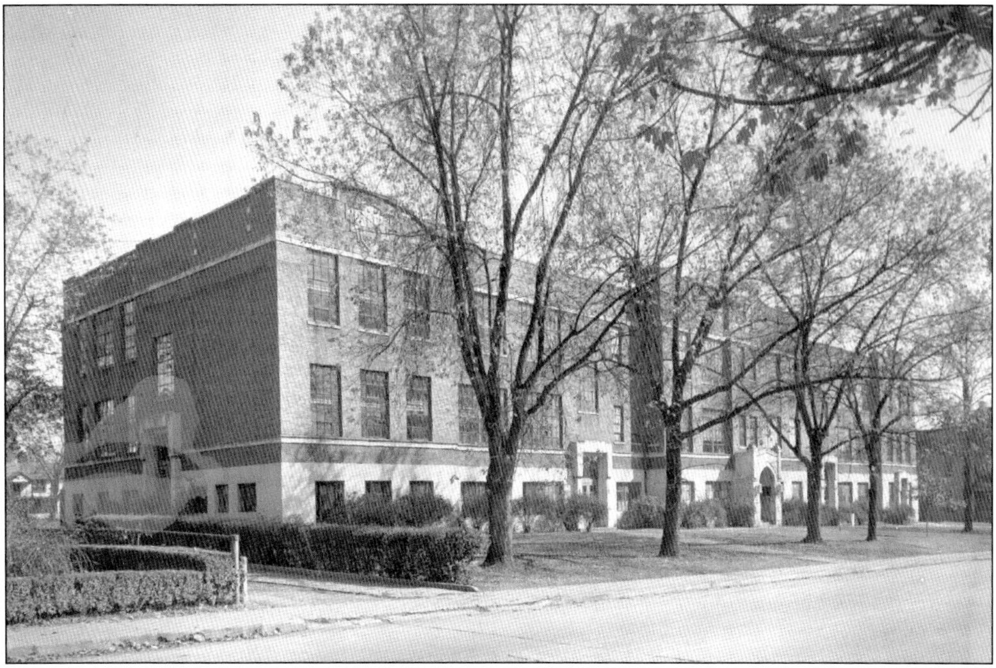

This is the Thomas Jefferson Elementary School, located on Mary Street in Bristol, Virginia. (Courtesy of Bristol Historical Association.)

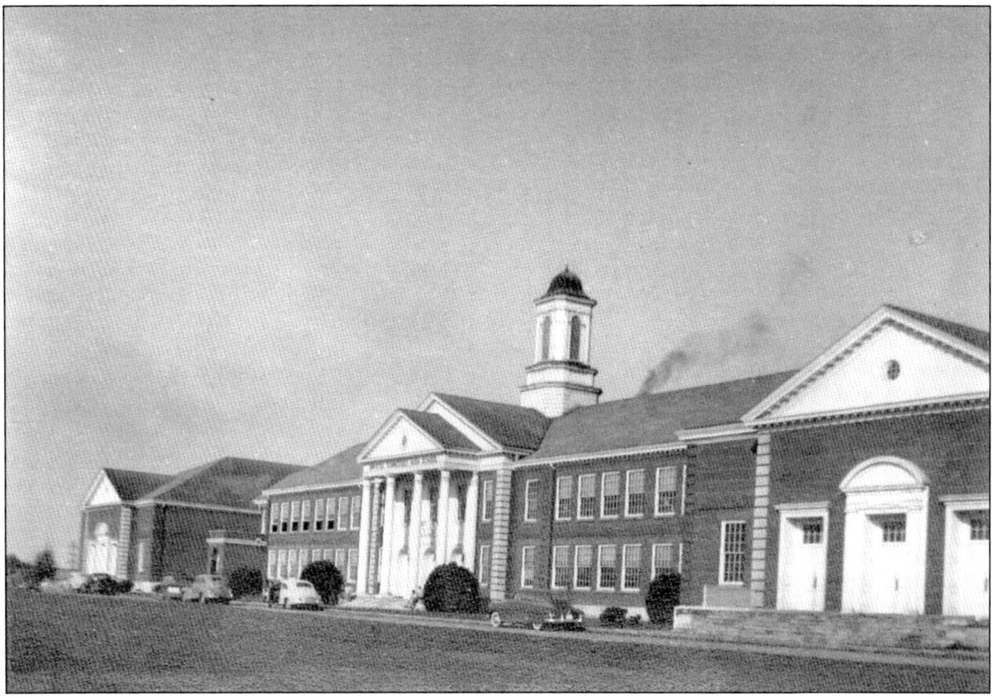

The Bristol, Tennessee, Public School System was organized in April 1888. Girls attended the Baptist Academy and boys attended what was generally known as "Cornfield Academy." The first official Tennessee High School opened in 1917. In the late 1930s, this building was erected on Edgemont Avenue. (Courtesy of authors' collection.)

Six

Religion

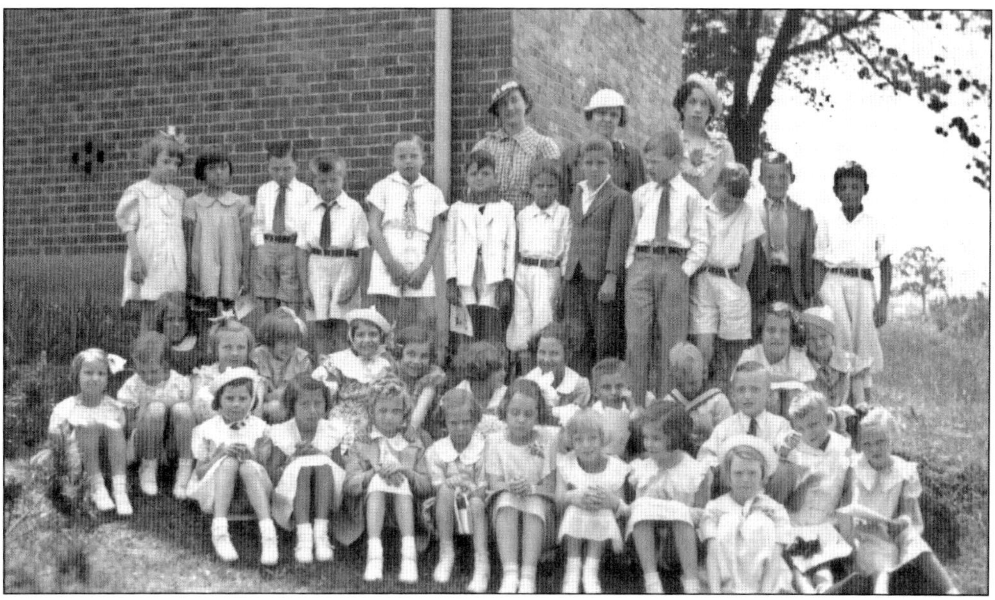

The Virginia Avenue Methodist Church Bible School class of 1934 is pictured here. Third from the left on the back row is Bob Broyles and fourth from the right on the back row is his older brother James. Lucille Swiney McHenry, standing behind the children, far right, is one of the Bible School teachers. (Courtesy of Bob and Marie Broyles.)

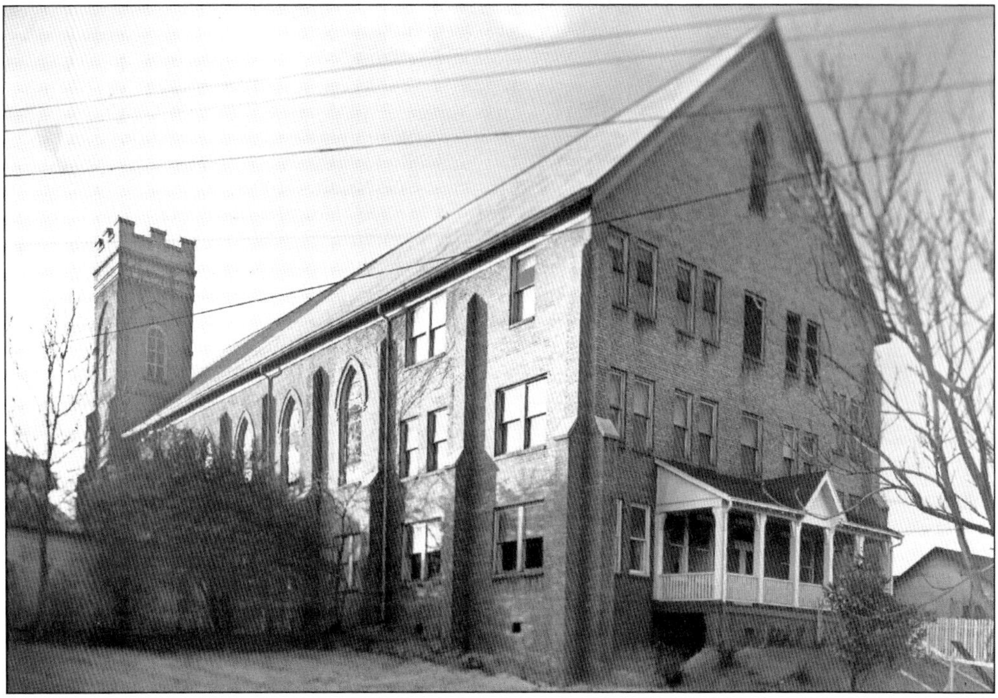

First Presbyterian Church began in 1854 when Joseph R. Anderson had Sunday school in his home. In 1857, a two-story brick building was erected at Fifth and Shelby Streets. A new church was built there in 1885, and over the years, it underwent several renovations. The back of that church is shown here. (Courtesy of Bristol Historical Association.)

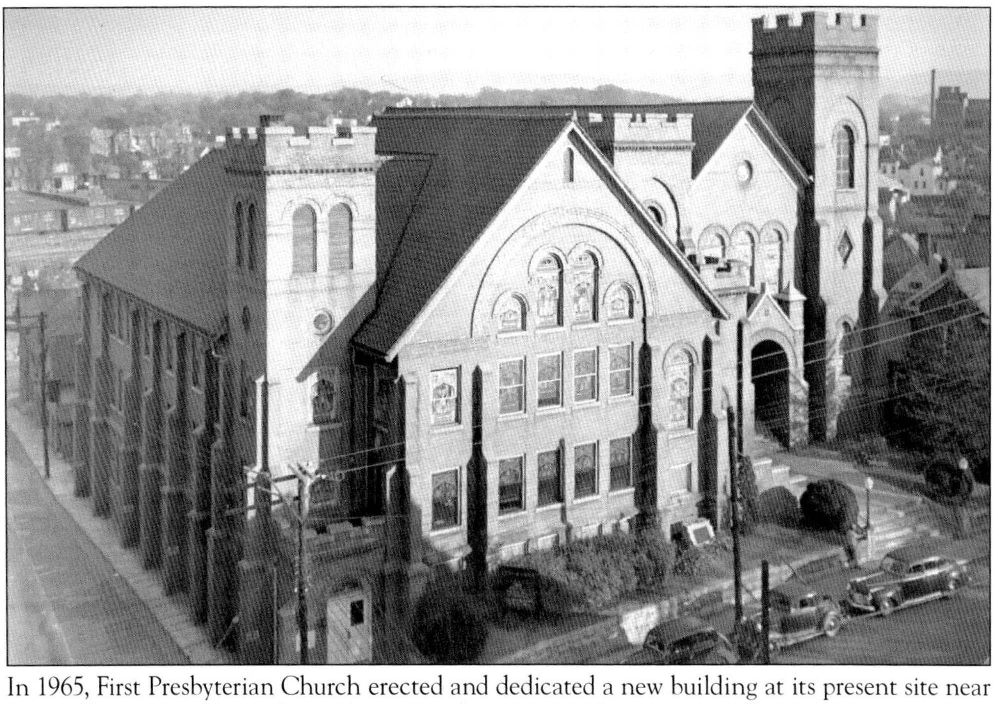

In 1965, First Presbyterian Church erected and dedicated a new building at its present site near King College. (Courtesy of Bristol Historical Association.)

Anderson Street Methodist Church began as Anderson Street Mission in 1893 and met in a brick schoolhouse on Anderson and Tenth Streets. As membership grew, a new building was erected in 1898. This building served the congregation for almost 30 years until it was determined that a larger church building was needed. While members worshipped in a tent, the present-day church was completed in 1930. (Courtesy of Tim Buchanan.)

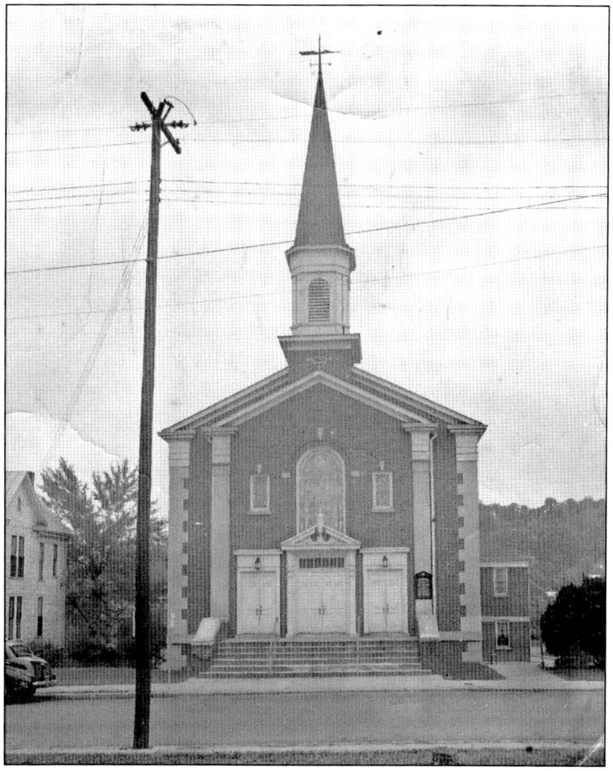

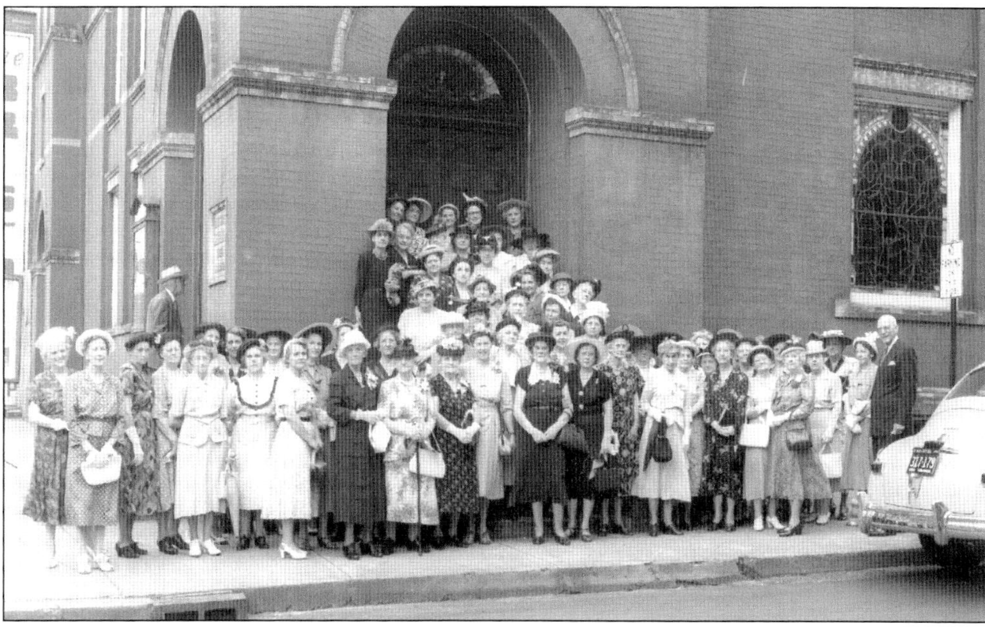

The ladies at State Street Methodist Church pose for this c. 1950 photograph. Dr. William F. Blackard (far right) was pastor at State Street Methodist from 1945 to 1955. The structure in the background was the old State Street Methodist, which was built in 1904 at a cost of $25,000. In 1956, a new building was erected in the Spring Garden section of Bristol, Virginia. (Courtesy of State Street Methodist Church.)

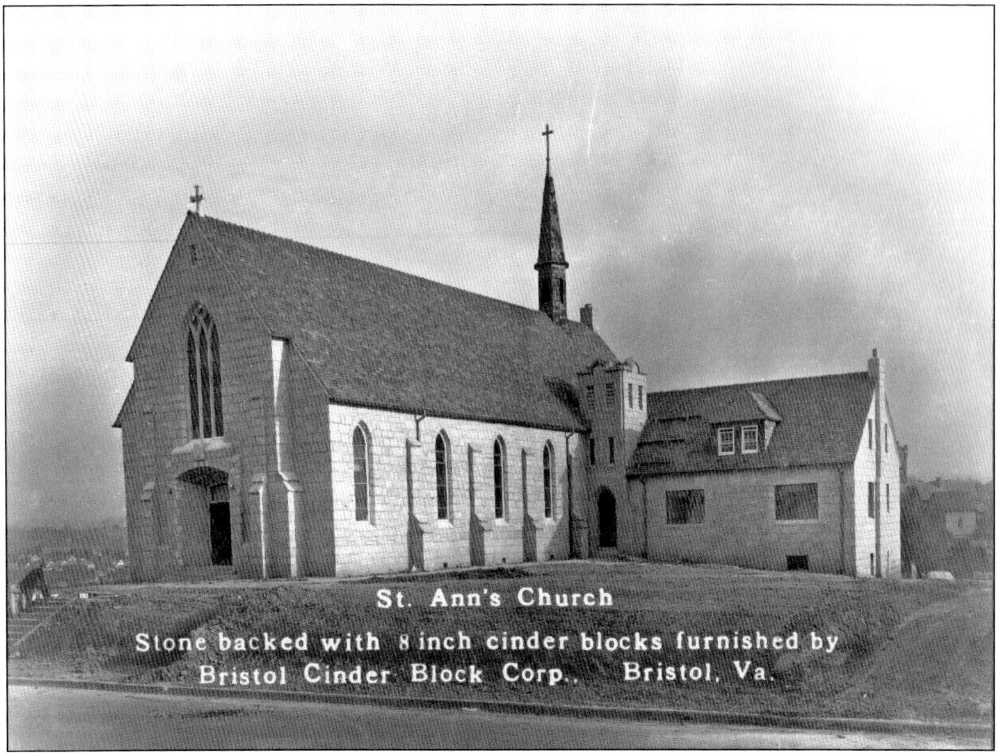

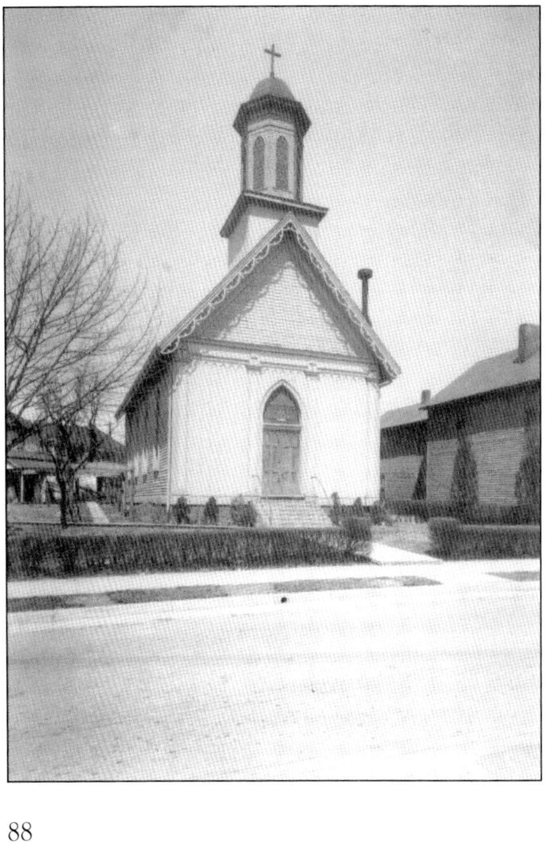

St. Anne's Catholic Church was founded in 1870 with a church building on Spencer Street. On November 22, 1936, a new church constructed of Georgia granite was dedicated on Euclid Avenue. Notice on this photograph from the late 1930s that St. Anne's is spelled St. Ann's. (Courtesy of Walter Doane.)

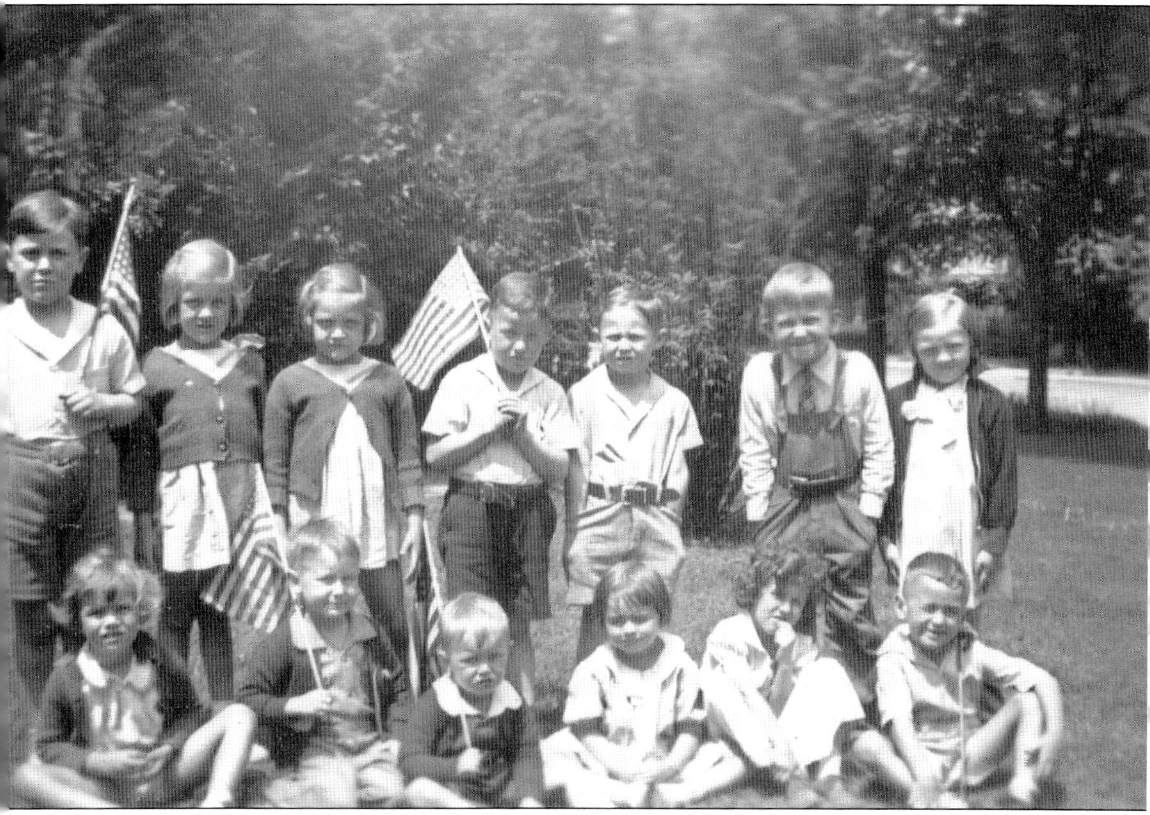

"Miss Maude" Kinkead began the kindergarten class for neighborhood children and years later organized the Anderson Street Methodist Church kindergarten class. This 1935 class was her first and includes, from left to right, (first row) Martha Hudson, King Rogers Jr., Bill Rogers, Billie Jean Carmody, Pat Kline, and Bobby Southerland; (second row) Jim McCord, Patsy Cole, Peggy Cole, Joe Fleenor, Paul Gunnings, David McClellan, and Peggy Smith. Miss Maude was very active at Anderson Street Methodist right up until the time of her death at the age of 89 in 1964. (Courtesy of King and Peggy Rogers.)

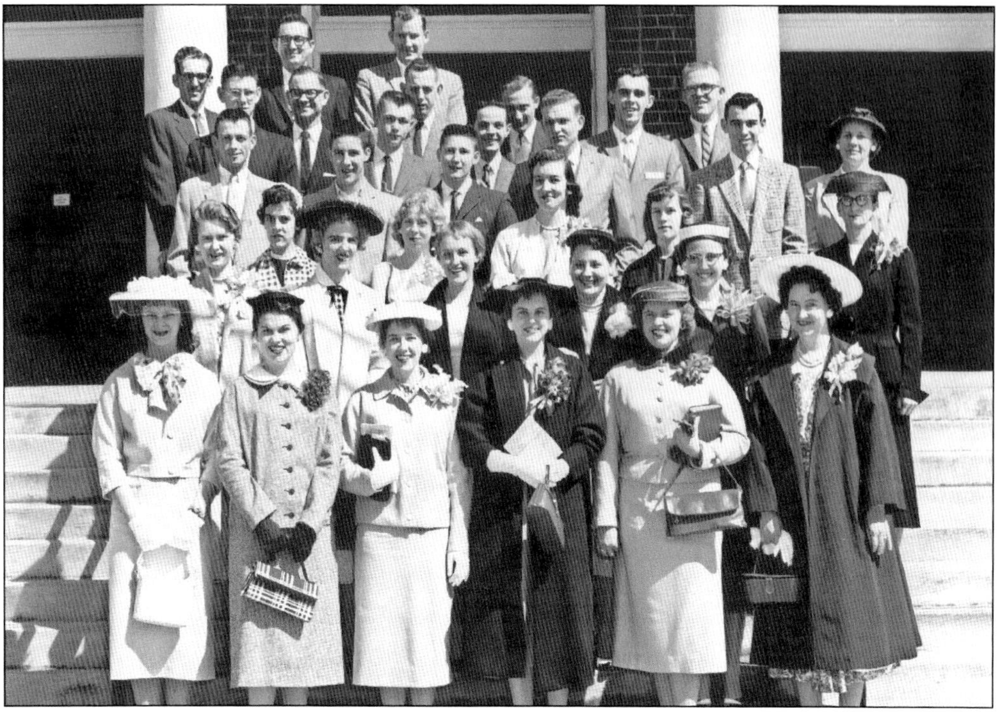

These men and women were the youth group leaders at Calvary Baptist Church in 1955. Also pictured in this photograph are the Reverend J. S. Aiken and his wife, Maxine. The Calvary Baptist Church building, which was erected in 1934, is located at Broad and Fifteenth Streets. The current structure replaced the Shelby Street church building, which was built c. 1900. (Courtesy of Joyce Kistner.)

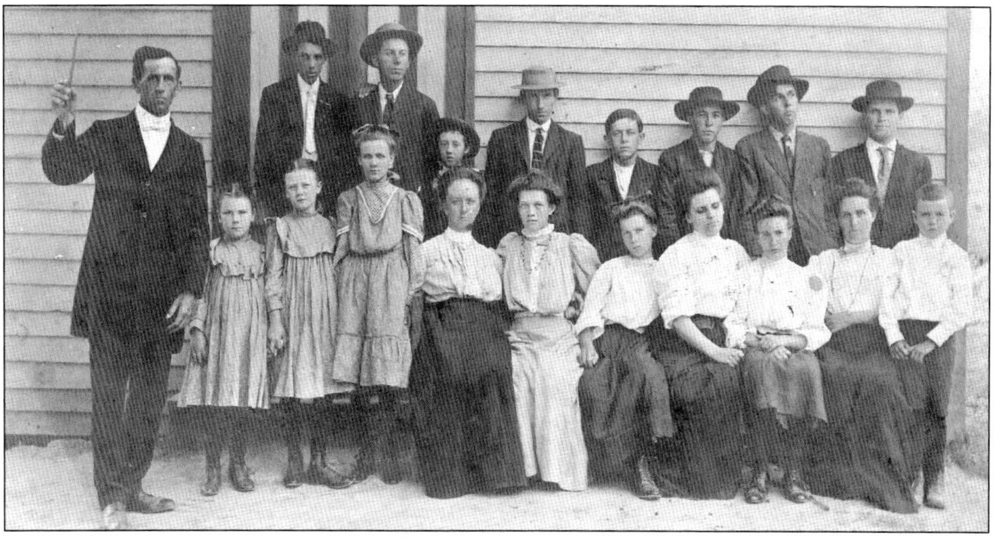

In the early 1900s many neighborhoods had small, one-room schools with various aged pupils. Pictured here is the one-room Chamberlain School, located on Walnut Hill Road close to the present-day Bristol Regional Medical Center. At times, teachers with musical backgrounds would visit the schools, as is the case in this photograph. Some of the students in this photograph are Jim Ed Harr, Tom Dishner, Hubert Spahr, and Daily Stone. (Courtesy of John Stone.)

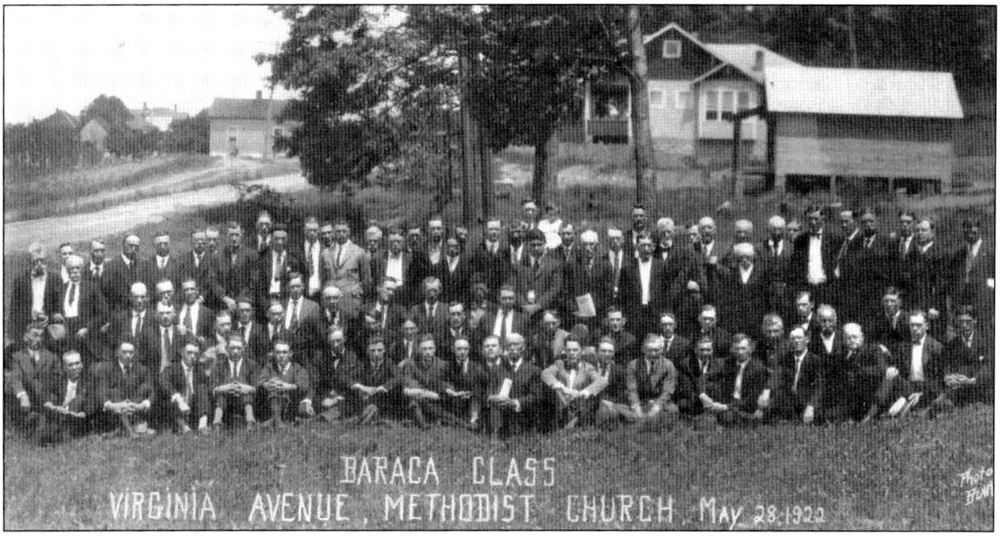

This photograph of the Virginia Avenue Methodist Church Men's Baraca Class was taken on May 28, 1922. Samuel Peters stands on the back row in front of the child with the white shirt. Peters owned the Virginia Avenue Coal Company and later the Carolina Coal Company. He also owned a store on the corner of Pennsylvania Avenue and Cedar Street. Peters died on November 12, 1969. (Courtesy of Bob Broyles.)

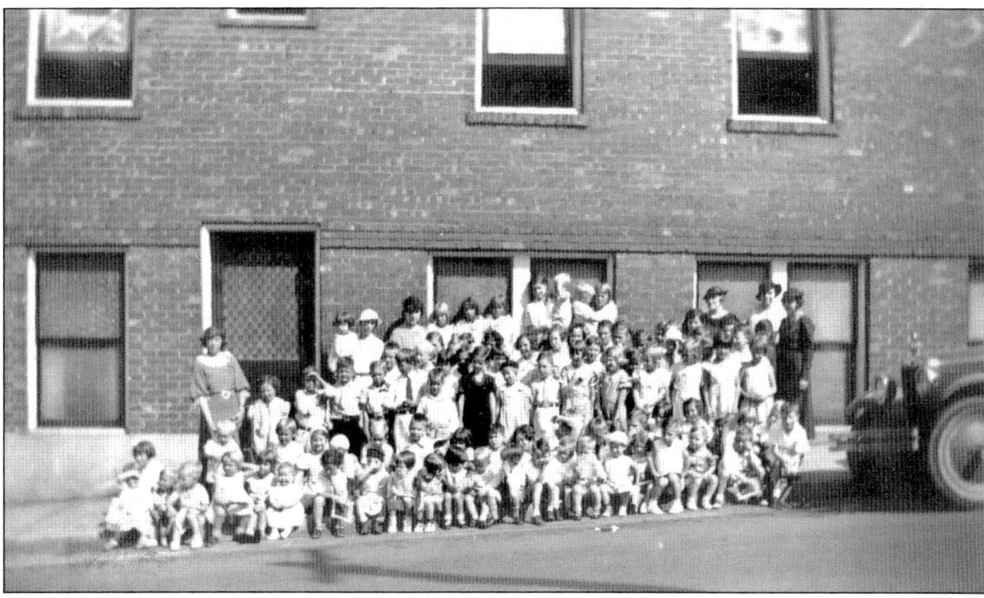

The Sunday school classes at Central Christian Church pose for this 1933 photograph in front of the original church located at Sixth and Broad Streets. Central Christian Church was organized in 1903, and the church's sanctuary was completed in 1906. The church would later be relocated to Melrose Street, and the first service in the new building came on June 30, 1968. (Courtesy of King and Peggy Rogers.)

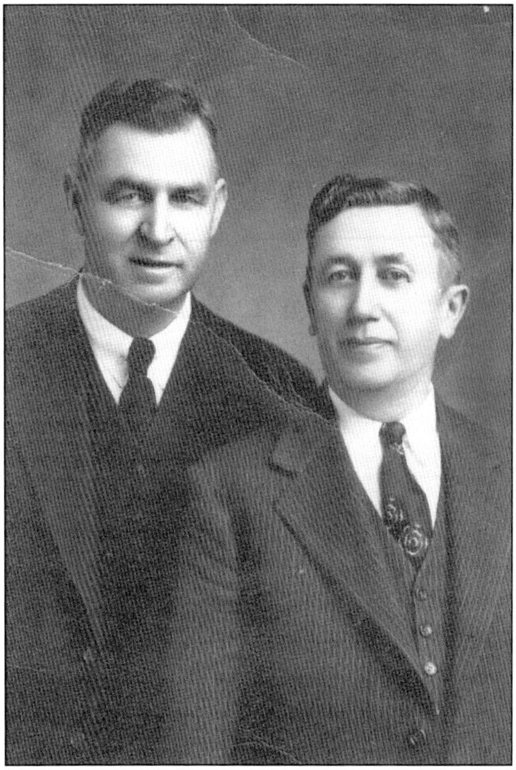

Dan Graham (left), shown here *c.* 1930, was known for his tent revival meetings and was recognized as a dynamic temperance preacher. When Graham went for revival meetings, Rhea Anderson (right) often played the piano. Years later, Graham had a local radio program on Saturdays. Graham, who retired from the pastorate in March 1972, died on January 14, 1975, just two days before his 86th birthday. (Courtesy of Walnut Hill Presbyterian Church.)

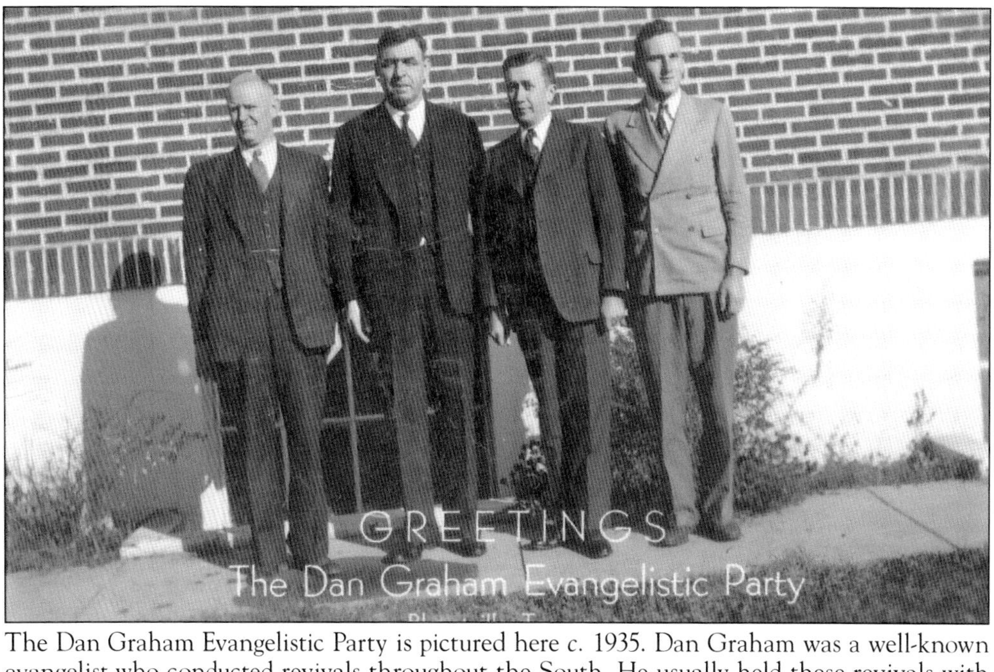

The Dan Graham Evangelistic Party is pictured here *c.* 1935. Dan Graham was a well-known evangelist who conducted revivals throughout the South. He usually held these revivals with other men of faith to assist him. Shown here from left to right are Alston Boyd, Graham, Rhea Anderson, and Jess Bellamy. Graham is responsible for starting 37 churches in Southwest Virginia and Northeast Tennessee. (Courtesy of Walnut Hill Presbyterian Church.)

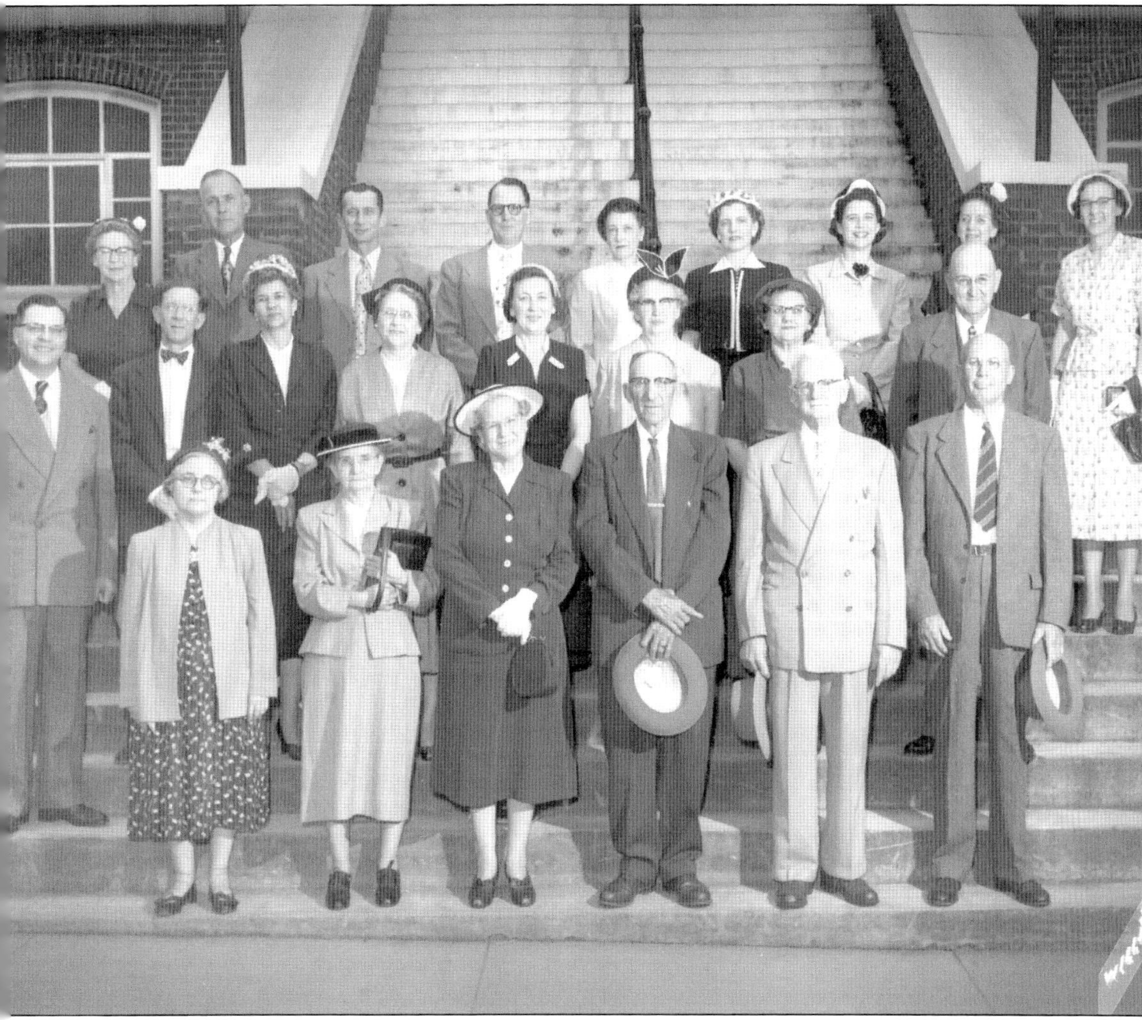

The remaining charter members of Euclid Avenue Baptist Church posed for this photograph on May 17, 1953. Pictured from left to right are (first row) Helen Cates, T. L. Cates, Mrs. C. F. Beaver, C. F. Beaver, J. B. Denton, and J. E. Marion; (second row) Rev. Raymond Smith (not a charter member), L. E. Barnes, Mrs. L. E. Barnes, Mrs. Will Pratt, Bernice Pearson, Mrs. Lewis Pitts, Mrs. Martin Lytz, and Martin Lytz; (third row) Mrs. Joe Plaskie, Joe Plaskie, Marion Miller, F. M. Worrell, Mrs. F. M. Worrell, Catherine Helton, Mrs. Carl Emmert, Jewell Beaver, and Laura Beaver. (Courtesy of Tim Buchanan.)

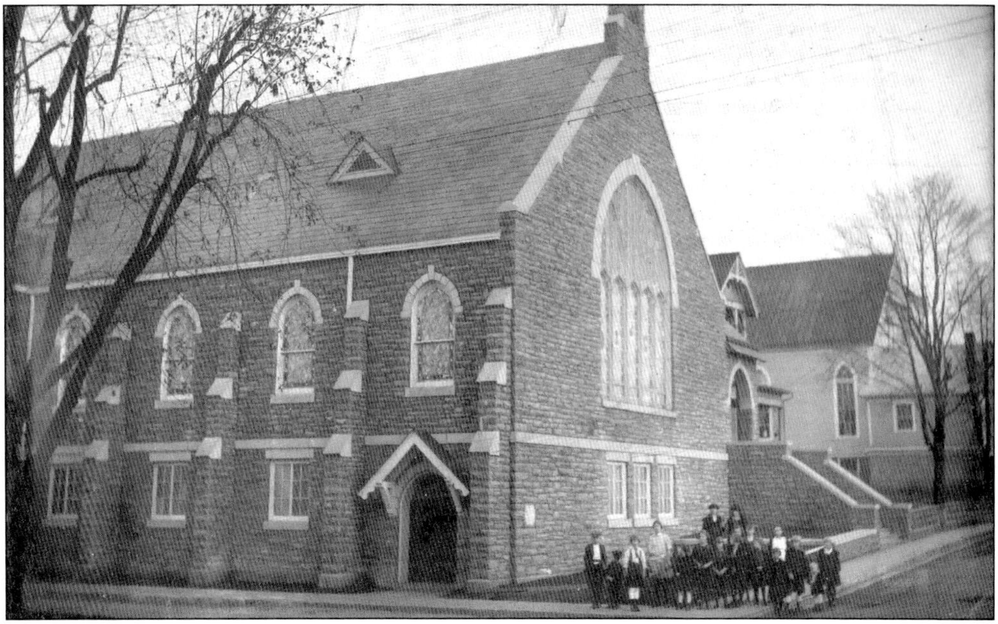

Mary Street Methodist Episcopal Church South was founded in 1880 and thus celebrates its 125th anniversary in 2005. The congregation first met in a simple cottage before moving into a church building in 1888. The building used today is shown in this photograph upon its completion in 1929. The church was renamed Reynolds Memorial United Methodist Church in 1929. (Courtesy of Reynolds Memorial United Methodist Church.)

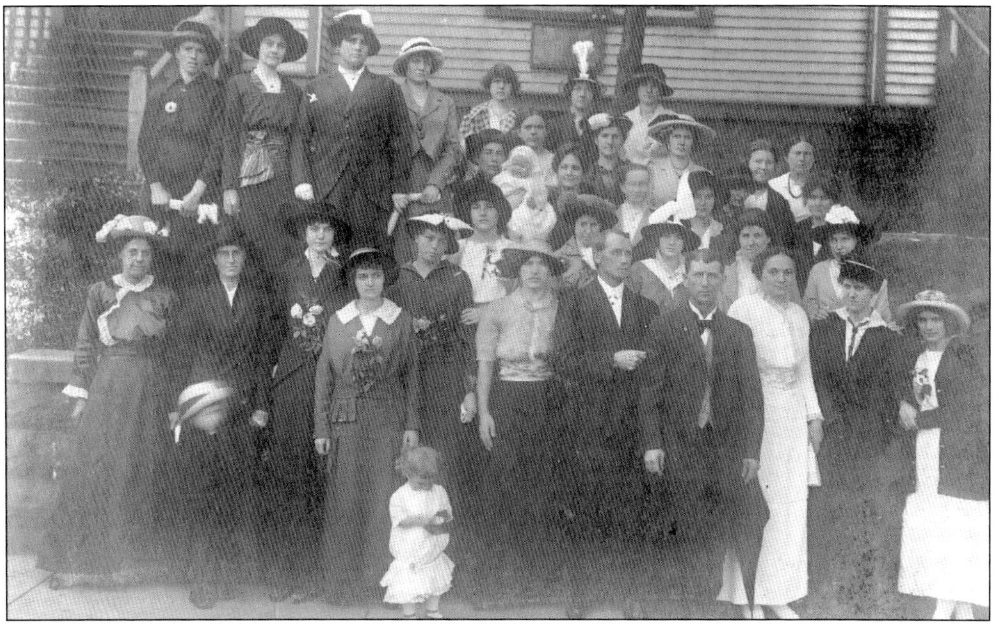

Interestingly, this photograph was discovered by construction workers above a ceiling during renovation at Reynolds Memorial United Methodist Church on July 16, 1997. The only people identified in the picture are the two men in front. On the right is John Everett Geagley, and on the left is the church pastor, Rev. Robert A. Hutsell (1903–1906). (Courtesy of Reynolds Memorial United Methodist Church.)

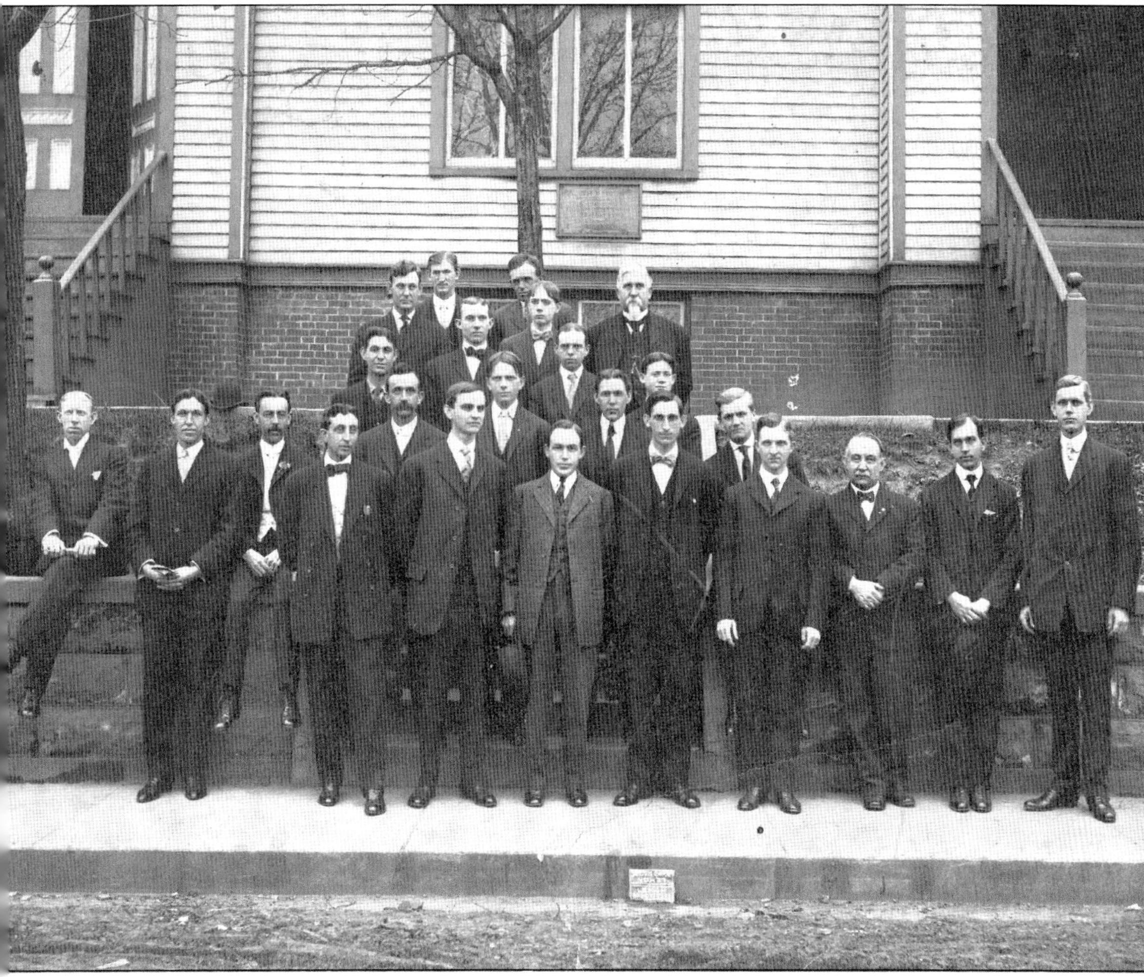

This photograph is dated April 5, 1908, and shows the Mary Street Methodist Episcopal Church South Baraca Sunday school class members. They are, from left to right, (first row) Thomas Gee, W. W. Senter, J. Ed Smith, Charles Kingsolver, Paul Kline, E. R. Shipley, Charles Brown, J. W. Mort, Ellis Pyle, and Paul Charles; (second row) Frank Walling, S. S. Kreger, Greever Dean, Joe McCrary, B. E. Ballard, G. Greek Henley, and Kyle Baldwin; (third row) J. E. Slaughter, William Crabtree, Raymond Fletcher, Benjamin Dean, Albert Killinger, and Maj. A. D. Reynolds. (Courtesy of Reynolds Memorial United Methodist Church.)

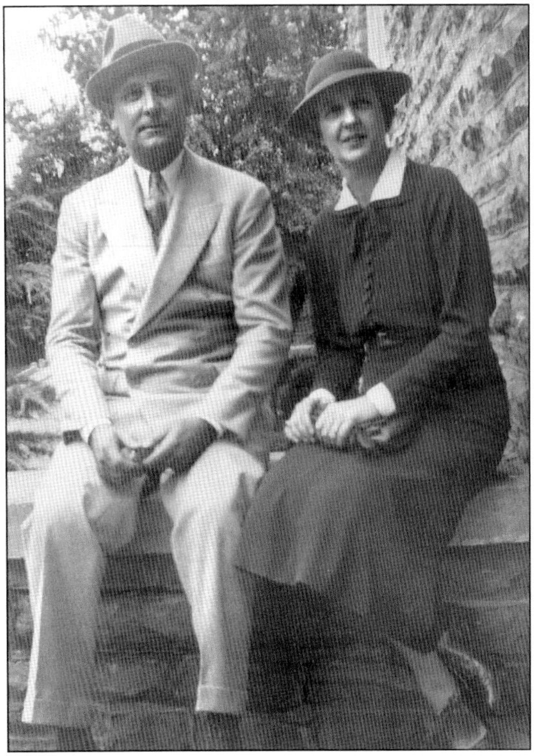

Rev. Sullins Dosser sits for a moment with his wife, Mary. Reverend Dosser pastored Reynolds Memorial United Methodist Church from 1933 to 1936. He was the grandson of David Sullins, who founded Sullins College. Sullins and Mary were married on August 3, 1910, and celebrated over 56 years together before Mary passed away. Reverend Dosser died on August 4, 1980. (Courtesy of Reynolds Memorial United Methodist Church.)

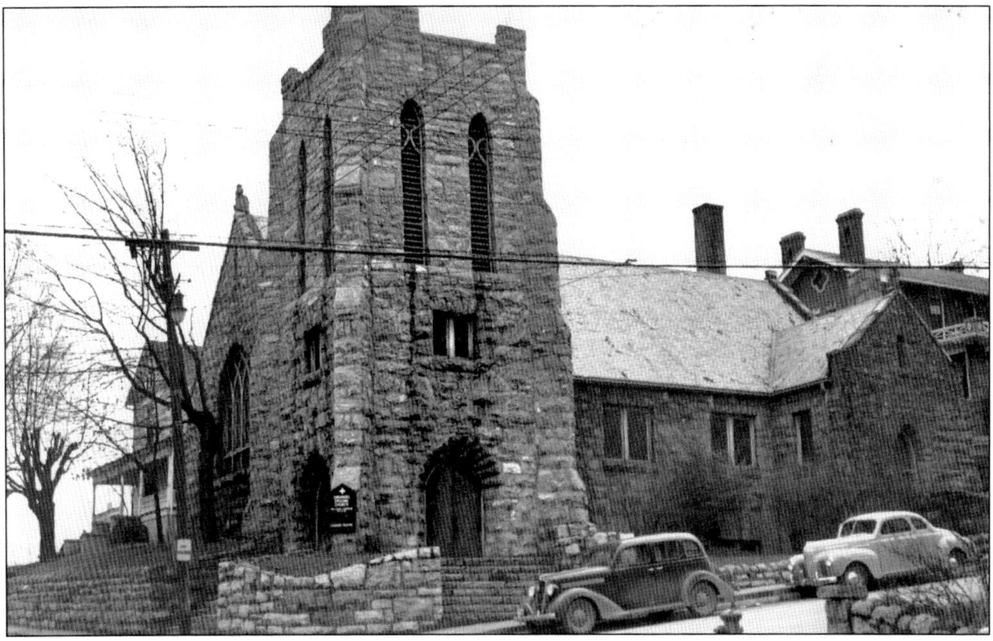

The original Emmanuel Episcopal Church was organized in 1862. The congregation had several meeting places until the present structure was built in 1921 on James and Cumberland Streets. The church is made of gray limestone in the Gothic style, modeled after the 13th-century Church of St. James the Less in Sulgrave, England. During construction of the church, the congregation met at the YMCA. (Courtesy of Bristol Historical Association.)

Seven

WORK

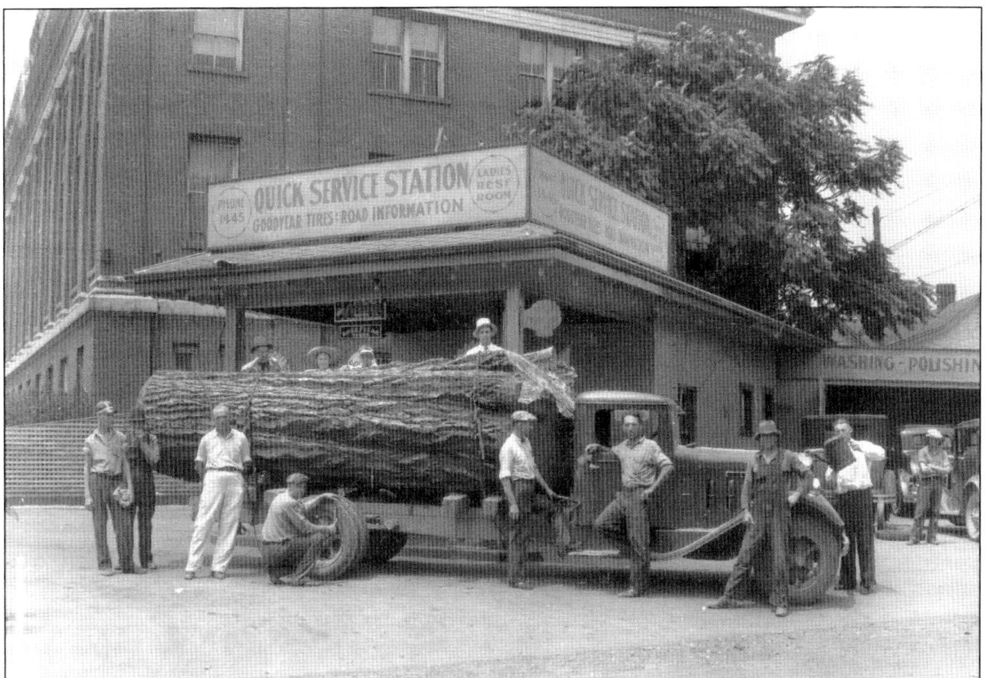

A logging truck receives water and gasoline at the Quick Service Station on State and Goodson Streets (behind the First Baptist Church). Notice the huge diameter of the giant red oak compared to the boys and men whose heads barely peek over the top. The tree was cut in the early 1930s on Holston Mountain, near where South Holston Lake is now. It took a truck and three trailers to haul the log. (Courtesy of Walter Doane.)

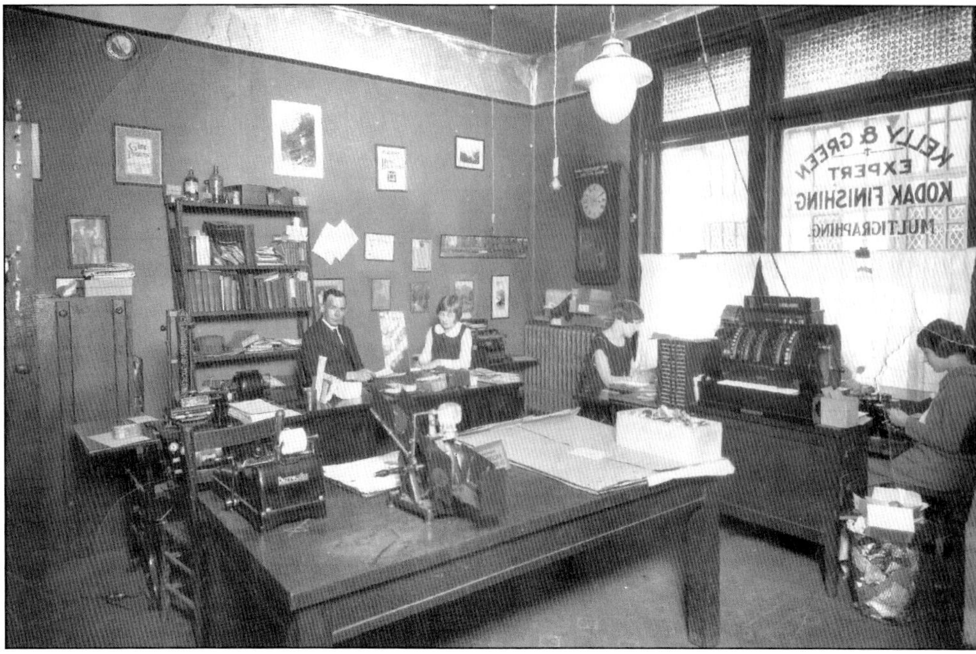

Kelly and Green Photo Craftsman, shown here *c.* 1925, was founded in 1920 by Albert Kelly Sr., who is believed to be the man sitting at the desk. Kelly and Green opened on Saturday, July 3, 1920, and was located at 514 Cumberland Street in Bristol, Virginia. The owners were A. (Albert) S. Kelly, Charles P. Kelly, and George L. Kelly. (Courtesy of Bristol Historical Association.)

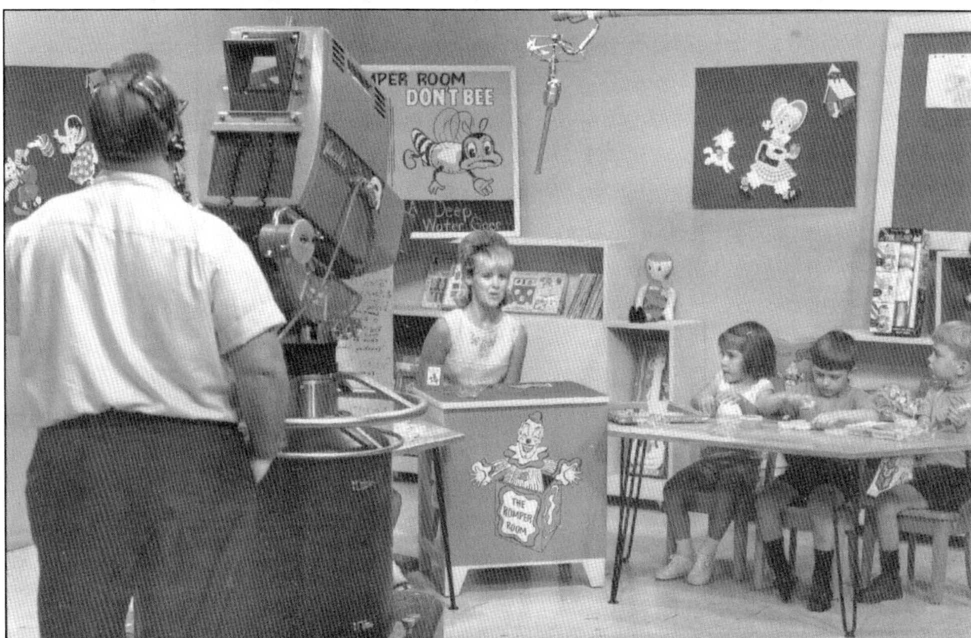

While the children play quietly at the table, "Miss Ann" Akard hosts the *Romper Room* show, which aired on WCYB in the late 1960s and into the 1970s. Most people who were children during that time are sure to remember watching Miss Ann and enjoying the fun and educational activities she showed on the program. (Photograph from the authors' collection.)

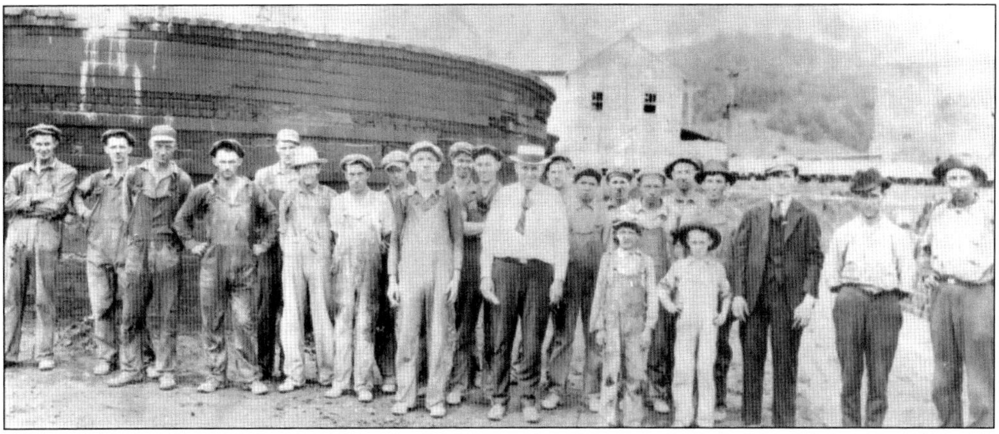

Alonzo Hyatt Kelly, center and wearing the straw hat, was superintendent of the Bristol Brick Corporation on Vance Drive. To his immediate right is yard boss Claude Helton. The other men in the picture, taken *c.* 1925, are laborers at the brickyard. Grover Campbell is on the far left. The Bristol Brick Corporation operated from about 1900 to about 1930, and the bricks made from here were used in construction of many of Bristol's structures. (Courtesy of Bristol Historical Association.)

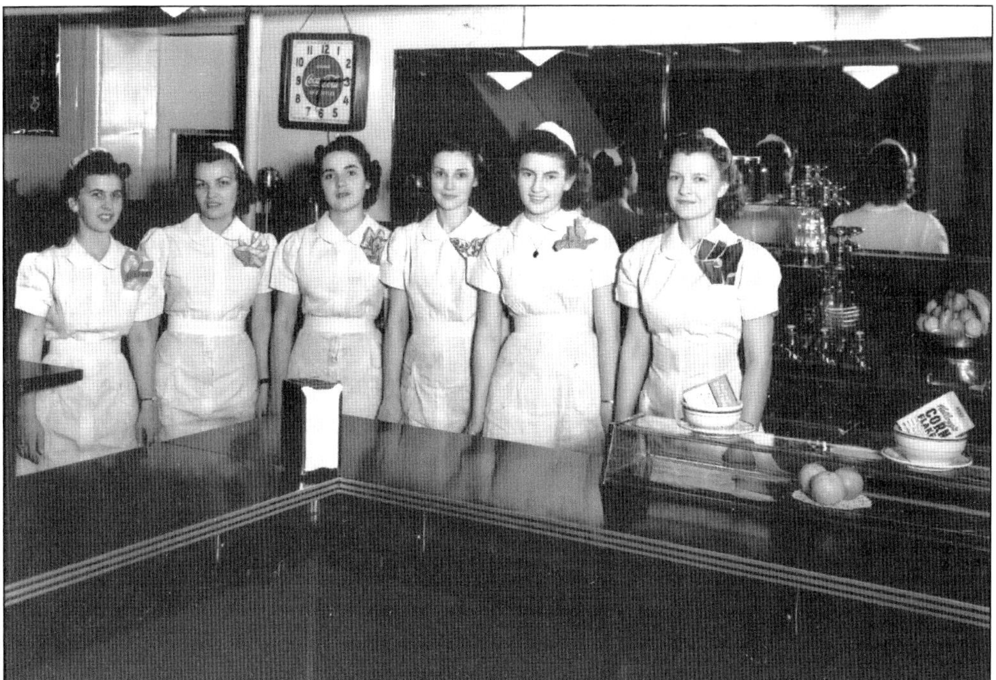

If you wanted a good lunchtime meal while shopping at H. P. King Department Store, you didn't have far to go because the Fountain served up some great food. Virginia Duncan Campbell, far right, was over the girls who took the orders and served the food in this 1936 photograph. The rest of the girls are unidentified. (Courtesy of Bristol Historical Association.)

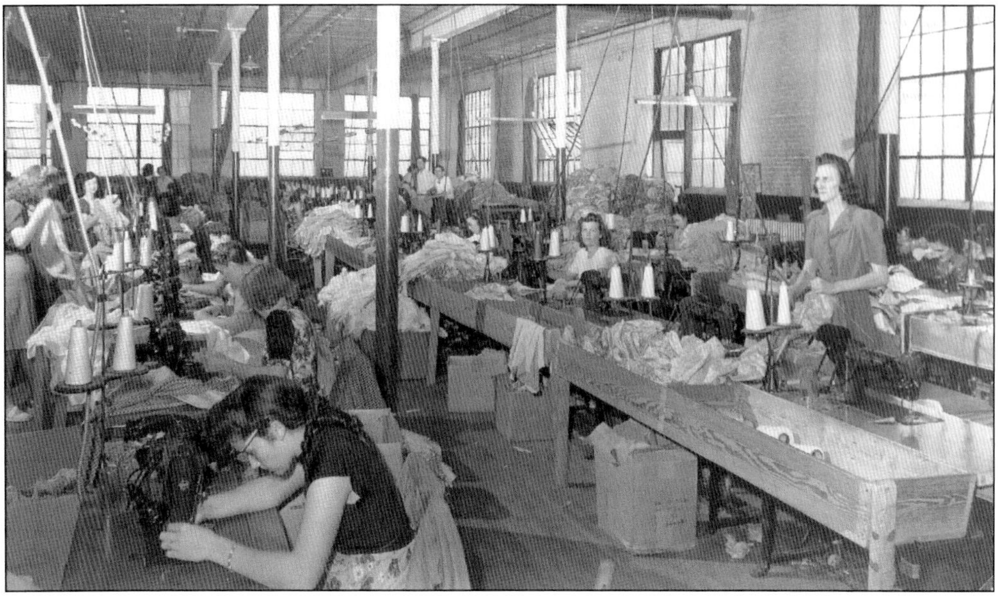

The Coronet Manufacturing Company, located on Pierce Street and a subsidiary of Luv-Lee Frocks, Inc., of New York, was the manufacturer of ladies' dresses. Coronet began operation in Bristol in 1943 with 80 employees and by 1955 had 335 employees. A $250,000 plant was built in the area of the old Combs Airport in 1956. As with most manufacturing companies of the early and mid-1900s, the ladies in this photograph probably worked long hours for low wages. (Courtesy of Bristol Historical Association.)

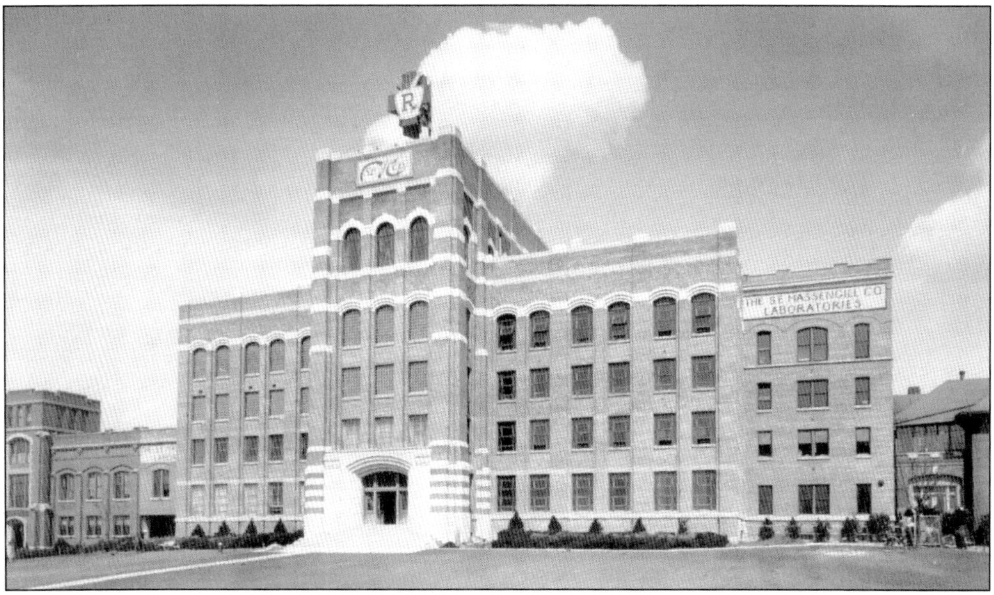

S. E. Massengill was originally located on Moore Street, and then the company moved to part of the old YMCA building on Fifth Street. The pharmaceutical business grew, and when larger quarters were once again needed, they rented a four-story building on Fourth Street. Finally in 1917, they moved to the old King College building shown on the far left of this photo. Employees of the pharmaceutical company are shown on the cover of this book inside S. E. Massengill. (Courtesy of Bristol Historical Association.)

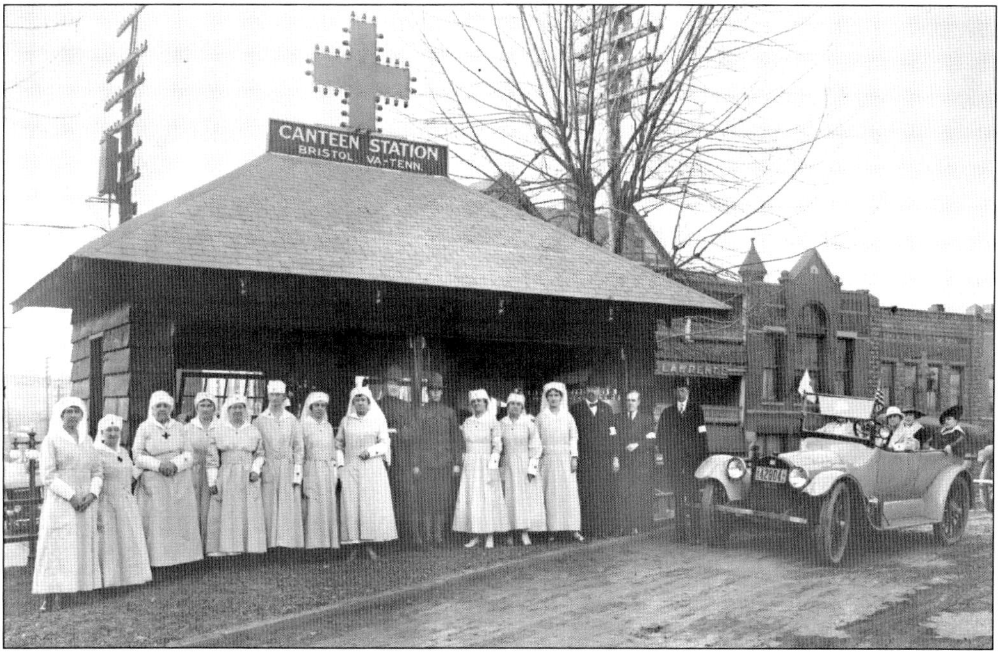

The Bristol Chapter of the American Red Cross made life a little easier for soldiers traveling by train during World War I. In 1917 and 1918, the Red Cross Canteen stood at the south end of the Union Station Depot, where it was stocked with sandwiches, hot coffee, candy bars, postcards, magazines, as well as homemade cookies, pies, and cakes donated by housewives around town. Trains with troops would stop in Bristol at all hours of the day and night, but the Red Cross Canteen was always open. (Courtesy of Bob and Marie Broyles.)

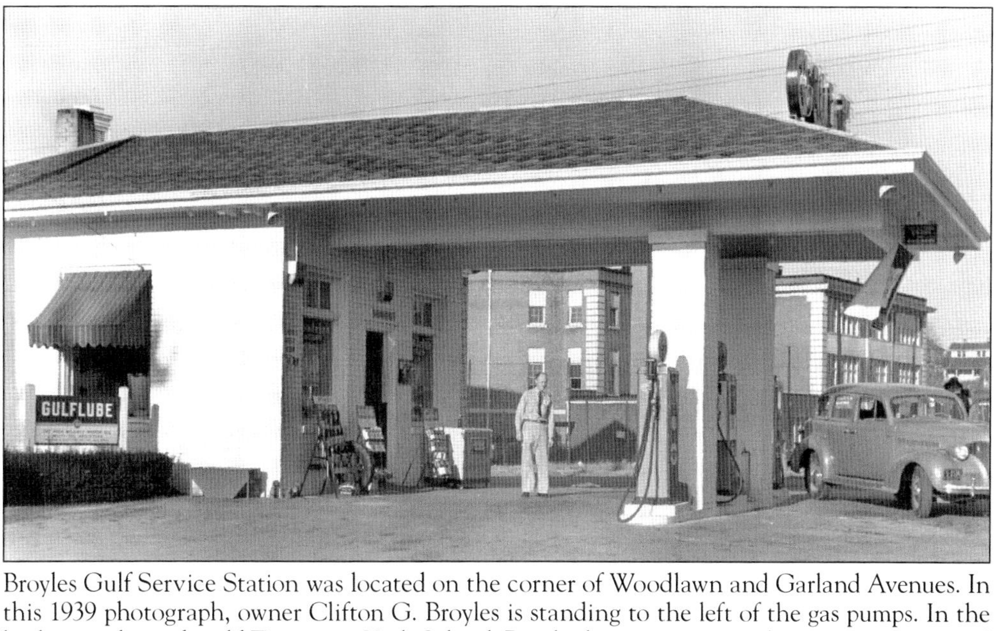

Broyles Gulf Service Station was located on the corner of Woodlawn and Garland Avenues. In this 1939 photograph, owner Clifton G. Broyles is standing to the left of the gas pumps. In the background was the old Tennessee High School. Broyles began operating the station in 1933 and ran the station until 1953. The station was torn down when Edgemont Avenue was widened into four lanes. (Courtesy of Bob and Marie Broyles.)

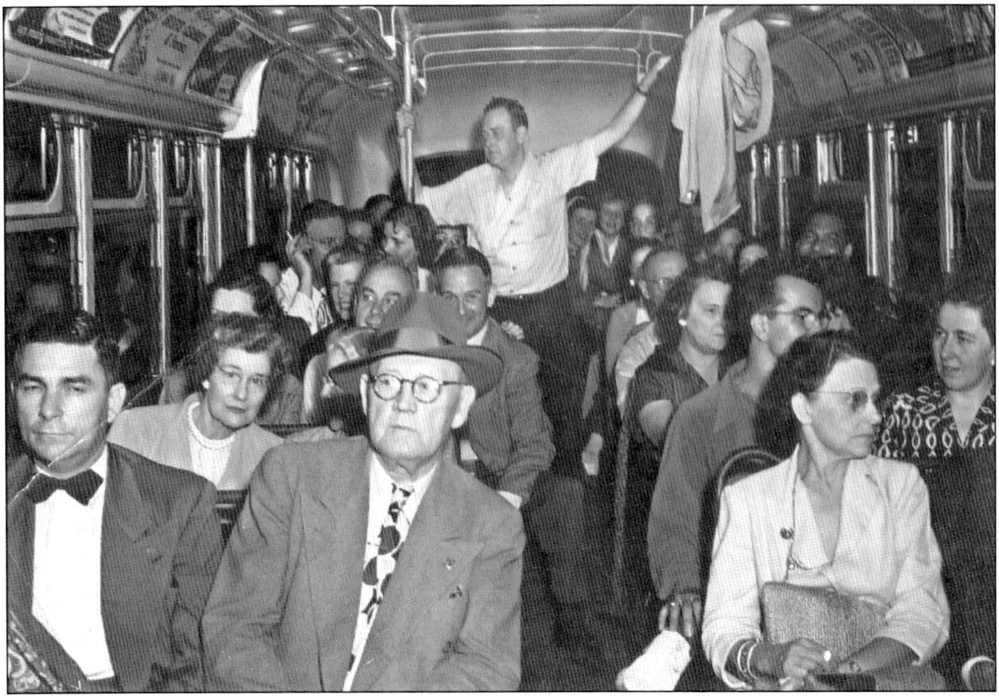

Bishop Osborne (center, in the hat) worked at H. P. King and was known over Bristol as simply Bish. Osborne lived at 348 Moore Street and enjoyed submitting comments to the peoples' column of the newspaper. In a 1949 article in the *Herald Courier*, he said: "I am a Democrat, a Methodist, an Elk, a T.P.A. and a U.C.T. but don't work hard at any of them." (Courtesy of Bud Phillips.)

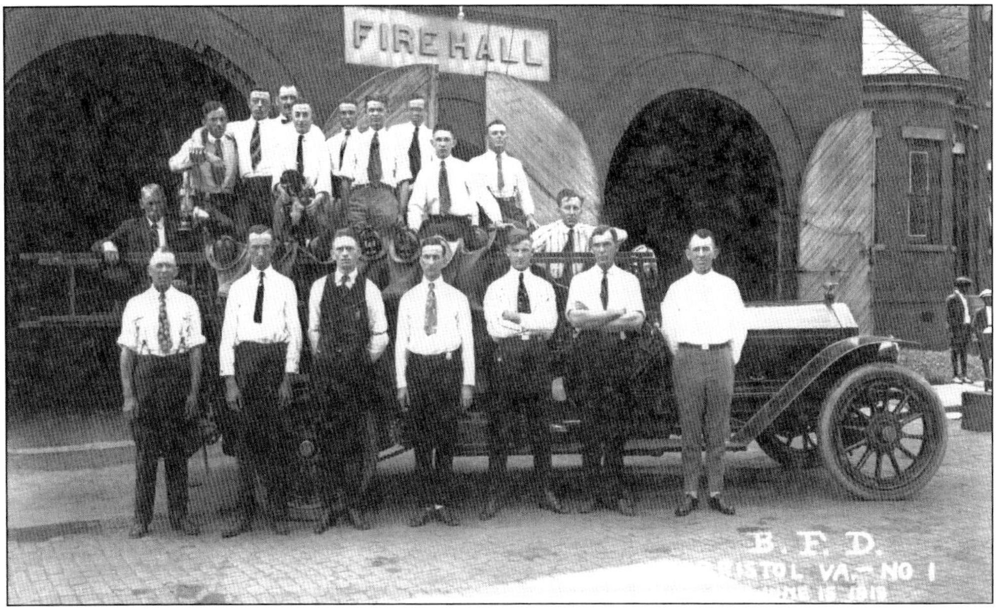

Members of the Bristol, Virginia, Fire Department shown in front of Pumper Number 1 on June 15, 1919, are R. C. Carter, Fred Millard, W. T. Crosswhite, Clarence Eades, R. W. Templeton, George Campbell, Clyde Barnette, Stackley Sure, Abe Perry, Bill Ellis, Bruce Ellis, Abe Bolling, Elmer Ager, O. L. Cross, and Lewis Keesling. (Courtesy of the Bristol, Virginia, Fire Department.)

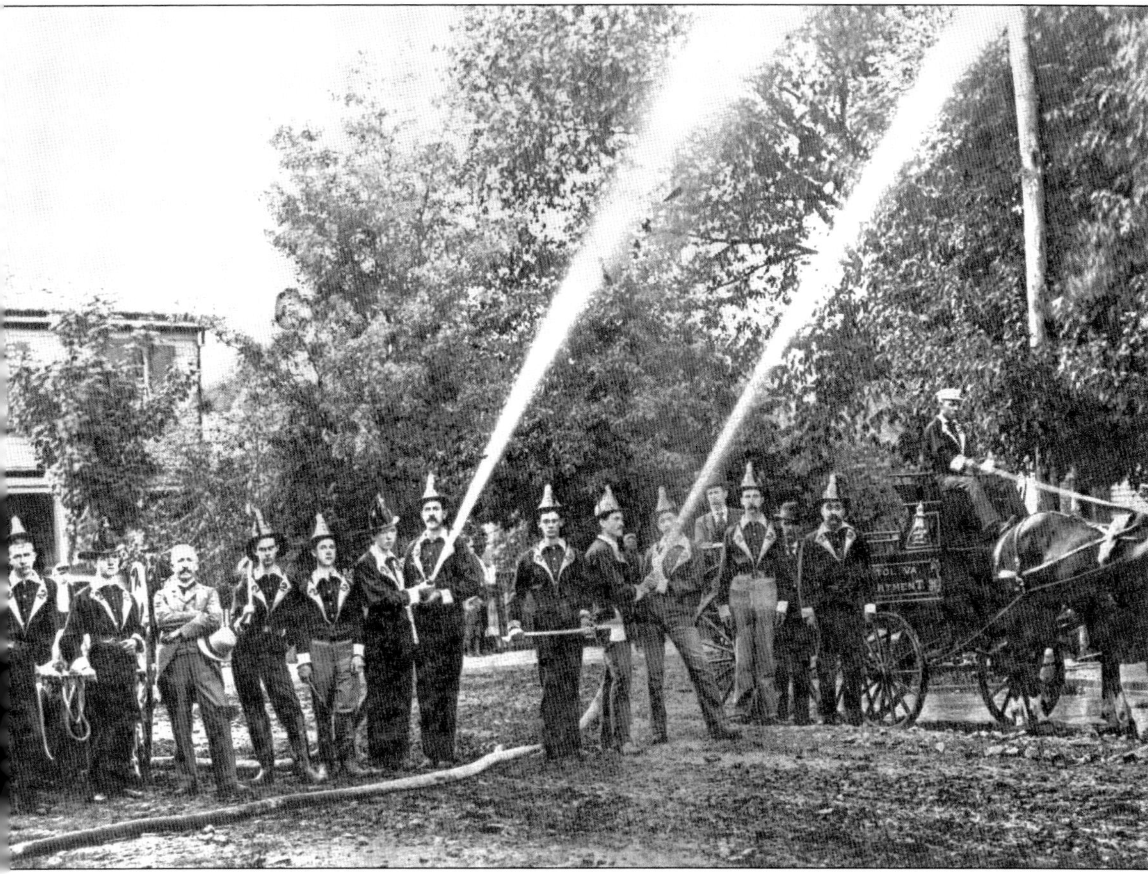

Taken in the summer of 1898, this is the oldest known photograph of the Bristol, Virginia, Fire Department. Shown here, from left to right, are Wilmer Frizzell, Karl Harmeling, Frank Coleman, John T. DeHart, Claude Hickman, Carroll L. Kidd, William McKamey, Samuel Keller, William B. Kelgore, Lang Lindsay, George Wolfe, John D. Witt, James Cox, Hugh Millard, and "Crum" Harrell. (Courtesy of the Bristol, Virginia, Fire Department.)

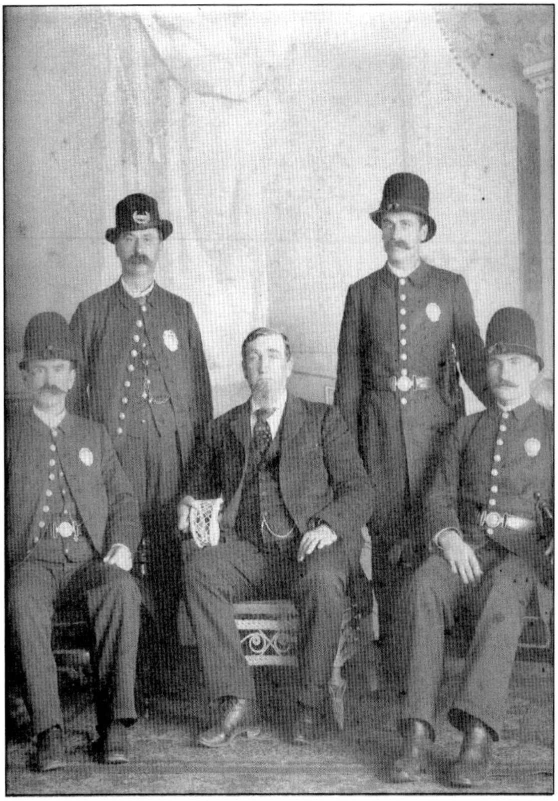

The average pay for police officers in 1890, when this photograph was taken, was about $30 per month. Pictured here from left to right are Hunter Price, W. J. Cox, W. A. Rader (mayor of Goodson and Bristol, Virginia, 1889–1894), ? Hill, and John Gore. W. J. Cox was the first police chief in Bristol, Virginia. (Courtesy of the Bristol, Virginia, Police Department.)

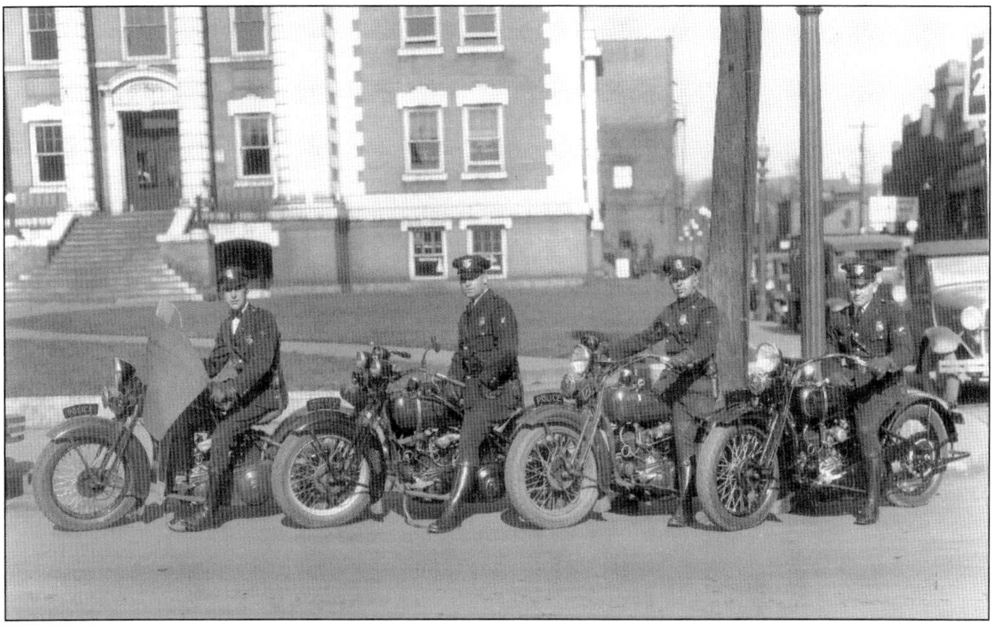

Bristol's finest policemen take time out to pose on their Harley-Davidsons in this 1930 photograph in front of the Bristol, Virginia, courthouse. The officers, from left to right, are Mark Kline (Bristol, Tennessee), Van Payne (Bristol, Virginia), George Houston (Bristol, Tennessee), and Nelson Ingoldsby (Bristol, Virginia). (Courtesy of Bristol, Virginia, Police Department.)

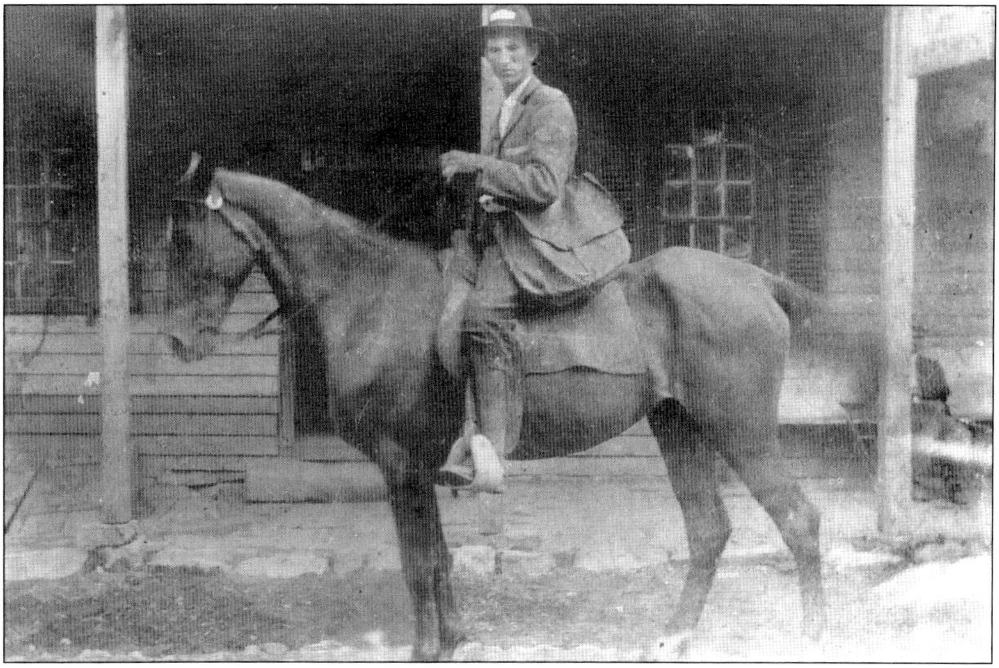

Andrew Marion was the area's first rural mail carrier. Marion's route covered nearly 30 miles starting in Blountville and going as far as the Boosey Creek community in what now is Bristol, Virginia. Sometimes it would be so cold that Andrew's shoes would freeze to the stirrups, and before he could dismount, someone would have to chip the ice away. Andrew died May 16, 1935. (Courtesy of Tony Marion.)

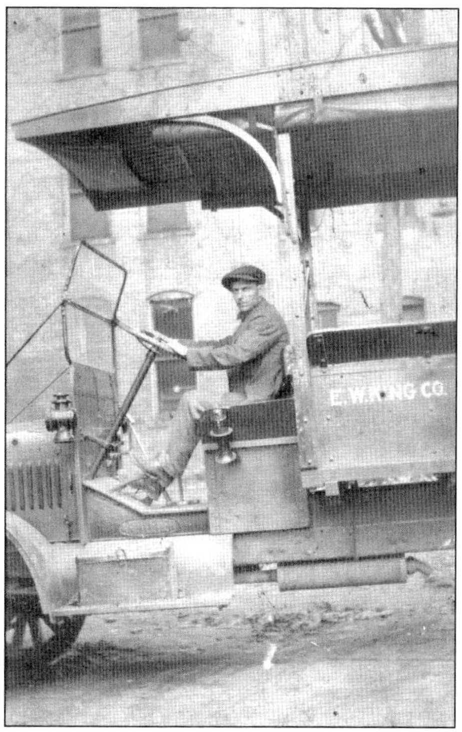

This delivery truck for E. W. King Company dates back to around 1915. E. W. King Company was founded in 1878 on Moore and State Streets. E. W. King, the company's founder, passed away on November 24, 1945. He was so well respected in the community that municipal offices and retail stores closed for funeral services. (Courtesy of Paul Stone Collection.)

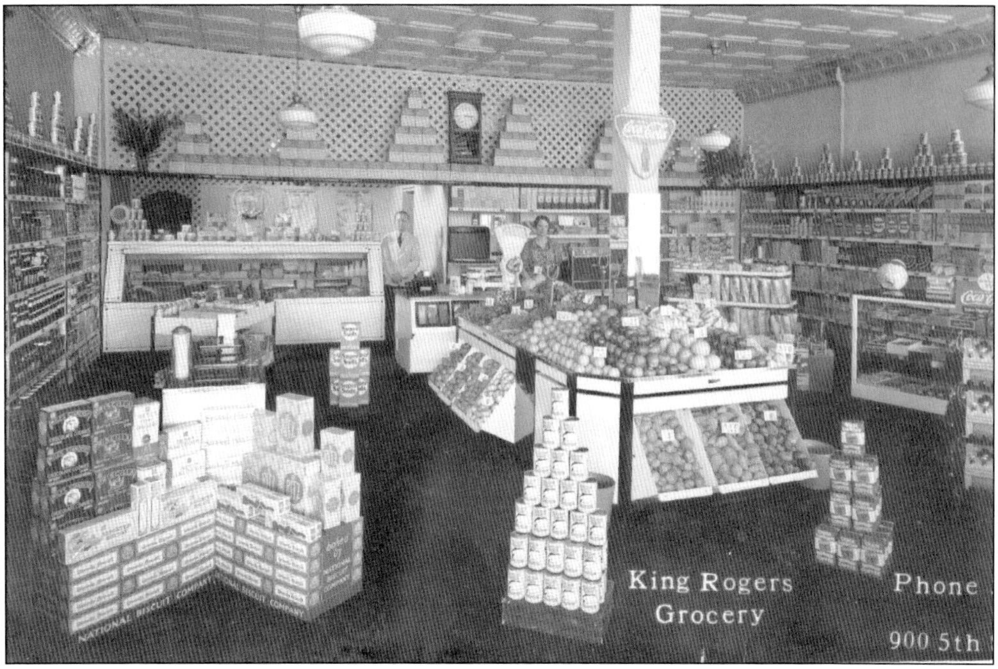

Jellies, jams, Chase Sanborn coffee, crackers, cookies, Super Suds, Oxydol, and other products lined the shelves at King Rogers Grocery. Grapefruit were only 5¢ apiece, while apples were less than a quarter. While many items could be taken off the shelves by customers, other items were carefully measured by King Rogers and his wife and placed into paper bags. (Courtesy of Paul Stone Collection.)

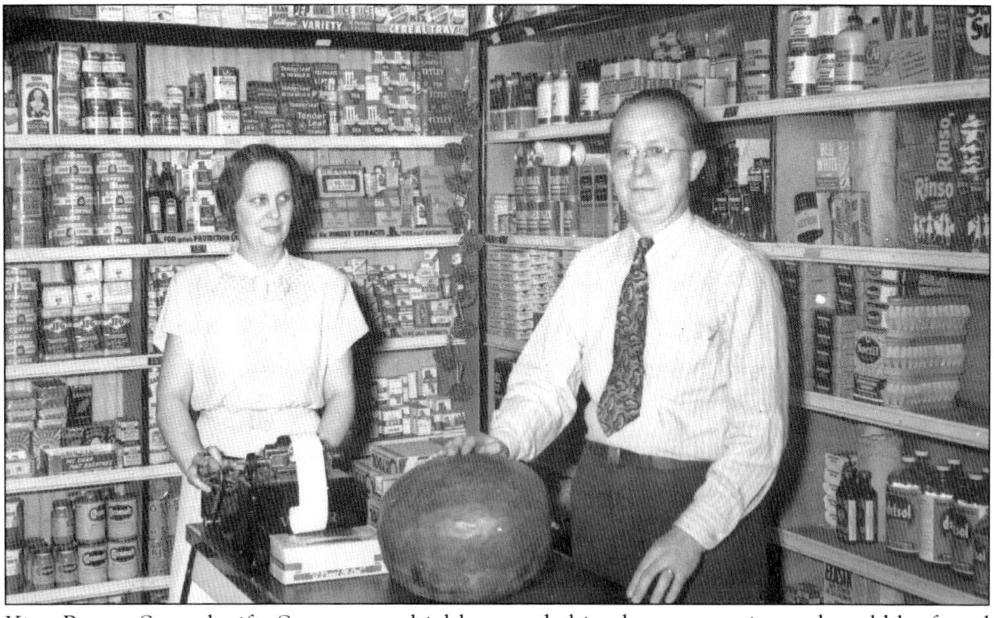

King Rogers Sr. and wife, Susan, were highly regarded in the community and could be found tending King Rogers Grocery located at 900 Fifth Street. King opened the store in 1923. Early on, Susan was busy raising a family, but later, she helped her husband in the store, which was open 53 years. King died in 1987 at the age of 79. (Courtesy of King Rogers Jr.)

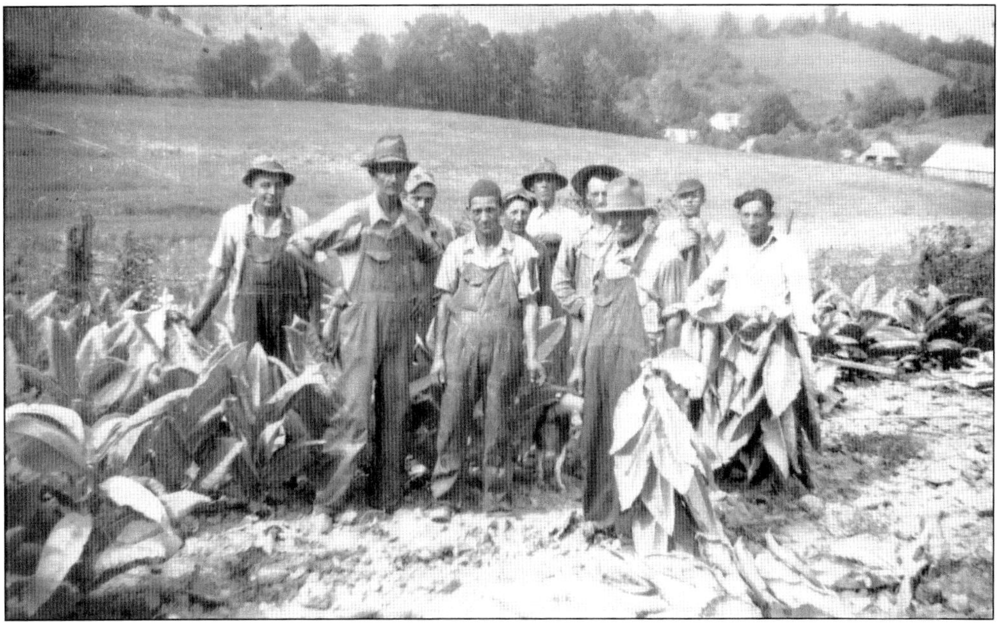

Tobacco was a huge money crop for many farmers around Bristol, and neighbors helped neighbors during the fall harvest. This crop, c. 1935, belonged to A. D. Stone. The field today would be less than a mile from Bristol Regional Medical Center. Pictured from left to right are Bruce Leonard, Harry Perry, unidentified, Erby Leonard, A. D. Stone, Jack Hagen, unidentified, Frank Leonard, Paul Stone Sr., and unidentified. (Courtesy of John Stone.)

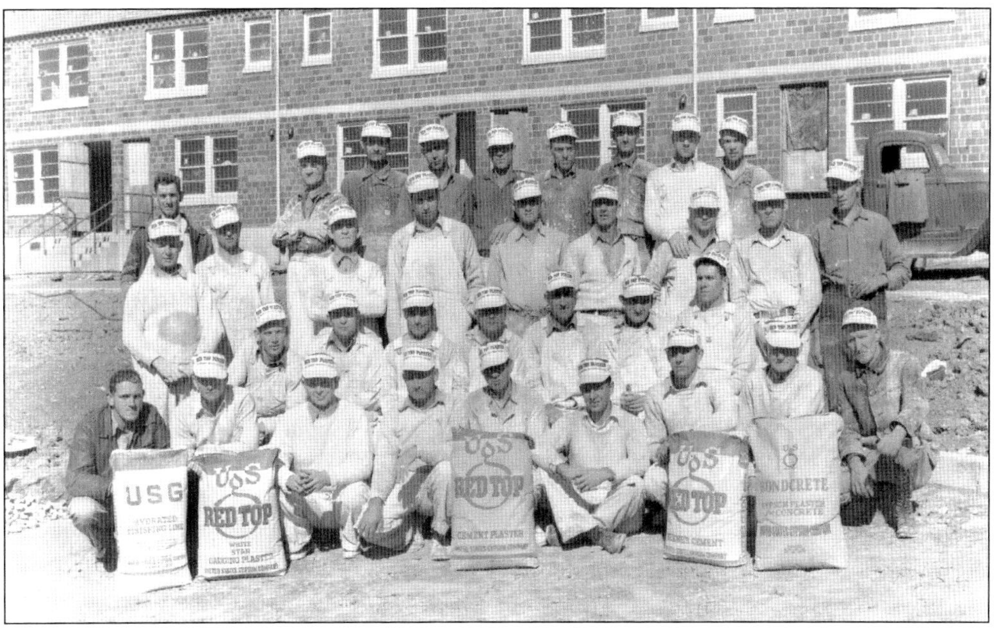

Workers with Red Top (a cement brand) caps pose in front of the newly completed William L. Rice Terrace in 1940. Rice Terrace, named in honor of Bristol's first mayor, was built for white families. Johnson Court, named after African American leader Rev. C. H. Johnson, was for African American families. In all, 216 families had new housing that cost Bristol Virginia Housing Authority nearly $800,000. (Courtesy of Walter Doane.)

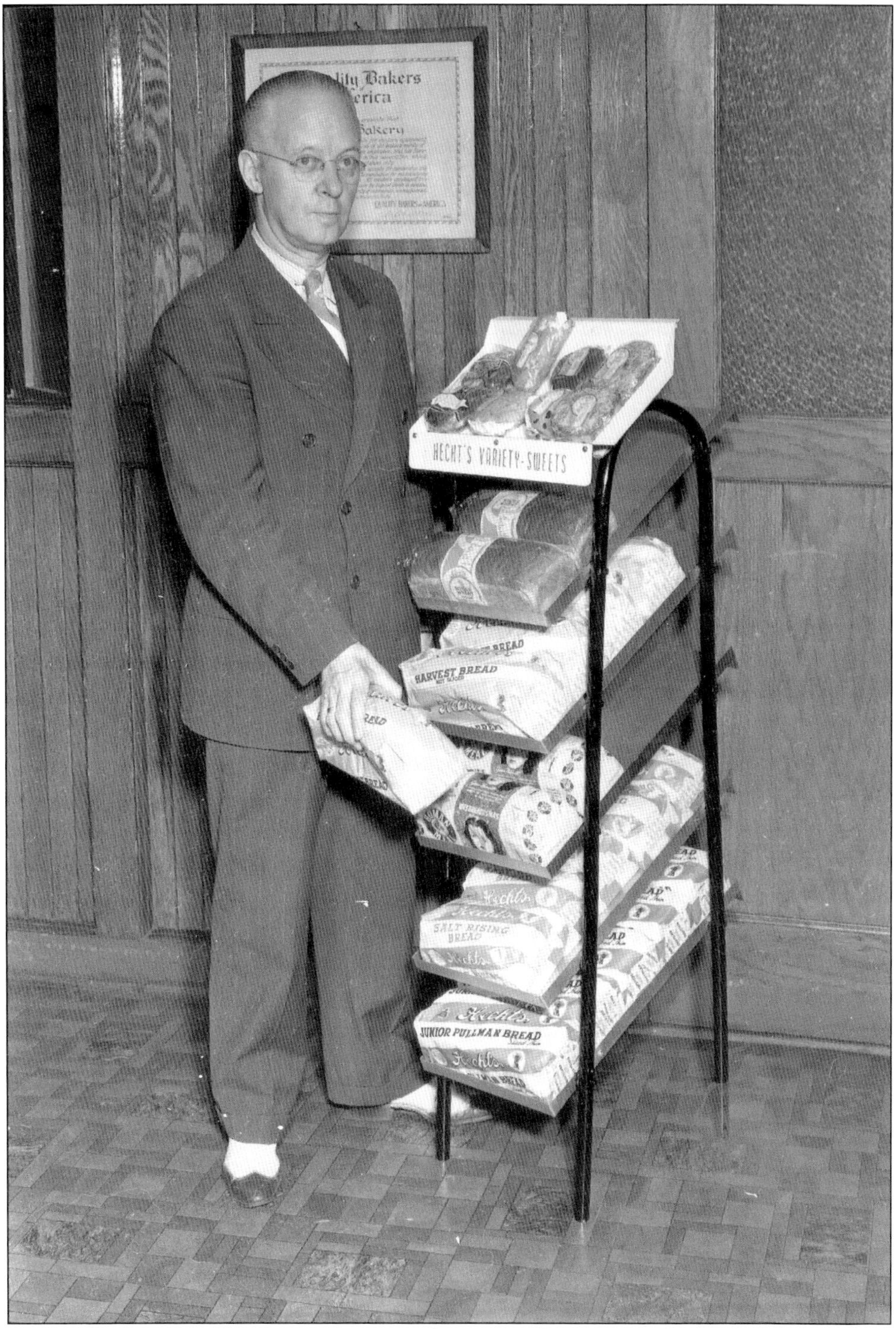

Armand Hecht, son of Herman Hecht who began Hecht's Bakery, located on the corner of Sixth and Shelby Streets, joined the business in 1920. Armand worked his way up to production manager and in 1937 became general manager. When Herman Hecht passed away in June 1948, Armand became president and general manager. (Courtesy of Walter Doane.)

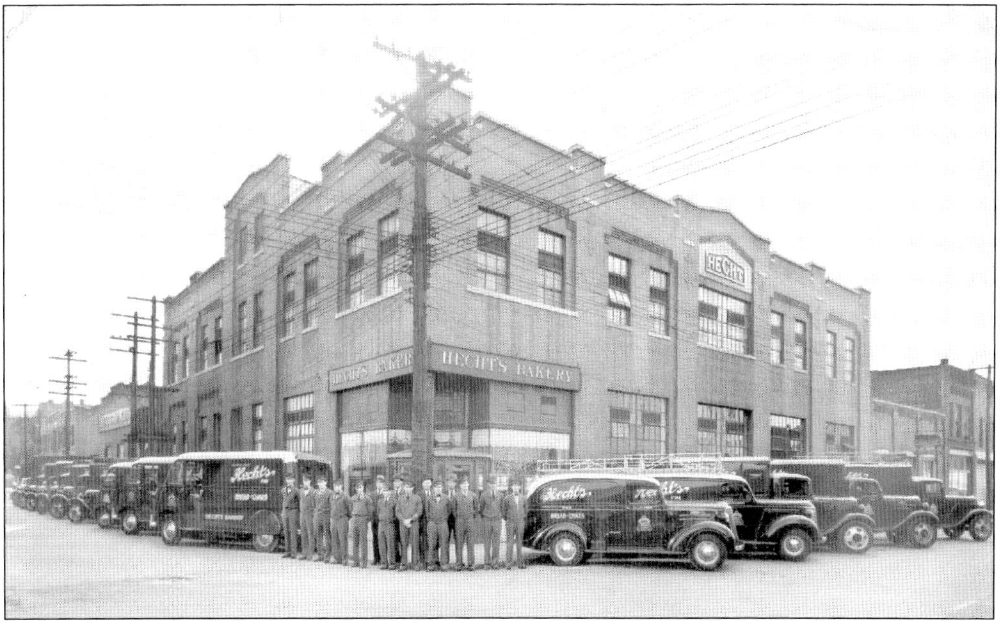

Mr. and Mrs. Herman Hecht opened Hecht's Bakery on the corner of Sixth and Shelby Streets on November 27, 1905. Bread sold for 5¢ a loaf, and the first day's sales totaled less than $11. Initially, the bread was delivered by horse and wagon. In this photograph, after automobiles were a common sight, Hecht's Bakery workers posed between delivery trucks in front of the company building. (Courtesy of Bill McKee.)

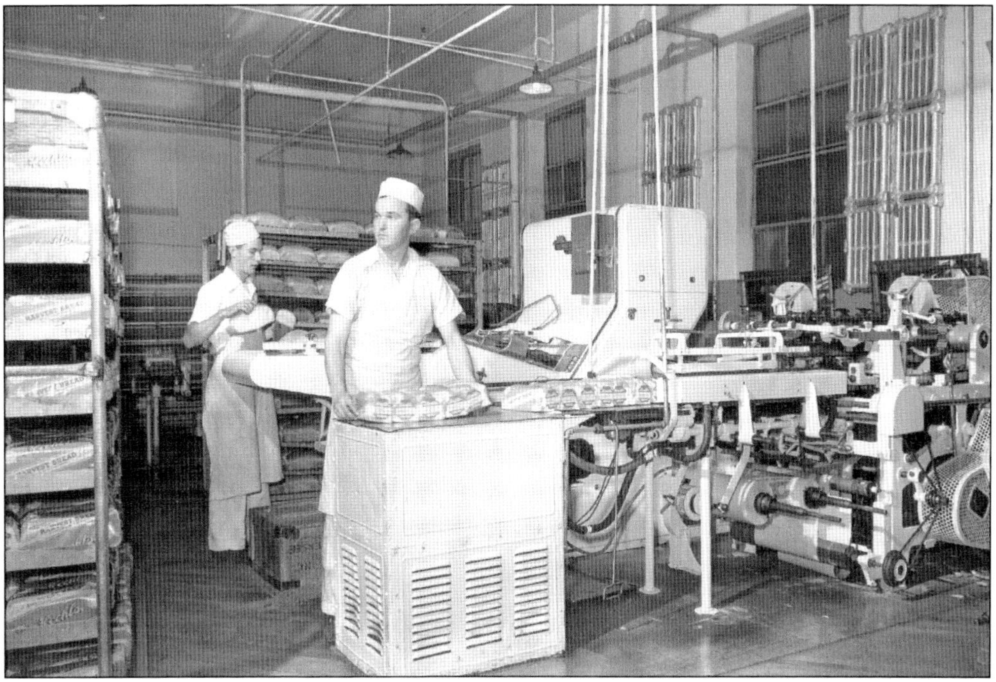

Two unidentified workers at Hecht's Bakery prepare bread that will be delivered to stores and restaurants throughout upper East Tennessee and Southwest Virginia. (Courtesy of Bristol Historical Association.)

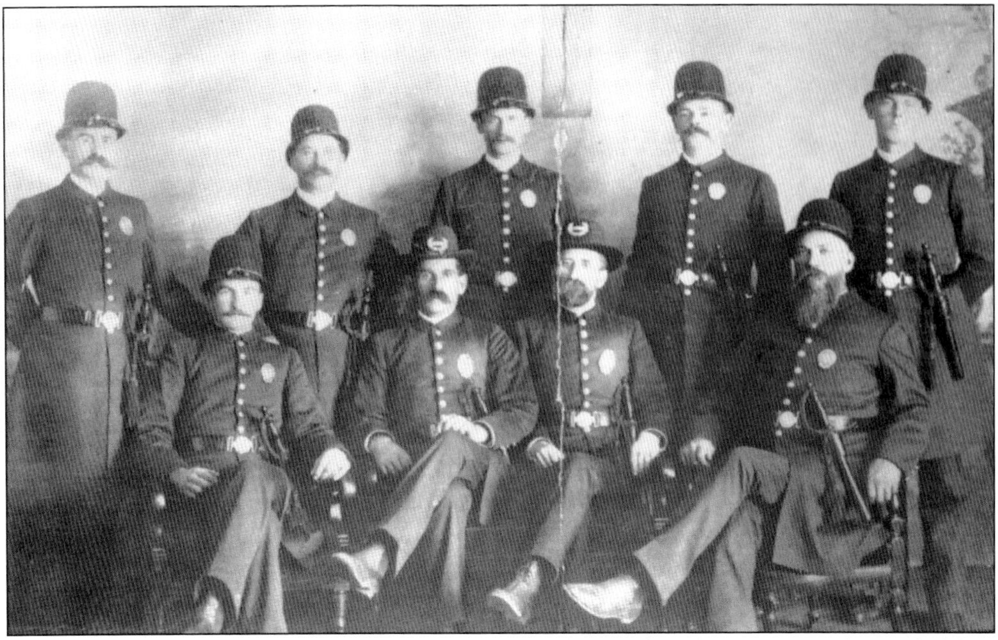

Members of the Bristol, Tennessee, and Bristol, Virginia, police departments of 1890 hold an intimidating pose. Pictured from left to right are (first row) John H. Gose (Bristol, Virginia), Jim Cox (Bristol, Virginia), Charles Caldwell (Bristol, Tennessee), and Bill Sullivan (Bristol, Tennessee); (second row) Hunter Price (Bristol, Virginia), Isaac Sharrett (Bristol, Virginia), George Jones (Bristol, Tennessee), Sam Hammer (Bristol, Tennessee), and Sam Slack (Bristol, Tennessee). (Courtesy of Walter Doane.)

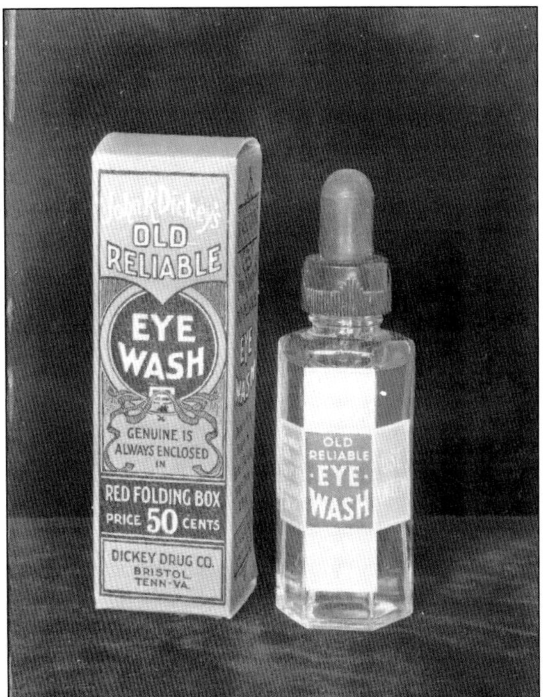

In 1870, Dr. John R. Dickey opened a drug store on Main Street and sold a prescription for an eye wash that had been created by Dr. J. F. Hicks. In the late 1870s, Dickey began his drug manufacturing business and the eye wash, known as Old Reliable, became his best seller. It soon became the only product he manufactured. (Courtesy of Walter Doane.)

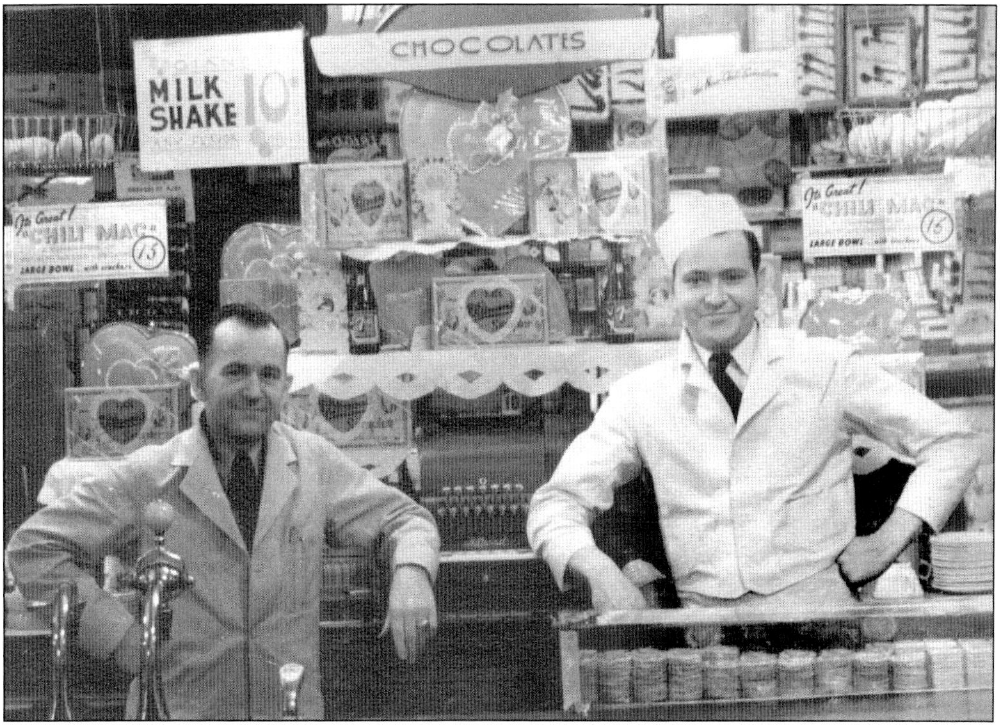

These pleasant-looking gentlemen in an unidentified Bristol store appear happy to mix up a giant milk shake for 10¢. Based on the large amount of Whitman's Chocolates and heart-shaped boxes on the display behind them, it certainly must have been near Valentine's Day. Also for sale is a large bowl of Chili Mac with crackers for 15¢. (Courtesy of Tim Buchanan.)

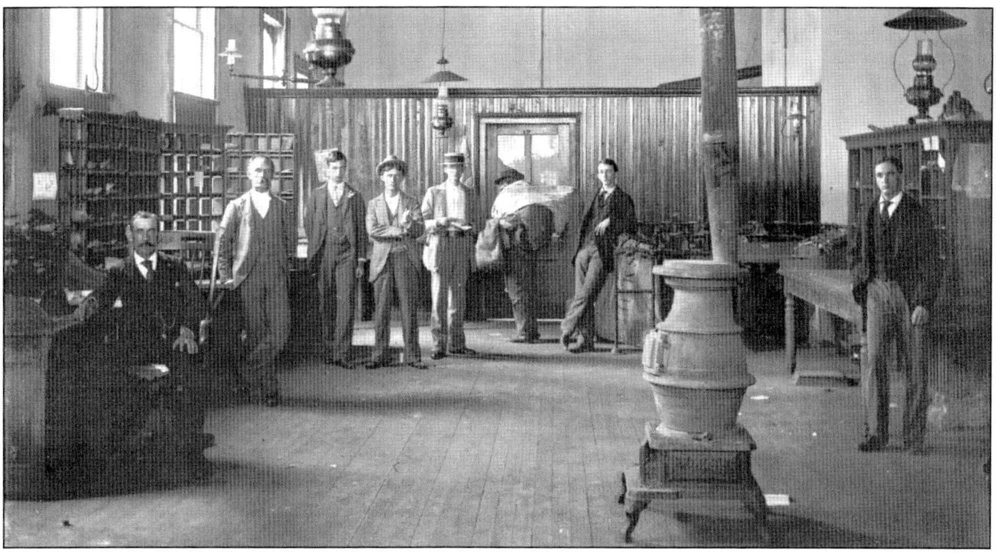

Post offices over the years have been in several locations around Bristol, but the one pictured here c. 1900 was located on the corner of Sixth and Shelby Streets. Eli A. Warren (far left) served as postmaster from 1898 to 1906. About the time this photograph was taken, the post office had seven clerks and seven letter carriers. This photograph was taken by S. C. Hodges. (Courtesy of Virginia Intermont College.)

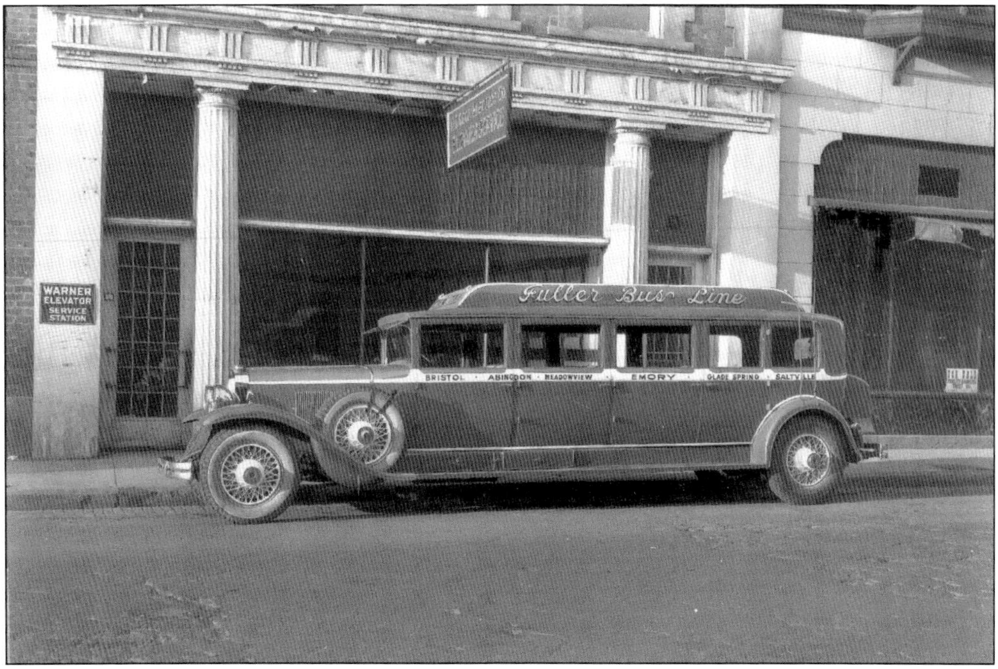

The Fuller Bus Line made two runs daily between Bristol and Saltville, Virginia, with stops in Abingdon, Meadowview, Emory, and Glade Spring (all in Virginia). The bus, shown here in May 1936, was constructed of two Cadillac automobiles cut apart and made into a 14-passenger vehicle. A one-way trip was $1.50. G. A. Fuller was the owner. (Courtesy of Walter Doane.)

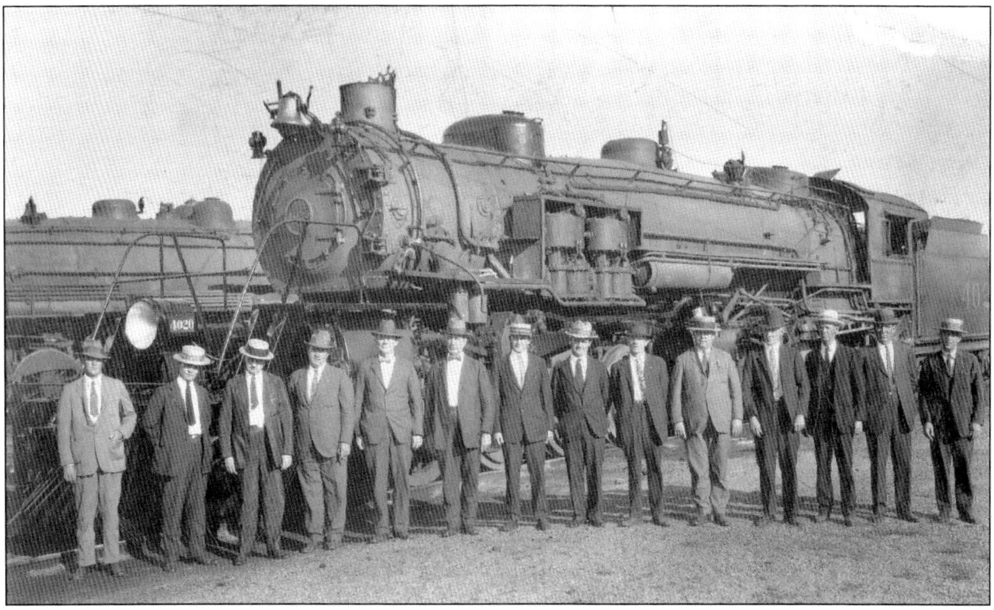

These were the men in charge who kept the trains rolling through Bristol *c.* 1920. Each man served as a foreman over car inspections, painting, repairs, yard laborers, blacksmiths, and boilermakers. Shown from left to right are Homer Collins, F. L. Anderson, Joseph Tevis, G. C. Rader, J. S. Brown, W. L. Cash, M. R. Brockman, S. W. Davis, H. J. Koester, E. F. Willis, J. F. McEver, W. E. Glover, H. L. Baker, and F. H. Blood. (Courtesy of the Bristol Public Library.)

Eight
The Birthplace of Country Music

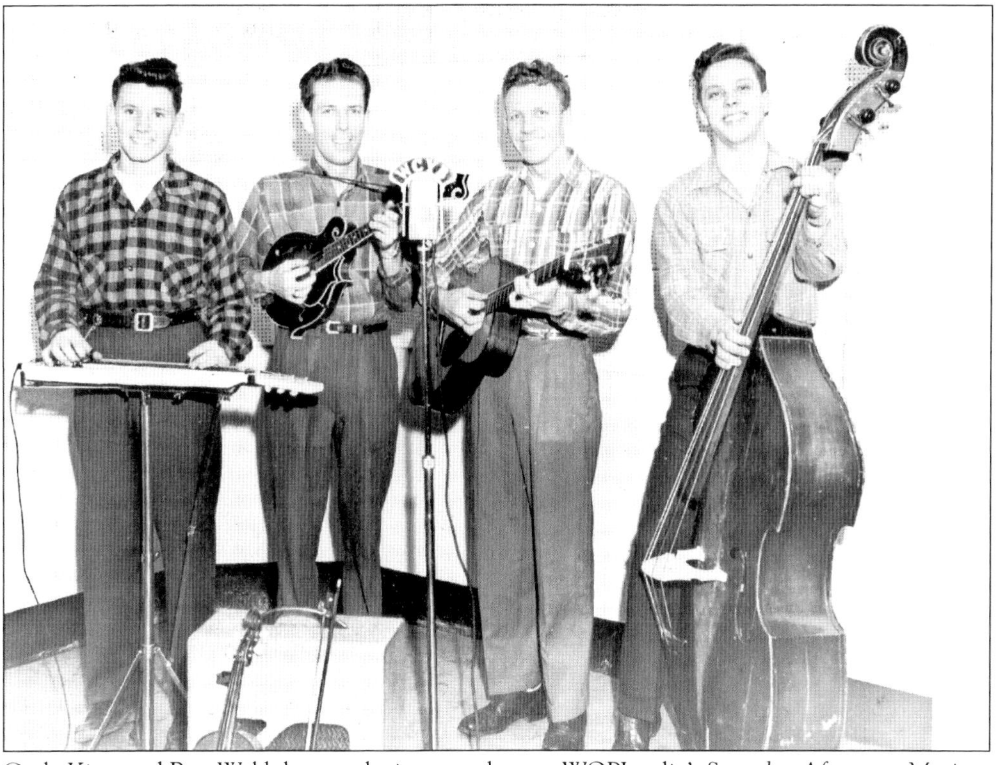

Curly King and Roy Webb began playing together on WOPI radio's *Saturday Afternoon Matinee* in 1938. The Hilltoppers got together as a group in 1940, but members changed over the years. In this shot, Curly King and the Tennessee Hilltoppers appear on WCYB radio's *Farm and Fun Time* c. 1947. Pictured from left to right are Don Campbell, Roy Webb, Curly King, and Zeke Leonard. (Courtesy of Joe Morrell.)

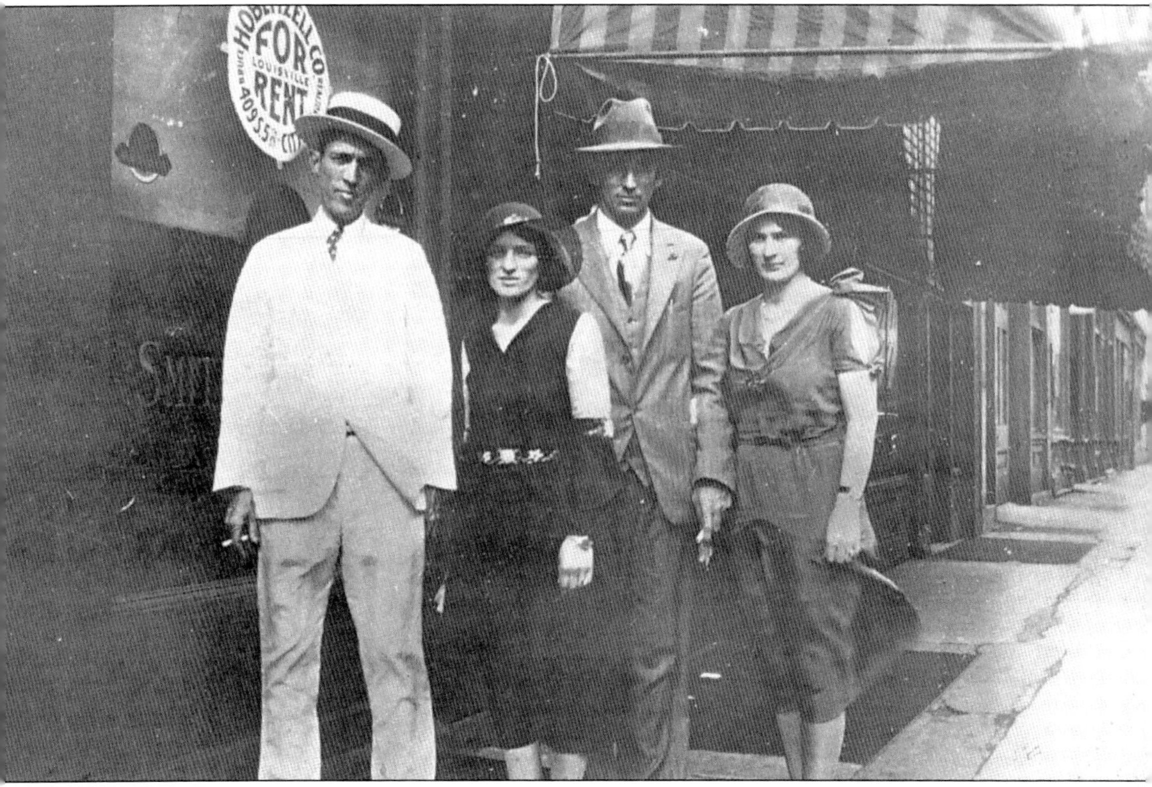

In a rare photograph together are Jimmie Rodgers and the Carter Family in 1930. From left to right, they are Jimmie Rodgers, Maybelle Carter, A. P. Carter, and Sara Carter. The Bristol Sessions is credited with launching the careers of Rodgers and the Carters, who became huge country music stars. Rodgers was born September 8, 1897, and died May 26, 1933, at age 36 of tuberculosis. He was the first inductee into the Country Music Hall of Fame in 1961, while the Carter Family was inducted into the Country Music Hall of Fame in 1970. (Courtesy of the Birthplace of Country Music Alliance.)

J. B. Litton and the Virginia Haymakers appear on a promotional songbook c. 1949. The group played on WOPI radio. Members of the group, from left to right, are: (first row) Lawrence Barnes (guitar) and Ralph Russell (mandolin); (second row) Charlie Nietch (bass), Luther Pennington (guitar), Roy Russell (fiddle), and J. B. Litton (steel). Luther Pennington, one of the few remaining survivors, lives in Bristol. (Courtesy of the Birthplace of Country Music Alliance.)

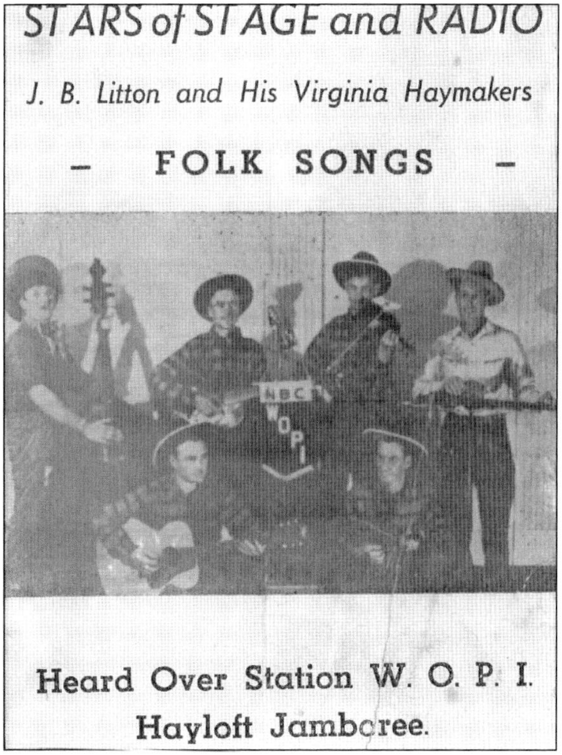

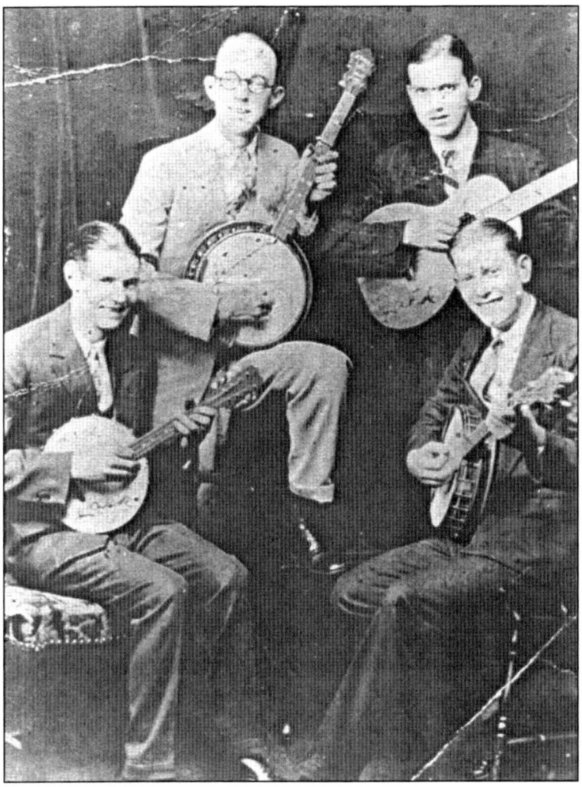

Jimmie Rodgers (standing left) performed with the Bristol musicians Jack Pierce (standing right) and Jack and Claude Grant (seated left to right). This group was called the Jimmie Rodgers Entertainers and is shown here in 1927 just before the Bristol Sessions in Asheville, North Carolina. Later, the group split up, and Pierce and the Grant brothers performed as the Tenneva Ramblers. (Courtesy of the Birthplace of Country Music Alliance.)

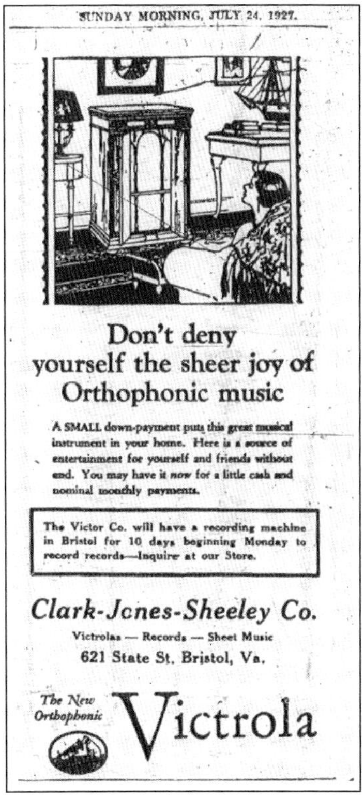

In 1927, the Victor Talking Machine Company hoped to enter the new market of hillbilly music. Ralph S. Peer, Victor's producer, came to Bristol and ran this ad in the *Bristol Herald Courier* on July 24, 1927. The ad invited musicians to audition to make field recordings of traditional mountain music that would later be known as the Bristol Sessions. Peer recorded 19 different bands and singers. (Courtesy of the Birthplace of Country Music Alliance.)

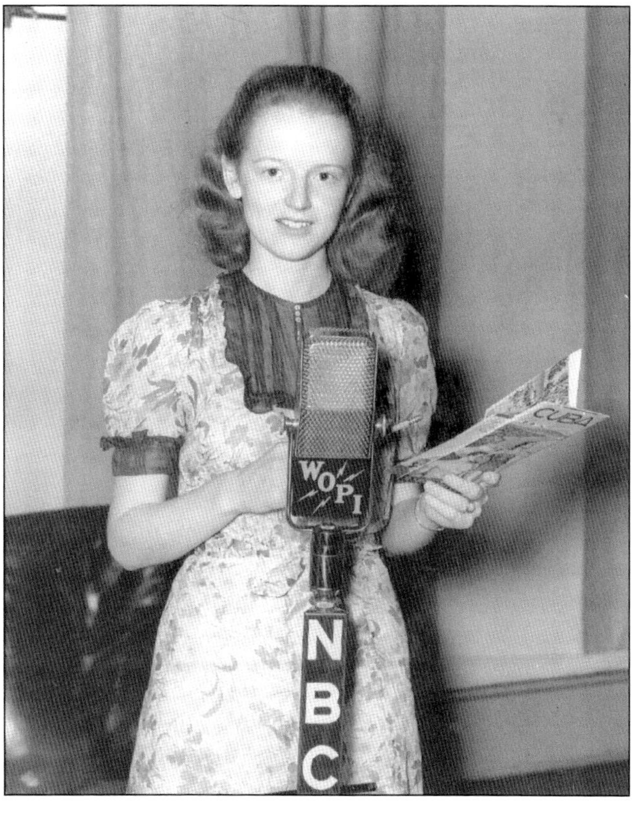

Young Margaret Freels reads from a brochure in front of a WOPI and NBC microphone. (Courtesy of the Birthplace of Country Music Alliance.)

WOPI-AM 1490 radio was the first station between Knoxville and Roanoke, signing on the air June 15, 1929. The first broadcast was at 6:30 p.m. and featured the Kingsport Concert Band performing live. Founded by W. A. Wilson Sr., the station's call letters stood for "Watch Our Popularity Increase." The station broadcast traditional mountain, hillbilly, and country music to be heard in homes around the area. (Courtesy of the Birthplace of Country Music Alliance.)

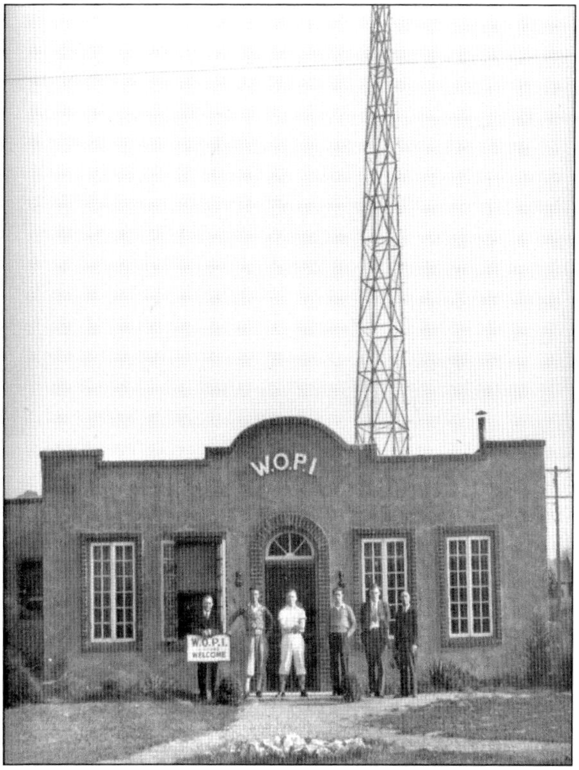

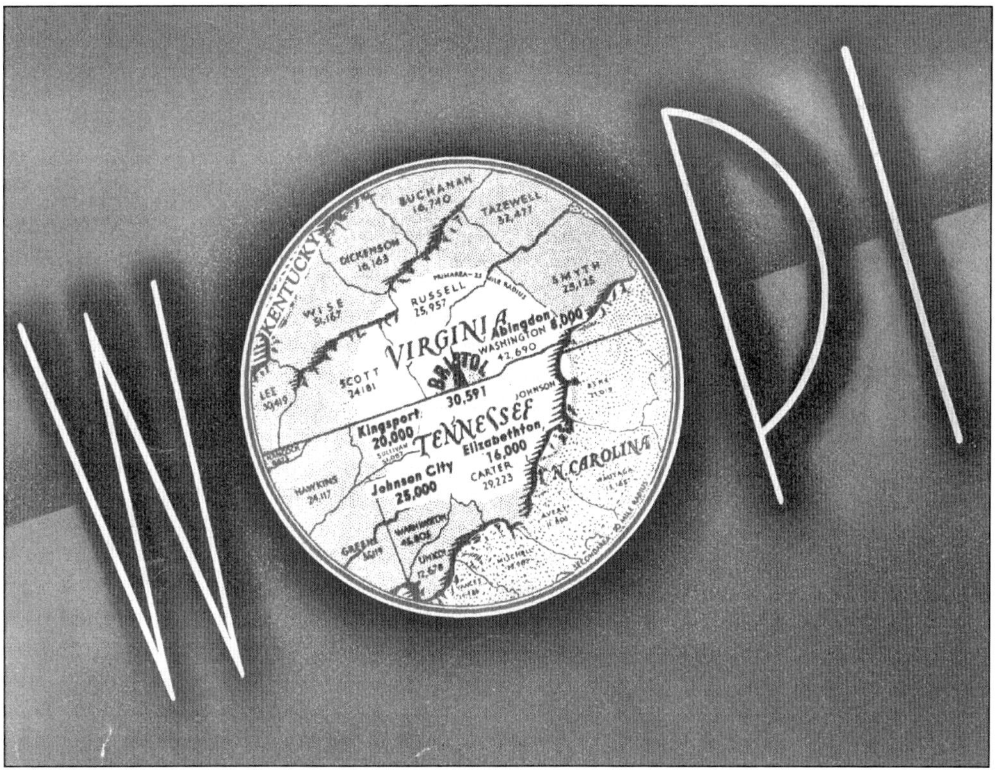

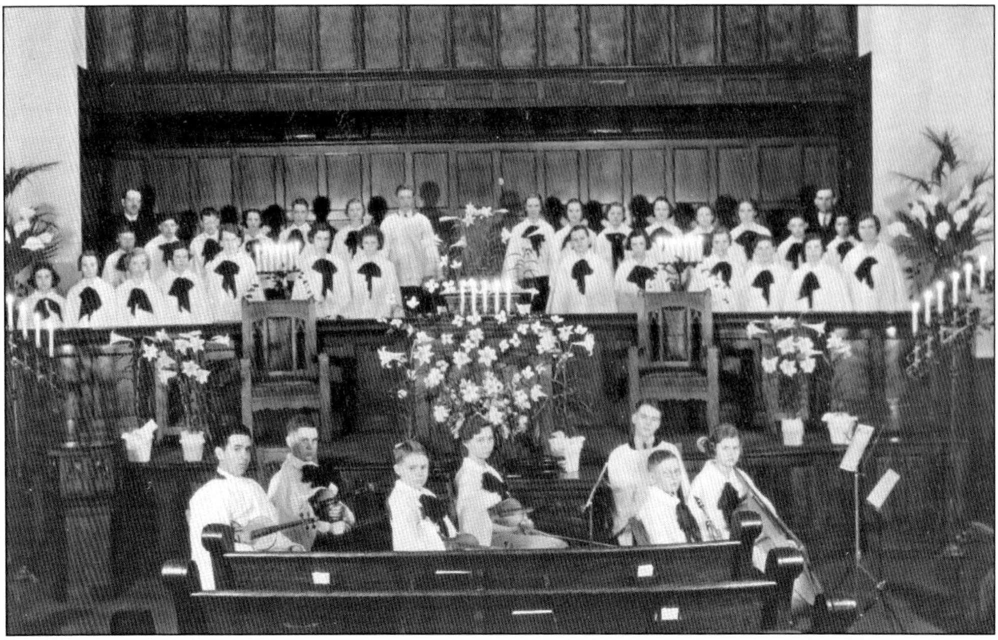

Ernest Jennings Ford was born February 13, 1919. Ford is shown above participating in his church choir, and below he is receiving an imprint of his first check from WOPI founder and announcer W. A. Wilson Sr. Ford went on to develop a legendary career and is still remembered for songs such as "Sixteen Tons." He passed away on October 17, 1991. (Top courtesy of the Birthplace of Country Music Alliance; bottom courtesy of Joe Morrell.)

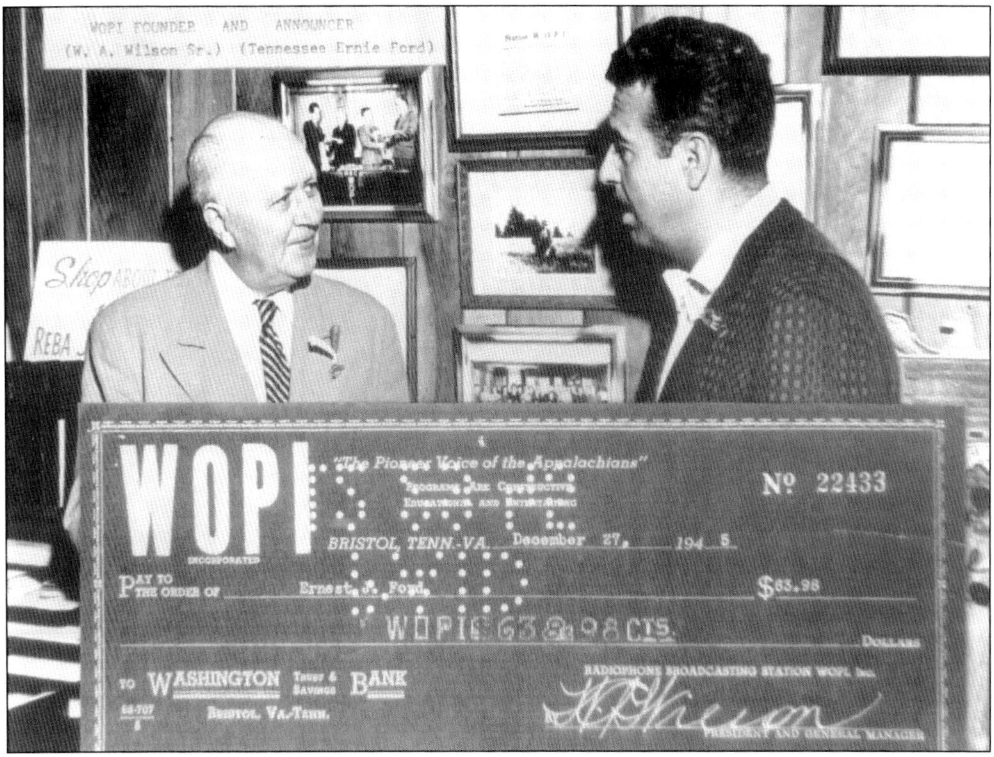

Nine

SPORTS AND COMMUNITY

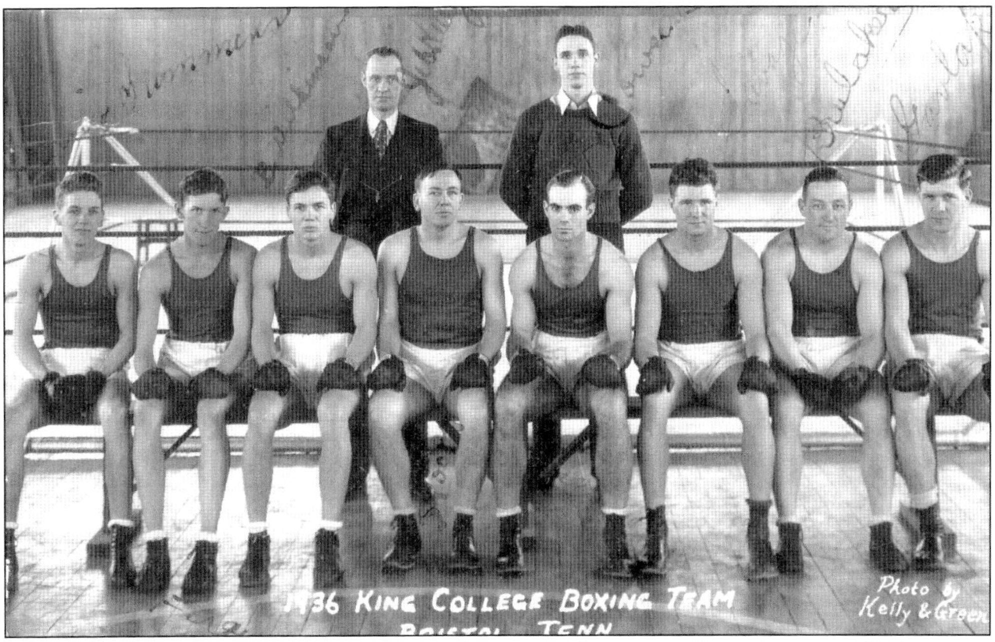

The King College boxing team was organized in 1935. The team is shown here in 1936 during an unbeaten season. Jack Kelly, standing left, was a local attorney who coached the team. Next to Kelly is team manager Charles Cowsert. Team members shown here, from left to right, are Lewis Summers (team captain), Paul Ferguson, Bill Wilkinson, Stoops Wilkinson, Fred Caldwell, Tony Savage, Steece Brubaker, and Emiel Gavlak. (Courtesy of Tony Marion.)

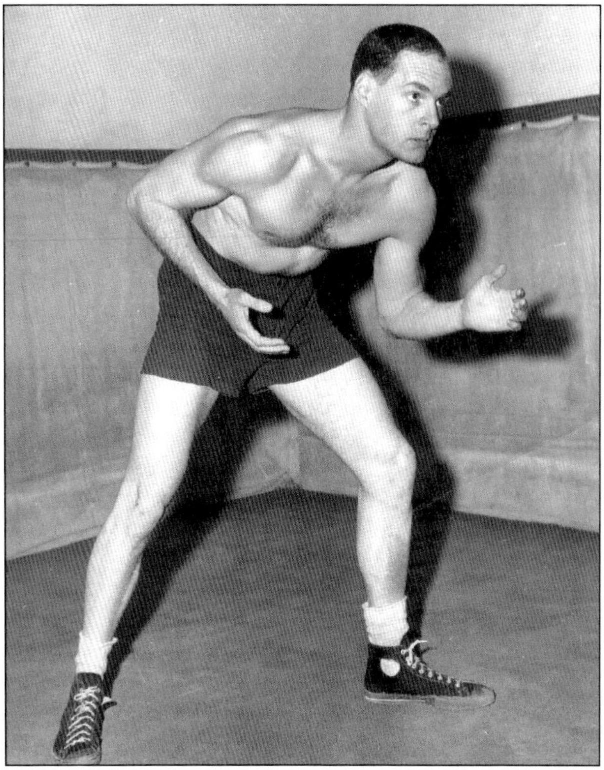

John R. (Dick) Easley poses in this photograph taken *c.* 1950. Easley wrestled for the Bristol YMCA and also at Davidson College in 1947, but then he transferred to the University of Tennessee. Easley entered the U.S. Army in 1944 for pilot's training before entering another branch of the service with the U.S. Navy. He was a well-known house builder in Bristol. Dick was born February 14, 1925, and died on November 29, 2003. (Courtesy of Mrs. Dick Easley.)

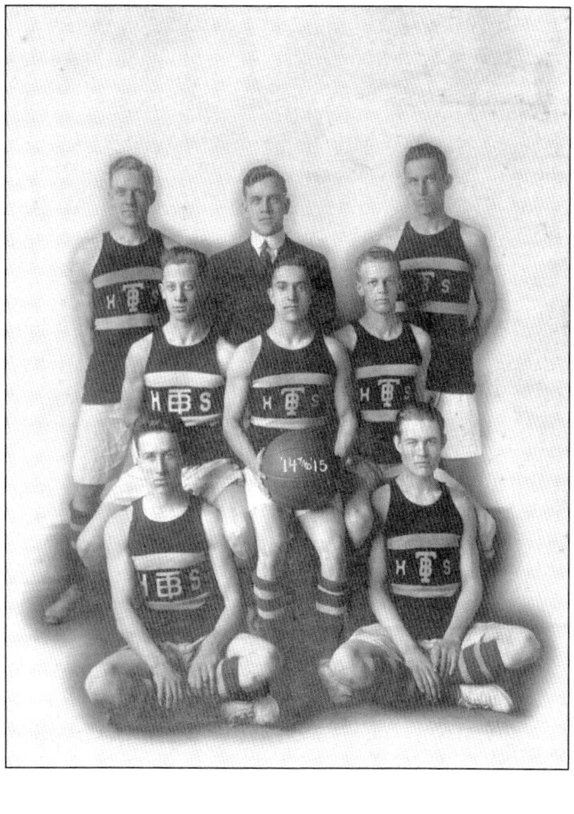

The Bristol Tennessee High School basketball team is shown in their 1914–1915 season with coach A. C. Adams (standing center in suit). Members of the team pictured here, from left to right, are (first row) Umstattd and McSpadden; (second row) King, Remine, and Hanson; (third row) Fain and Painter (team captain). Known as the Vikings now, Tennessee High's early nicknames included the Warriors, the Maroon and White Machine, and the Adamites. (Courtesy of Bud Phillips.)

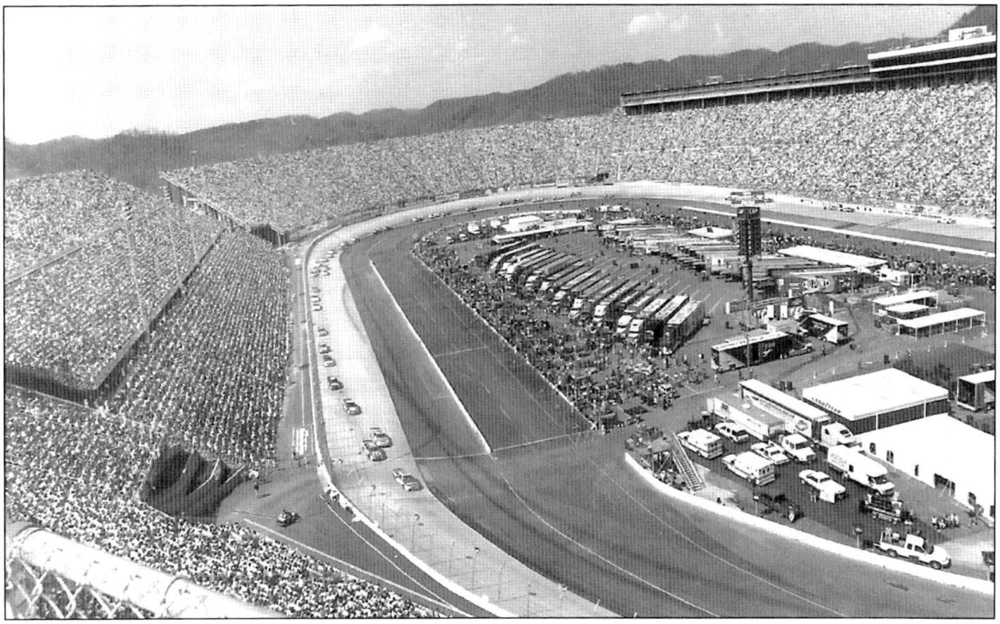

The Bristol Motor Speedway was initially constructed in 1961. Over the years, it has undergone numerous changes and additions and now holds a prominent status among the millions of NASCAR stock car racing fans. Shown here in the earlier years, Bristol Motor Speedway has been a platform in the community not only for NASCAR, but other events such as concerts and Speedway in Lights. (Courtesy of David McGee.)

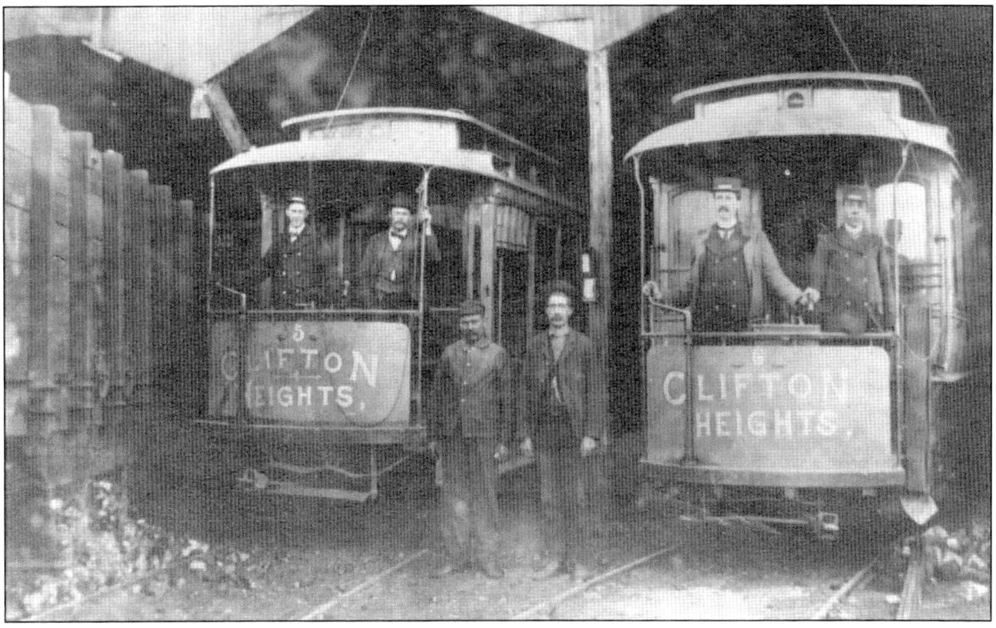

In the early 1900s, a dancing pavilion was built on a high knob near the ends of Hill Street and Windsor Avenue. The area was called Clifton Heights and was once a center of social activity until more accessible centers developed. The Clifton Heights pavilion seated 600 to 800 people and was reached with streetcars such as the two shown here on January 4, 1903. (Courtesy of Julia Wade.)

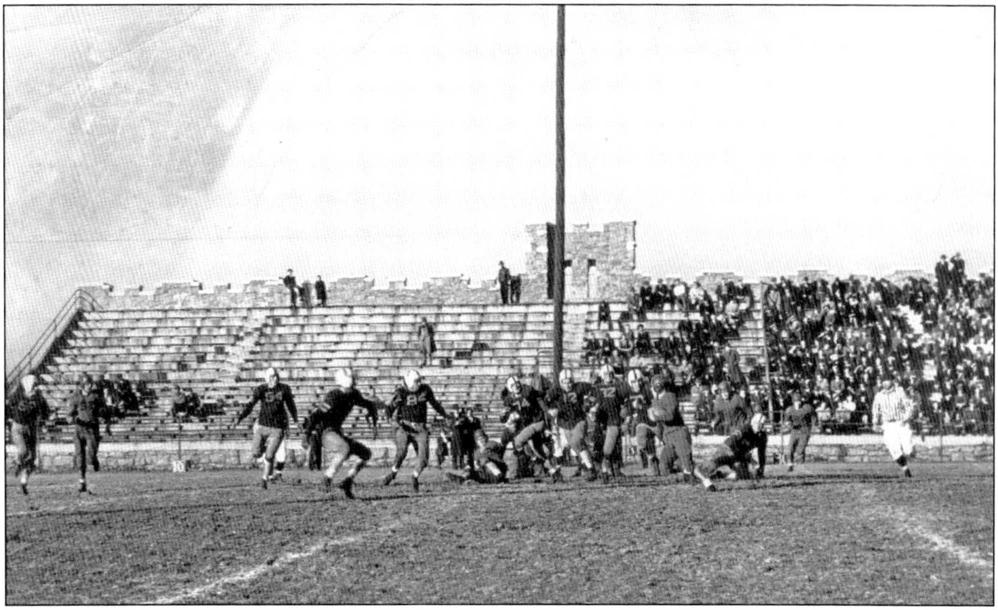

The Tennessee High School Vikings are in action in this late-1930s photograph against an unknown opponent. The Stone Castle was built by Pres. Franklin D. Roosevelt's Works Progress Administration, which was formed to provide economic relief to citizens across America who lost jobs during the Great Depression. The Stone Castle was constructed between 1935 and 1936 and is still packed on Friday nights almost 70 years later. (Courtesy of Tim Buchanan.)

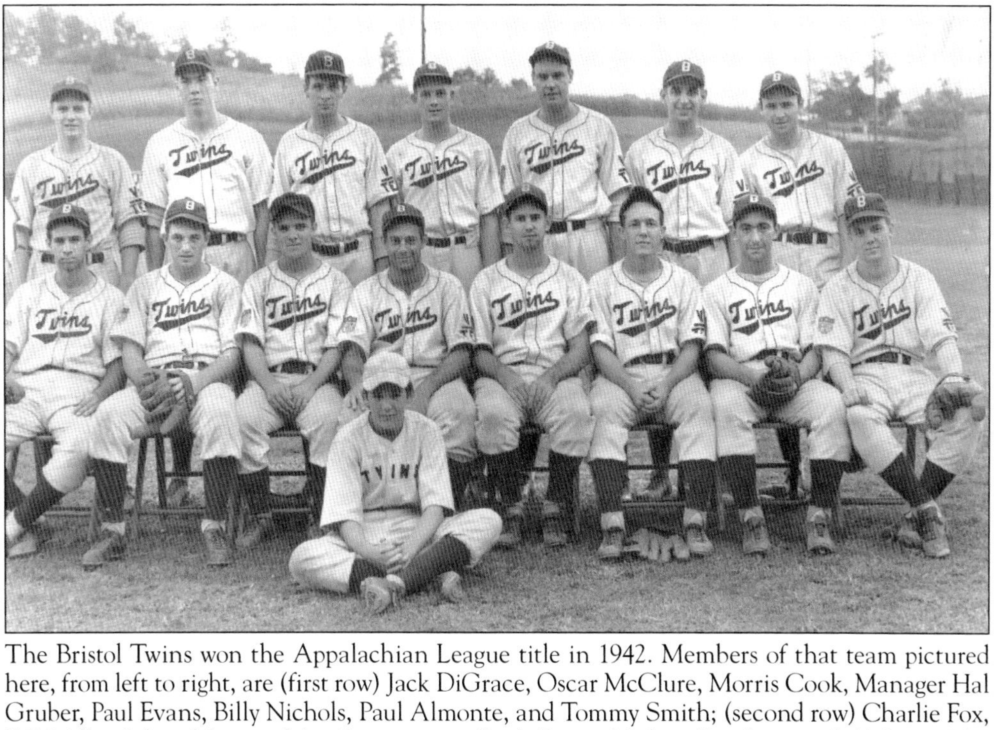

The Bristol Twins won the Appalachian League title in 1942. Members of that team pictured here, from left to right, are (first row) Jack DiGrace, Oscar McClure, Morris Cook, Manager Hal Gruber, Paul Evans, Billy Nichols, Paul Almonte, and Tommy Smith; (second row) Charlie Fox, Bill Miller, Julian Morgan, Max Pennington, Buck Zeiger, Nishan Bendian, and Al Sima. The batboy (seated on the ground) is Gene Hamlin. (Courtesy of Bristol Historical Association.)

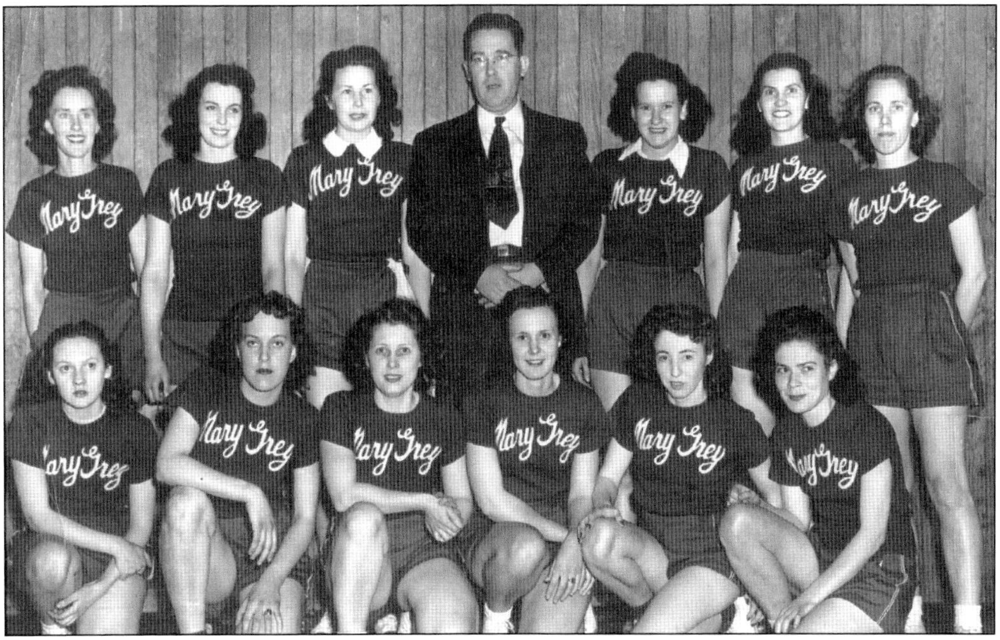

Many industries around Bristol sponsored teams in the YMCA Industrial League. Pictured here is the Mary Grey Hosiery Mill basketball team *c.* 1948, with Doris Nichols, Helen Lester, Vivian Phelps, and Lucille McCroskey among the players. Grey Hosiery, a manufacturer of ladies' stockings, was organized in 1920 and, by 1959, had sales organizations in 42 states. The company closed in 1974. (Courtesy of Tim Buchanan.)

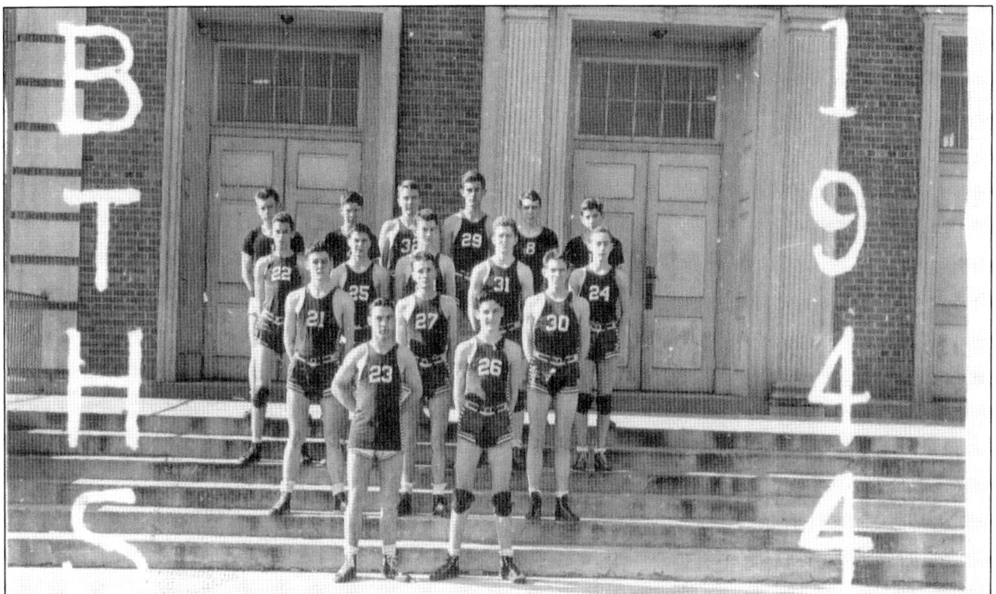

The Tennessee High School boys basketball team of 1944 finished a lackluster 4-10, but athletics were a break from talk of war. Identified by their uniform numbers are Jack Cross (23), Mack Fain (26), Randy Blevins (21), Jack Smith (27), Bob Millard (30), Charlie Harkins (22), Joe Eldridge (25), Bill Pippin (31), Dan McCrary (24), Frank Winston (32), Sam Stevenson (29), and Hugh Harr (8). (Courtesy of Paul Stone Collection.)

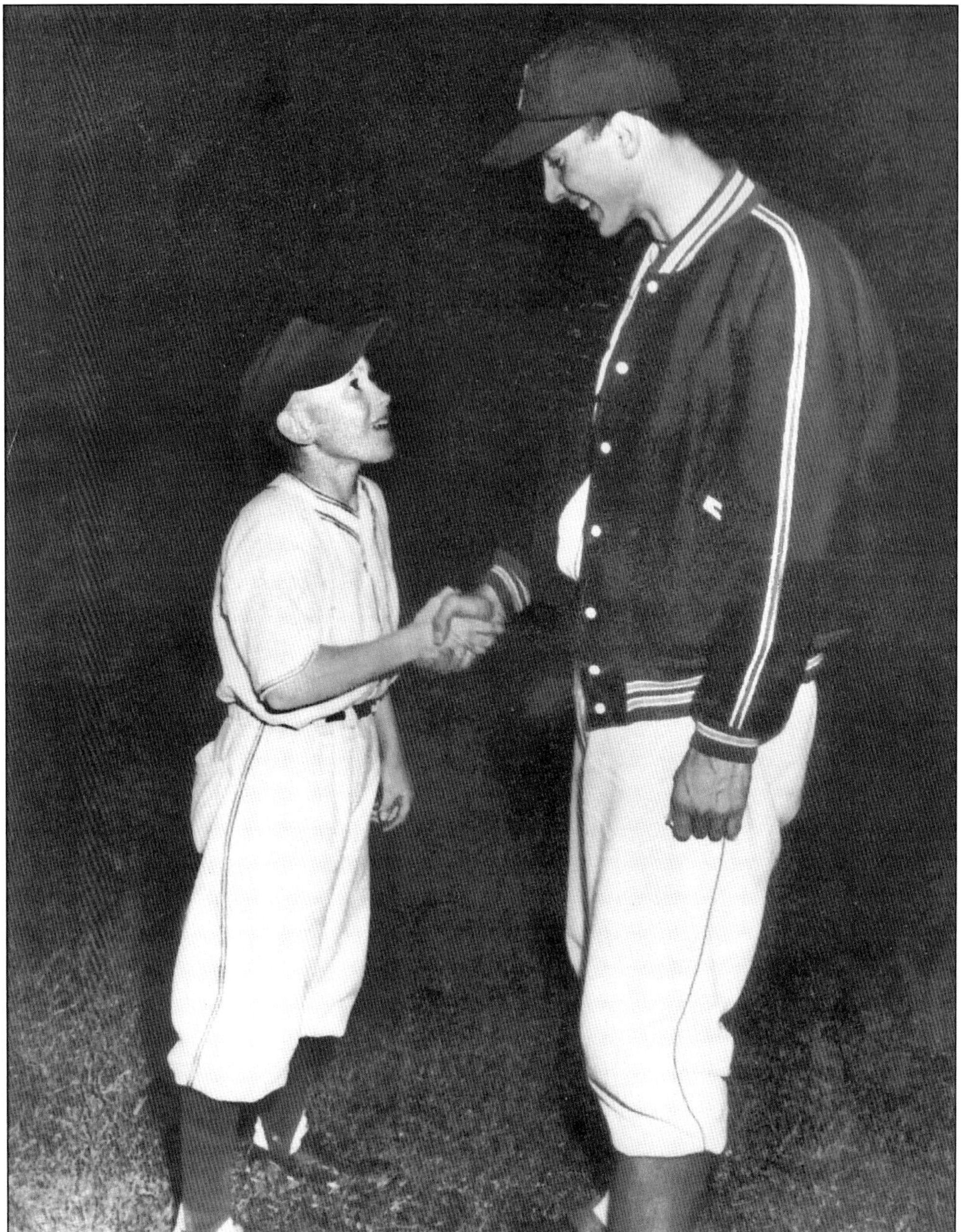

Ronnie Odum, 13-year-old batboy for the Bristol Twins, shakes the hand of his hero Ron Necciai in this 1952 photograph. Necciai, only 19 years old, struck out 27 batters in a game on May 13, 1952, against the Welch (West Virginia) Miners in an Appalachian League game at Shaw Stadium. He is the only pitcher in a professional baseball game to strike out 27 batters in a game. By August, Necciai was pitching for the Pittsburgh Pirates in the National League. After this photograph, Necciai was moved from Bristol to Burlington, North Carolina. (Courtesy of Ronnie Odum.)

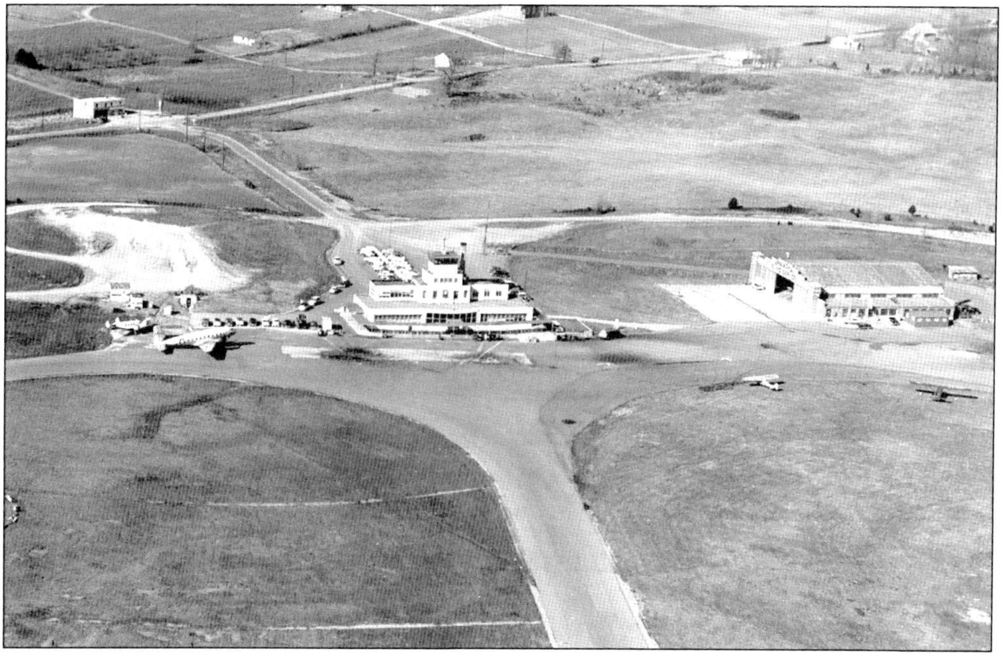

In 1934, a group of prominent men began discussing the common interest of creating an airport that would serve the tri-cities area. By October 1935, construction on the airport had begun, and by September 1937, two small runways, a terminal building, and an aircraft hangar were ready for service. The airport was initially called McKellar Field. (Courtesy of Bristol Historical Association.)

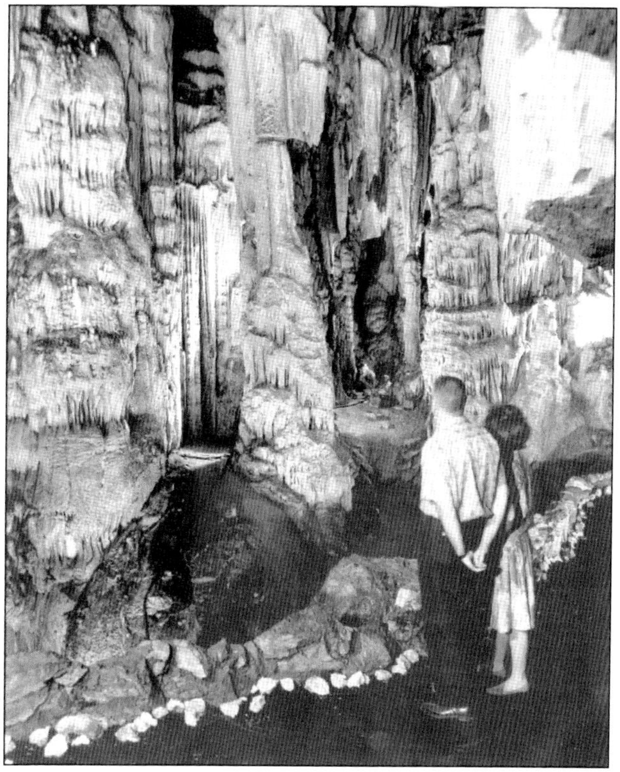

Stalactites and stalagmites, "some larger than tree trunks and others smaller than straws" create beautiful underground formations of solid stone in one of Bristol's most commonly visited tourist attractions, called Bristol Caverns. Created naturally by an underground river and used as a route for the Native Americans for raids on unsuspecting settlers who thought the Native Americans disappeared into the earth, the caverns are worth visiting for beauty and history alike. (Courtesy of Bristol Historical Association.)

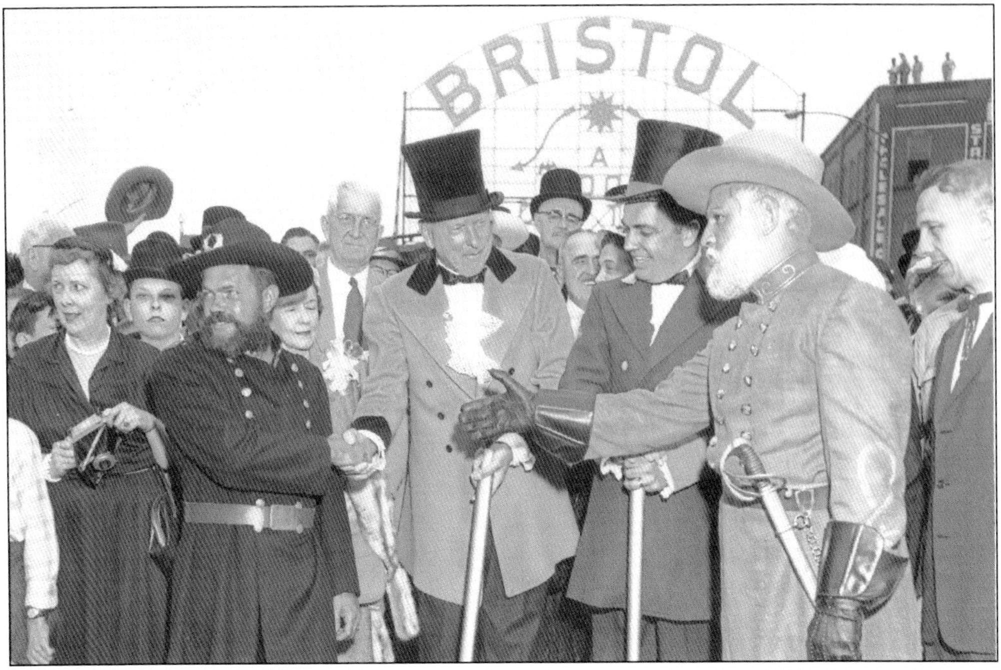

The railroad from Lynchburg, Virginia, to Bristol was completed in 1856. During Bristol's Centennial Celebration in 1956, Virginia governor Thomas B. Stanley (center left, in top hat) and Tennessee governor Frank Clement (center right, in top hat) shake hands amidst a crowd of supporters in front of the Bristol sign. (Courtesy of Bristol Historical Association.)

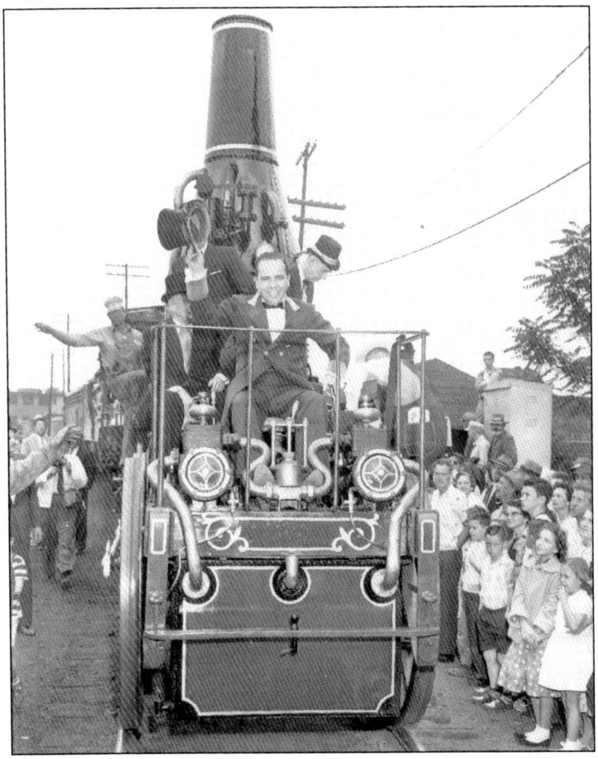

Tennessee governor Frank Clement made a grand entrance into Bristol during the city's Centennial Celebration on May 26, 1956. Clement is the engineer on this old wood-burning Southern Railroad locomotive. (Courtesy of Bristol Historical Association.)

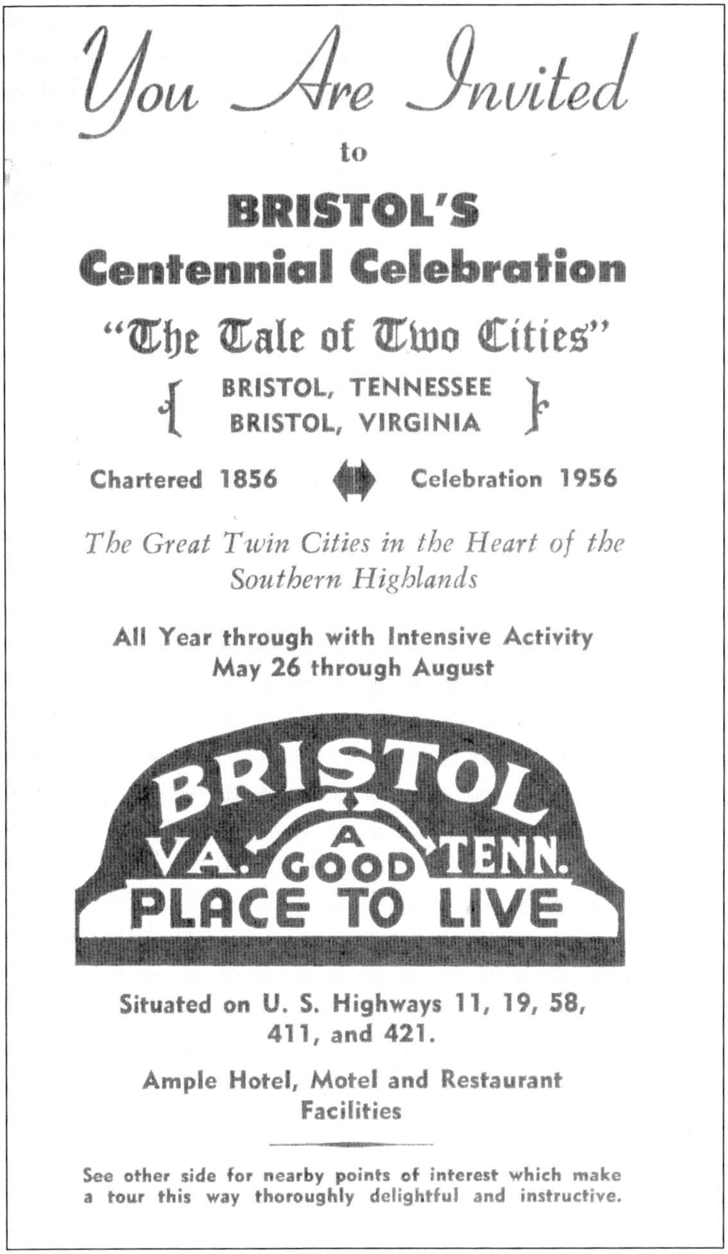

The 1956 Bristol centennial was one of the largest events in the history of both cities. A Centennial Committee was headed by Dr. Guy Richardson, and Mac King became the president of the board of directors. The giant celebration was under the direction of a professional production company, the John Rogers Producing Company, and climaxed for a 10-week celebration, May 26 to August 4. The theme was "The Tale of Two Cities," taking the title from *The History of Bristol*, a book written by newsman Robert Loving. The centennial highlighted three major events with three parades, the Southeastern Band Festival, and hundreds of events. The opening activities on Governor's Day featured the Century of Progress Parade, driving the Golden Spike with both governors present, a horse show, a citywide barbeque, and a street party emceed by Archie Campbell. (Courtesy of Tim Buchanan.)

BRISTOL'S SESQUICENTENNIAL

As we peruse through the images of our past, we quickly identify the special flavor, the unique heritage, we have in Bristol. The state line, the twin governments, and the varied landmarks and attractions confirm the remarkable tradition that we have built upon over the years. Though as important as that tradition is, the treasure of the Twin Cities is our people and the generations of our forbears that had a dream and dared to make their mark. There's not one story of Bristol, but as many versions as there are people, generations of people. This includes those for whom Bristol was a stopping off place rather than a permanent home. Our common heritage is understated but identified on our Bristol sign, "Bristol—A GOOD Place to Live" and also by the indiscernible blurring of the lines between progress and destruction. Bristol, both Bristols, are unique to themselves and also share a common heritage and destiny. Bristol is an absolute treasure!

This pictorial edition gives you a glimpse of the special flavor of our city and serves as an invaluable resource during our sesquicentennial year, 2006. Our 10-month celebration will highlight the many special aspects of our heritage, culture, and our optimism for the future. The theme is "Celebrating 150 Years of Heritage and Harmony." Participate and enjoy the unique inheritance that made Bristol the jewel of the Mountain Empire.

—Tim Buchanan
Bristol Sesquicentennial Committee Chairman

ABOUT THE AUTHORS

George Stone attended King College and East Tennessee State University. He began his journalism career as a sports writer for the *Johnson City Press-Chronicle* from 1975 to 1978 before joining the *Bristol Herald Courier* in 1979 and serving as sports editor from 1995 to 1999. He is currently a freelance writer having written for various magazines and newspapers, and in 2003, he self-published *Muscle: A Minor League Legend*, the story of minor league baseball home-run legend Leo "Muscle" Shoals. Stone lives in Bristol with wife, Marcia, son, Michael, and daughter, Katye.

Sonya Haskins has a bachelor's degree in English from King College in Bristol, Tennessee. She has written hundreds of articles for newspapers and magazines, including *Writer's Digest, Guideposts for Teens, Decision, Physician's Practice Digest, College Bound, Educational Dealers,* and *Homeschooling Today*. Sonya is also the author of two other Images of America books—*Jonesborough* and *Johnson City*, which are available online or at your local bookstore. She lives in Upper East Tennessee with her husband, Chris, and children, Sarah, Micah, Christopher, Daniel, and Hannah.